ᕈᕈ IN THE ᕈᕈ

MAINE
WOODS

Also by Alice Arlen

Nonfiction
Half a Mind: Hashing, the Outrageous New Sport
A Taste of Hallowell

Poetry
"2096," Journal of Indian Literature

IN THE MAINE WOODS

THE INSIDERS' GUIDE TO TRADITIONAL MAINE SPORTING CAMPS

Second Edition, Revised and Expanded

ALICE ARLEN

THE COUNTRYMAN PRESS
WOODSTOCK, VERMONT

A Note to Our Readers

Although we update this guide every time it goes to press—about once a year—there is no way we can guarantee its accuracy. Change is inevitable, and what's more, we are human and may overlook something. We hope you will help us by contributing your knowledge and experience to this guide. Send us a postcard or letter with corrections, comments, or stories; or even send us a photograph. We wish we could include a photo of every camp in the book, but we simply don't have room. In future editions, photos will be added or replaced. Address your correspondence to:

In the Maine Woods editor
The Countryman Press
PO Box 748
Woodstock, VT 05091

Copyright © 1994, 1998 by Alice Arlen

First Countryman Press edition, 1998

Library of Congress Cataloging-in-Publication Data
Arlen, Alice
    In the Maine woods : the insiders' guide to traditional Maine sporting camps / Alice Arlen.
        p.   cm.
    Includes recipe index
    ISBN 0-88150-417-3 (alk. paper)
    1. Hunting lodges—Maine. 2. Fishing lodges—Maine. I. Title.
SK85.A75 1998
796.5'741—ds21

                                                                    98-3276
                                                                    CIP

Cover and text design by Julie Duquet
Maps by Paul Woodward, copyright © 1998 The Countryman Press
Cover photograph by Alice Arlen.
Interior photographs by Alice Arlen unless indicated otherwise.

Published by The Countryman Press
PO Box 748, Woodstock, VT 05091

Distributed by W. W. Norton & Company, Inc.
500 Fifth Avenue, New York, NY 10110

Printed in Canada
10 9 8 7 6 5 4 3 2 1

*For all those who
work, live, and play
in the Maine woods*

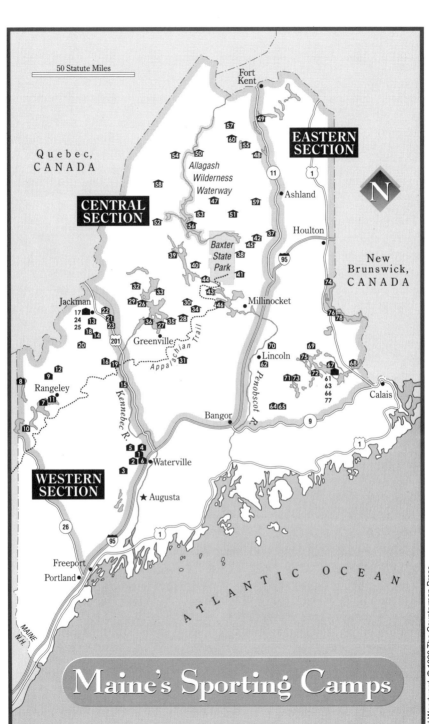

50 Statute Miles

Fort
Kent

EASTERN
SECTION

Quebec,
CANADA

57

60   55

49

54   50

48

Allagash
Wilderness
Waterway

11

1

58

47

59

Ashland

53

51

Houlton

52

56

Baxter
State
Park

42

45

37

CENTRAL
SECTION

39

38

New
Brunswick,
CANADA

40

41

95

44

32

33

43

74

Jackman

29 26

30

46

Millinocket

17
24
25

22
21
23

13

36

27

35

34

28

76
78

18
14

201

Appalachian Trail

70

69

20

Greenville

31

Lincoln

62

75

67

68

16 19

Penobscot R.

71 73

72

61
63
66
77

15

Calais

9
12

Rangeley

7   11

64 65

Bangor

8

10

Kennebec R.

9

1

5   4
1
2   6

Waterville

3

WESTERN
SECTION

★ Augusta

26

95

1

Freeport

Portland

ATLANTIC OCEAN

MAINE
N.H.

Maine's Sporting Camps

Paul Woodward, © 1998 The Countryman Press

CONTENTS

. . . none of us ever thought that there was any place in the world like that lake in Maine. I guess I remembered clearest of all the early mornings, when the lake was cool and motionless, remembered how the bedroom smelled of the lumber it was made of and of the wet woods whose scent entered through the screen . . . those summers had been infinitely precious and worth saving.

—E.B. White, "Once More to the Lake"

AUTHOR'S NOTE

In the fall of 1992, after a lovely anniversary stay at a Maine sporting camp, I arrived early at L.L. Bean for my author's signing session of *A Taste of Hallowell* because I wanted to purchase at least one of their sporting-camp books. After searching in vain, I approached a salesperson. "You know," she said, "in all the years I've been here, I've never seen a book on Maine sporting camps." Gee, I thought, if there isn't one here, there probably isn't one anywhere! (This I subsequently found to be true.)

Several months later I found myself standing before a group of strangers at a Maine Sporting Camp Association meeting attempting to share my idea of writing a book that would feature them, the sporting-camp owners, in a series of interviews. Little did I anticipate where this notion would take me. Specifically, two weeks later I was driving down a series of logging roads, miles from anywhere, seven hours from home (still in Maine!), in the middle of a snowstorm, for a rendezvous with a Maine guide at Dead Horse Gulch. This was the prelude to a wonderful few days of winter camping, a first for me.

In fact, my sojourns at sporting camps catapulted me into many firsts. One spring day, the wilderness scene before me was transformed as I learned to "read" rocks and really see ground cover and wildflowers. On a drizzly summer morning, I learned to fly-cast for bass as our solitary canoe hugged the misty shoreline of a pristine lake. Several months later, on a crisp fall morning, I crouched motionless, waiting for the dawn. Our guide, perched in the "waiting tree," made grunting noises while the sunrise set the autumn foliage aglow. Suddenly the squish and tunk of a moose walking through a muddy bog grew louder, then stopped . . . grew louder. Magical moments. And there were many, many more. One week I drove 873 miles and, for the most part, never saw a telephone pole or power line, a tarred road, or a vehicle other than a pickup or pulp truck. Dotting this landscape were the sporting camps, welcome oases of warmth and hospitality.

The first edition of *In the Maine Woods*, published in 1994, sold out quickly. Clearly, a second edition was needed, full of new and updated information. In the spring of 1997 I looked at the old car that had carried me 6,500 miles the first time around and begged, "Please, once more." Together we bounced along over 10,000 miles with nary a hitch. This time was like coming home, over and over again. There

The author at work

were changes: new owners, new buildings, people and places I had missed before. But there was also a sense of permanence and continuity. On a day with distant, ominous clouds, I strapped into a Piper Cub floatplane and was given an exhilarating view of the network of roads, forests, and waterways I had just traveled. We floated in to another sporting camp and, later, as we left, dipped our wings to the 18 bear hunters out on the dock waving. A pocket-sized beach sheltered a midday skinny-dip, peregrine falcons floated in updrafts, strangers shared their hearts' desires. More magical moments.

In the Maine Woods is a look at this sporting-camp world through facts (guidebook data), flavors (recipes), and most of all through the words of camp owners, which is only fitting since this book is really their story. Guests return to their chosen sporting camp year after year not only because the layout and location suit them, but also because the owners have created a little community that "feels right." Camp owners really make the place for many people: Witness the exodus of clientele after new owners take over, the migration of guests when an owner purchases a different camp, the outpouring of affection from long-term visitors, the "camp hopping" until a guest finds the right spot and settles in. Sporting-camp owners truly know the meaning of the word hospitality, and I want to thank them here for their help and generosity. This book commemorates the sporting-camp industry, a Maine tradition that, through the dogged determina-

The author and her vehicle, deep in the Maine woods

tion of a few individuals and their families, hasn't vanished.

So, dear reader, before you peruse these pages, I offer several overall suggestions. Please realize that this book is a series of snapshots. These interviews were generally conducted during a one-hour to two-day visit. What I offer here is an image of the camps and their people at one moment in time, and as we all know from looking at family albums, things change. Sporting camps are sold, go under, rise like the phoenix. If, in the course of reading this book, you find camps that interest you, by all means write to them for information. But also call and talk to the owners. Calling can itself be an adventure, since many camps use radio phones. It is in the owners' interest, as well as yours, that your stay at their camp is a happy one and not derailed by unmet or unclear expectations. Sporting camps, or what some think of as "hunting and fishing lodges," are rustic, some more so than others. This book should help give you an idea of what to expect, but if you have a question, ask the owners in advance of your stay.

For people who would like a cabin in the woods without having the responsibilities of actually owning it, or for those who would like to explore remote areas in a congenial atmosphere, this book will open up a wonderful world. Folks who love sporting camps will tell you that they are a point of reference for them—a place and time for peace, companionship, and beauty that enrich their lives immeasurably. I hope this becomes the case for you. Happy reading!

INTRODUCTION

In addition to my own thoughts, the following incorporates information from Gary Cobb's *The History of Pierce Pond Camps* and Stephen Cole's manuscript *Maine Sporting Camps* (see Further Reading).

There is a grand tradition that has become an integral part of Maine's heritage: Unique to the state, and over 140 years old, it is called the Maine sporting camp. Some people think of these camps as "hunting and fishing lodges." They are that, but they are also much more. Nearly all sporting camps are on a lake or river, generally in a remote area of forested land. Most have buildings made of peeled and chinked logs with porches looking over the water. The guest sleeping cabins are clustered near the shore around a central dining lodge. Plumbing was (and often still is) "out back." Primitive, and in harmony with their surroundings, sporting camps have the appearance of having grown out of the ground. New Hampshire and Vermont have private hunting and fishing clubs and game preserves. New York, in the Adirondacks, has private camps and rustic estates. But Maine sporting camps are open to paying customers and are a cultural and entrepreneurial resource distinctive to the state.

Several factors came together to produce the Maine sporting camp. The post–Civil War transition into the Victorian era saw tremendous industrial and economic expansion and the development of technologies such as the internal-combustion engine and electricity. The iron and steel industries flourished, and the railroads entered their golden age. The high economic growth rate in the Victorian era created a substantial upper-middle class. At the same time, intellectuals and writers such as Henry David Thoreau decried what they saw as society's growing alienation from nature and expressed general uneasiness about the direction of American culture. Life in polluted eastern cities during the Industrial Revolution was felt to be "undermining character, taste, morality, and the health and welfare of individuals and the family." As a result, those who could sought escape from the questionable influences and pollution of the cities, as well as from the summer heat. (Ironically,

COURTESY OF TIM POND CAMPS

many who "took the airs" were the families of magnates and managers whose factories were causing the pollution they were escaping.)

Recreational sailing and canoeing are lasting legacies of the Victorian era. Hunting, fishing, and hiking took on a certain cachet as sporting pursuits instead of merely functional activities. Not only did people have motives for escape (aesthetics, expendable income, leisure time, status, health concerns), they also had the means. It is no coincidence that the heyday of fishing and hunting in Maine was also the golden age of lumbering and railroading. The very rail lines that were bringing trainloads of Maine timber to fuel factory burners also carried trainloads of vacationers fleeing back to the source of all that smog! With the growth of a national rail transportation network, an extended family vacation at one of the much-publicized public sporting camps in the Maine wilderness became possible and desirable. The Bangor, the Aroostook, and the Central Maine Railroads all offered direct service to Brownville in 1881, to Presque Isle in 1882, to Katahdin Iron Works in 1883, and reached Moosehead Lake in 1884. The Somerset Railroad came to Bingham in 1890; the narrow-gauge trains got to Rangeley and Carrabassett by 1895; and the Katahdin, Allagash, and Fish River areas were opened by 1900. Before Henry Ford put his first automobile on the road, place-names such as Sysladobsis, Oquossoc, Nesowadnehunk, and Munsungan were part of

COURTESY OF TIM POND CAMPS

the vocabulary of hunters, anglers, and vacationers from Boston to Philadelphia.

In 1904 there were at least 300 sporting camps in operation in Maine. In 1997, there were few more than the 78 herein recorded. After World War II, Americans could no longer spend the time or money on a monthlong vacation at a Maine sporting camp. The railroads were in decline and automobiles and "motor coaches" were on the increase. The road system in Maine was poor and people stayed close to the tarmac, where motels and motor-coach campgrounds were now the rage. And finally, air transportation took travelers out of New England altogether. Over the years, many camps burned, some became resorts, some sold as condominiums or individual cottages, and others simply rotted away to become part of the forest.

But good things die hard. In spite of these changes and setbacks, tucked away here and there stand sporting camps whose owners proudly struggle to maintain a tradition that may very well be the only stabilizing factor in the Maine woods. Fortunately, these few hardy souls have held on long enough to witness a renewed interest in Maine sporting camps. We have come full circle. We need what sporting camps have to offer, now more than ever. There are precious few places where we can feel the fundamental connections with nature and with one another. Sporting camps still provide solace for urban refugees (meaning most of us), and a wilderness playground for those who love the outdoors. Most of all, they still provide a much-needed "port in the storm," far from the fractured, mobile, frenetic, and alienating forces that impose on our humanity.

How to Use This Book

In the Maine Woods is largely anecdotal. Along with guidebook data is information about the region's flora and fauna, geology and history, ecological policies, and the business of recreation. The owners' comments give insights into the workings of specific sporting camps as well as impressions about the individuals who run these camps. My purpose in compiling this book is to provide a resource for the present and an oral history for the future. Some themes that came up in my interviews are specific to the sporting-camp industry, but many are universal. Thus, you can read the book purely for enjoyment—a camp or two before bed—or you can study it with the intention of finding a future vacation spot.

How to find an appropriate camp

The first thing you need to decide is whether or not you want to cook your own meals. Next, depending on your recreational interests, ask yourself what time of year you want to go. Then, consider how you feel about reading by gaslight, stoking a woodstove, or using an outhouse or central shower. How much do you want to spend? Do you want to bring a pet? The headings for each camp answer these questions and can help you narrow your search. Once you've found several camps that fit your logistical needs, the full text should help you assess other considerations.

Understanding the terms

Underneath the chapter heading for each sporting camp you'll find one or more codes in capital letters. Here's what they mean:

AP   American Plan: three meals served as part of the price.

MAP   Modified American Plan: one or two meals, usually part of the price.

HK   Housekeeping: You supply the food and cook your own meals.

HK/AP   When a combination is noted, the first abbreviation is most prevalent (for example, the camp is primarily housekeeping but meals are also available, perhaps only at certain times of the year).

SCA   Maine Sporting Camp Association: Members adhere to certain standards, make referrals to each other, and act together in regard to legislative issues. Nonmembership is not necessarily an indication of inferior quality.

Where in Maine?

Is there a particular area of Maine you want to explore? I have provided a map with the state divided into three sections, each corresponding to a part of the book: western, central, and eastern. The number for each camp corresponds to the location of that camp on the map. The chapter camps within each geographical region are listed in alphabetical order. In addition, an introduction gives an overview of each region and indicates where you can call or write for further information. I recommend getting a copy of the DeLorme *Maine Map and Guide.* You can order a map from DeLorme Mapping, PO Box 298, Yarmouth, ME 04096; 1-800-452-5931, or 1-800-227-1656. In addition, you may want to contact the Maine Publicity Bureau, PO Box 2300, Hallowell, ME 04347-2300; 207-623-0363, and ask for the free pamphlets "Maine Invites You," "Maine Guide to Hunting and Fishing," "Maine Camping Guide," and "Exploring Maine." The local chambers of commerce put out good guides to their areas, and I have listed these contacts in the introduction to each region.

How much is it?

The prices I've listed are generally a range of low- to high-season daily and weekly rates, either per person or per cabin. Boat rental is extra, unless I've indicated otherwise. Most camps offer package deals for hunting, fishing, off-season, and families, and some sponsor special-

Float planes are a means of transportation . . .

interest programs, so be sure to find out what is available. And finally, the rates listed in this guide are primarily for purposes of comparison and are subject to change. When you call or write for brochures, you will get the most up-to-date rate schedule.

How do I get there?

Once you've decided on an area, how are you going to get there? I have included general driving times under the sectional introductions and have also indicated air-transportation options. I've given general driving directions to each camp under the heading "Access." These assume you will be traveling from the south. To drive or not to drive, that is the question. The answer, of course, is, it depends. A 14-hour ordeal for a New Yorker might be a half-hour jaunt for a Canadian. A 14-hour drive, seen as part of the adventure, is preferable to flying for someone who loves back roads (or hates to fly).

It also depends on how much gear and how many people are involved. You will have more supplies going to a housekeeping establishment than to an American Plan camp. How much are you planning on using a car once at camp? If you choose a camp near population

no matter what the season.

centers and cultural activities, you will probably want a vehicle (which can be a rental car from an airport if you fly in). If you plan to go to a remote American Plan camp and then return home, you can do as many do: Fly in and leave your car and worries behind.

If you drive, your chosen camp will give you detailed directions, but I recommend getting DeLorme's Maine Atlas and Gazetteer, which shows all the major back roads in Maine (see page 21 for address). Keep in mind that a new logging road can pop up in a matter of days and so may not be on the map. Major logging roads have mile markers—little rectangular number plates—tacked up on trees. Be aware also that there may be a logging company gatehouse along your route. You will be charged a usage fee for each person in your vehicle (a reduced fee for those going to sporting camps). There are restrictions on bringing in bicycles or motorcycles, so you'll need to check this out with your chosen camp ahead of time. Some sporting camps have private gates. Be sure to ask what time their gate closes. How hellacious to drive 12 hours only to find the gate closed and gatekeeper gone!

Be sure to check the status of your spare tire and tools, fill up with gas, carry something to eat and drink, and in all seasons have some-

thing for extra warmth (in winter I throw in a sleeping bag, small shovel, and jumper cables). Logging roads, it is important to remember, are for logging trucks, and trucks have the right of way. It is not only a convention of the back road, but also a smart lifesaving maneuver, to pull over to the side and slow way down when a pulp truck comes at you. Keep alert for telltale dust clouds ahead, and don't cut the corners. If this sounds serious, it is.

In addition to being alert for logging trucks, you'll need to watch out for pedestrians—the four-legged kind, that is. It is better for everyone's health to count how many different critters you spotted, rather than splatted, along the way. However, if you're careful, driving around the back roads of Maine can be a wonderful experience. You certainly get an appreciation for how much of Maine lies beyond the coast, and how vast and beautiful are its timber resources and varied topography.

What should I bring?

Aside from the items mentioned above (sleeping bag, tools for emergency car repair, road map), you will want (per person) a flashlight, warm clothes (even in summer), rain gear, bug repellent, sunglasses (even in winter), a visor hat, as well as personal items and toiletries.

You may want a small medical kit and, naturally, any personal medication. If you bring anything that requires batteries, bring backup batteries. If you bring a radio, bring earphones (a major reason most people go to sporting camps is to get away from noise). Many camps, but not all, have libraries, and most have board games. Some camps rent mountain bikes; nearly all rent boats. For most camps, there's no point in packing a hair dryer or electric razor or anything else electrical. Most of all, don't forget to bring your sense of adventure, sense of humor, and sense of wonder!

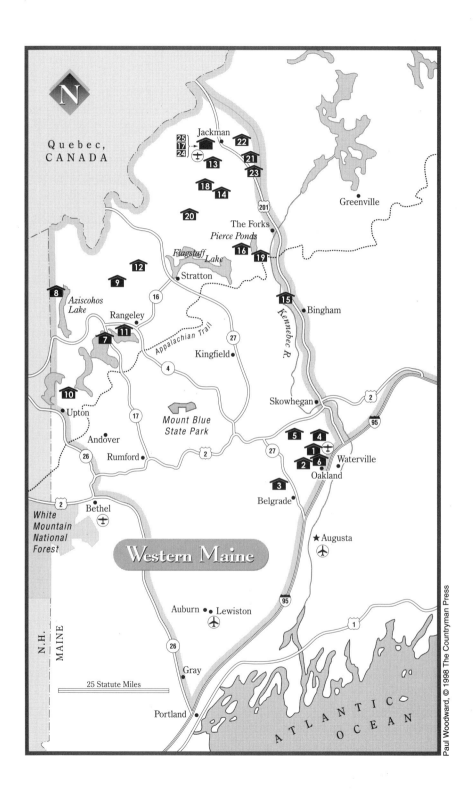

PART ONE
WESTERN MAINE

This region includes the Belgrade Lakes region to the south, the Rangeley Lakes region in the west near the New Hampshire border, and the Dead River–Jackman region between ME 27 and US 201.

The Belgrade Lakes Region

This region is the "southern" area of our sporting-camp inventory. Located about half an hour north of Augusta, Maine's state capital, it is made up of a chain of seven lakes and gently rolling hills and fields, and it is near many cultural and tourist attractions. All the sporting camps listed here are easily accessible by car or regularly scheduled plane flights.

The area was once the fishing, hunting, and farming terrain of the Abenaki Indians and was settled by Europeans in the 1700s. Belgrade mills, orchards, and farms provided goods that were carried by train to cities. By the early 1900s, those railway lines brought children to one of the couple of dozen summer camps ranged around the various lakes. Sporting camps and grand hotels popped up to service the rich and famous (and not-so-rich-and-famous). The area inspired the film *On Golden Pond* (parts of the movie were shot at Great Pond and Long Pond).

The Belgrade chain—East, North, Great, Long, McGrath, and Salmon Ponds and Messalonskee Lake—is part of the 177-square-mile Messalonskee Stream drainage, a tributary of the Kennebec River, which flows into the Atlantic. The lakes range in depth from 133 feet in Messalonskee Lake to 20 feet in North Pond. At least 20 different species of fish can be found in the Belgrade Lakes, including large- and smallmouth bass, pike, perch, brown trout, salmon, and brook trout.

Visitors to the area will find opportunities for hiking (Mount Pisgah, Mount Philip, Mount Tom, French's Mountain, Blueberry

Hill), golfing, cultural events, and festivals all within a half hour's easy drive. Highlights of a Belgrade summer include a children's pet show and a loon-calling contest, a ride on the mailboat that tours Great Pond daily, and outdoor concerts at the New England Music Camp on Messalonskee Lake.

Getting there: Augusta is the nearest airport to the Belgrade Lakes region (with connecting flights from Boston; rental cars available). Driving time from Augusta is 35 minutes; from Portland, 1.5 hours; from Boston, 4 hours; from New York City, 8 hours.

Guidance: For further information, contact Belgrade Lakes Region, Inc., PO Box 72, Belgrade, ME 04917; 207-465-3406. During the summer, there is an information booth on the right side of ME 27 as you drive north from Augusta, about 3 miles from the village of Belgrade.

1. ALDEN CAMPS

AP, SCA

OWNERS: Vesta and George Putnam

ADDRESS: RFD #2, Box 1140, Oakland, ME 04963; 207-465-7703

SEASON: May 17 through September 27

ACCOMMODATIONS: 18 log cabins (one to three bedrooms) with indoor plumbing, shower, screened porch, woodstove or Franklin fireplace, electric lights, small refrigerator

RATES: $50–130 per person per day; $300–780 per person per week; canoes free

ACCESS: I-95 north to exit 33. Take a right onto ME 137 west and go 2 miles into the town of Oakland. Go straight through town (between the Mobil gas station on your left and Charlie's Log Cabin on your right). At the four-way stop sign, continue straight on ME 137 west. In about 4 miles, you will see the D&L Country Store on your right. Alden Camps is 1 mile past D&L on the right.

Vesta and George Putnam's pale blue farmhouse, surrounded by flowers, sits close to ME 137, just 7 miles—but a world away—from I-95. A screened-in porch takes up the entire side of a long ell. There, white wicker chairs and sofas provide a place for guests to gather and visit. Inside is a small living room adjacent to the pine-paneled dining room and the office where you sign in. Opposite the house is a long, mowed field with a basketball court in the distance and a swing set in

The porch at Alden's

the foreground (baseball, volleyball, badminton, tetherball, croquet, and horseshoe equipment are available). A red barn provides the setting for weekly lobster dinners. Beyond the barn is a clay tennis court and vegetable garden "for the enjoyment and education of the children who come here from the city," the Putnams explain.

Down the driveway, the guest cabins are set among a grove of old pines. In 1911, two years after Fred Allen, Vesta's uncle, bought the 40-acre site, he built four cabins and some tent platforms and opened up for business.

Vesta: "My uncle was killed in an automobile accident in 1922 when his family was very young. So my aunt ran the camps for quite a long time when she was left a widow. Then her eldest son ran it. But after she passed away, he decided that he didn't want to run the camps anymore. That's when his sister, Ellen Reed, and I started out."

George: "Vesta and I met at Colby College [15 minutes away], where I majored in chemistry. I then went on to MIT and became a chemical engineer working for an oil company in New Jersey. We were married in 1937 and didn't come here until 1956."

Vesta: "When Ellen and I took over, George was still working and we needed to have a man to help with things. Our current manager is Wendy Coons Wentworth, and her father was our first manager. We moved here full time in 1967. We have five children and they've all worked here. Four of our grandchildren, Carter, Chris, Garret, and Melissa, have worked here; Carter is assistant manager. We plan to keep the business in the family."

Vesta: "East Pond is the headwaters of the Belgrade Lakes. When people are from out of state, we call it East Lake so they don't think it's a puddle. People came here to fish primarily for smallmouth bass. We have largemouth now, too." *George:* "Largemouth are supposed to be the gamiest. When they hit, you know it. They're a lot of fun. We also have perch, pickerel, and bullheads or horn pout."

Alden's has seen four generations of management, guests, and staff. *Wendy:* "I try to hire by attitude. You can show somebody how to wait on a table or make a bed, but you can't show somebody how to give a darn that guests have a good time—you know, how to pick up what to do to make it special for them. I always try to encourage initiative. You try to hire people you're going to be able to trust and then you go ahead and trust them. You have high expectations, which people will try to live up to, and you point out what they do right. If they do something wrong, you don't pick the one little thing and criticize it, you give them an overview. I think the whole idea of the hospitality industry is to make people feel comfortable. At camp we're laid back enough so that people can relax, but we do things nicely. The cabins are rustic and simple but we have maid service. People come up to breakfast and when they go back they have fresh towels and their beds are made. It's civilized.

"The regulars come here and they 'instant relax' because they know this is the place they do that. The new guests, who have often come from an urban area, have been traveling for hours, usually on a Saturday in heavy traffic, maybe with screaming children. When they get here they sometimes are stressed out, hot, tired, maybe angry. But if you can please them on Saturday night, they are, in fact, going to be happy. So you try to do back handsprings to accommodate these people and usually by about Monday they start to loosen up. A lot of people—we're in such a competitive society—think you've got to be hard-nosed to get what you want. Whereas with us, if you just say please, you're going to get it as fast as if you slammed your fist on the counter. With our staff, you can pass them on the path and they'll be all ready to go on their water-ski run for their break, but if they notice your water jug is empty, they'll go get you some ice. That's what I mean by hiring by attitude."

East Pond is the locale of several children's summer camps, and seasonal private cottages dot the shoreline. Moose frequent a boggy area beyond camp, and where East Pond flows into North Pond is a meandering waterway rich with wildlife called the Serpentine. The camp offers waterskiing every afternoon (weather permitting). Two golf courses (one 18-hole, one 9-hole) are 15 minutes away.

Most sporting camps serve one or two entrées a night. Alden's has six or more on the menu and serves dinner for people in the area. Chef Ellen Kiser always prepares a vegetarian dish.

Vegetable-Stuffed Portobello Mushrooms

¼ cup oil, 2 T minced garlic, ¼ cup minced shallots, 1 cup grated carrot, 10 broccoli flowerets, ½ cup diced celery, ½ cup diced sweet red pepper, 4 cups bread crumbs, ½ cup grated Parmesan cheese, 6 large portobello mushrooms, ¼–½ cup vegetable broth or white wine

Sauté all vegetables in oil. Add the cheese and bread crumbs. Add broth or wine to moisten and hold together. Stuff mushrooms with mixture. Bake at 325 degrees for 30 minutes. Serves 6.

2. BEAR SPRING CAMPS

AP, SCA
MANAGERS: Ron and Peg Churchill
ADDRESS: RR 3, Box 9900, Oakland, ME 04963; 207-397-2341
SEASON: May 15 through October 1
ACCOMMODATIONS: 32 log and cedar-clapboard cabins with indoor plumbing, shower, electric lights, automatic heat, small refrigerator, woodstove
RATES: $425–1,600 per cabin per week
ACCESS: I-95 to exit 31B. Follow ME 27 north for 17 miles through Belgrade (last stop for shopping before camp). Turn right onto ME 225 east (sign will say TO ROME, where camps are located; mail goes to Oakland). Follow ME 225 for 4.5 miles to Jamaica Point Road. Turn right. Camp is ¼ mile on the right.

As you descend the hill and round the curve into Bear Spring Camps, a pastoral view opens up before you. A rambling, white-clapboard farmhouse is set amid 400 acres of woods and lush green fields. Its red roof and pots of flowers color the landscape. Bluebird boxes and a swing set stand ready for occupants. A long dirt road leads down the field on the left, past a clay tennis court, to dark brown cabins and an expanse of lake. Stop at the farmhouse, go into the screened-in porch, and check in with Peg at the office. *Peg:* "I see what people have in mind so I can help them with a fishing license, or general information. Then they follow my car down to their cabin. Each cabin has its own dock and boat."

The cabins range around the North Bay of Great Pond—at 9 by 6 miles, the largest of the Belgrade Lakes. The shoreline is grassy, with about 2 feet of sand that continues underwater in a gentle slope for easy swimming. *Ron:* "We have 2800 feet of continuous shorefront. Then we own another 900 feet which goes to Meadow Stream. Beyond that is bog which can't be developed, so this all looks pristine and will stay that way." Meadow Stream—a marshy area full of wildlife—is navigable, in a ribbon-candy kind of way, for some distance. "People fish for bass here primarily, and in the last few years, they're also fishing for pike. Pike are bony but very sweet, like a pickerel. In the early spring, if they're not using live bait, they'll use just the biggest, ugliest lure they've got in their boxes. They're big, so they're fun to fish for."

Peg's mother, Marguerite Mosher, offers insight into the camp's history: "My husband Burt's father and his grandfather, George, came up here in 1910. George Mosher went to Connecticut, made and lost a fortune, came back, and bought the original old farmhouse here. Within a year or so they had built a couple of camps and rented them. Up where our dining room is now there was a summer kitchen. Probably put wood in it in the winter. I came here in 1942. Waited tables. Back in the '30s and '40s, all the young people in the area worked at local jobs: canning factories and sporting camps. Every town, nearly, had a canning factory. Around here they canned vegetables. And there were a lot of sporting camps then, an awful lot. There are housekeeping camps still around. But the old resorts like ours mostly have been made into condos."

Ron: "Peg and I came here in 1984 because Peg missed the sunsets and sunrises and evenings on the porch." *Peg:* "I was literally crying to get back. I was brought up here so I knew what I was getting in for. But Ron didn't." Ron laughs. "No, I didn't at all!"

Ron says he trailed Marguerite's late husband around for several years and learned on the job. Now, with two young children, up to 130 guests, three dozen boats to maintain, and 25 staff to oversee, that early training has proved invaluable.

Ron and Peg's children, Abby and Spencer, are an integral part of the camp scene. *Peg:* "Families love it here. We have swings, a driving range, tennis court, badminton, volleyball court, horseshoes, basketball, walking trails, and the swimming and boating. Also, a lot of people come in the spring for a month before most of our families arrive and again for another month in the fall after school starts. It's pretty much the same people from all over New England, and recently folks from Maryland and Virginia."

Ron: "This area of Maine has a true chain of lakes." *Marguerite:* "They used to do a tour of the lakes. Alden Camps is on East Pond, so that's the headwaters right there. That dumps into North Pond, which flows down here into Meadow Stream, which you can portage to. McGrath and Salmon Ponds come into this lake halfway down." *Ron:* "Great Pond then flows into Long Pond, which leads to Belgrade Stream and Messalonskee Lake, and then Messalonskee Stream, which leads to the Kennebec River, which flows into the Atlantic Ocean!"

Ron: " The only thing that upsets me is fear of being sued. People seem to take less and less responsibility for their own actions. They feel that if something happens to them, it's someone else's fault instead of just an accident. If we have to start locking doors, or whatever, I think that's the thing that will close Bear Spring. It won't be because we're tired of the work or anything, it'll be because of the liability."

Peg: "It's expensive to run a camp. We spend around $100,000 a summer, just on payroll. And we're being overregulated. We've had to make ourselves handicapped accessible, we've had water regulations, and the big issue is that property taxes are going up all the time. We are the stewards of a lot of land. What with inheritance taxes and property taxes and offers of huge sums by developers, what are the incentives to keep these large parcels of land undeveloped?"

Ron: "So we've set up a fund for unexpected expenses. It's like our kids' college fund—we're putting a little into it each year. That way, if something happens, you don't go into shock and get depressed, and you don't resent the guests or have to take out a loan or close up. But you can't focus on the bad or you wouldn't stay in business at all, because there's so much crazy stuff that happens. But so much good happens, you just go on from there."

Marguerite: "We're trying to maintain a good way of life. Our guests feel that when they come here. In 1942, when I was first waiting tables, I remember I went down to the lake to sit on a cabin porch one afternoon. Nice day, just like this. And I said, 'Oh God, I wish I could live here the rest of my life,'" she laughs. "And I guess God heard me!"

Chocolate Denver Pudding

> ¾ cup white sugar, 1 cup flour, 2 tsp. baking powder, 1 ounce unsweetened chocolate (or 3 T unsweetened cocoa), 2 T melted butter, ½ tsp. vanilla, ½ cup milk

Sift sugar, flour, baking powder (and salt to taste if desired). Melt butter and chocolate (or cocoa) together. Add to flour mixture. Add milk and vanilla and pour into a 9x9-inch buttered pan. Combine and scatter over the top: ½ cup white sugar, ½ cup brown sugar, 4 T unsweetened cocoa. Pour over top: 1½ cups cold coffee or water. Bake at 350 degrees for 40 minutes. Serve warm with ice cream or whipped cream.

3. CASTLE ISLAND CAMPS

AP

OWNERS: Horatio and Valerie Castle
ADDRESS: PO Box 251, Belgrade Lakes, ME 04918; 207-495-3312
WINTER ADDRESS: 1800 Carambola Road, Lake Clarke Shores, West Palm Beach, FL 33406; 561-641-8339
SEASON: May through October
ACCOMMODATIONS: 12 cabins (painted white, with gray paneling on the inside), with indoor plumbing, shower, screened porch, automatic heat, electric lights, small refrigerator, bottled water
RATES: $58 per person per day; $399 per person per week
ACCESS: I-95 to exit 31B. Turn left onto ME 27 west and go 12.3 miles to a left-hand turn, where a sign reads CASTLE ISLAND CAMPS. Go straight at an intersection, then down the hill through a grove of pines. The road narrows as it crosses the water; the camps come up quickly on the right.

Castle Island Camps nestle in a causeway between two sections of 12-mile Long Pond. Picture them in the middle of a figure 8 and you'll have the idea. Everything is within easy reach, including the Castle's solicitous hospitality. The atmosphere is homey and the attention to detail evident.

Horatio: "When my father, Leighton Castle, bought this 1-acre parcel from the state there was nothing on it. This was back in the mid-1920s. He was brought here by his parents from Brooklyn, New

Ready for fishing at Castle Island Camps

York. They wanted to get out of the city and buy a farm and become farmers. And they did. Their farm is right up the road here. My father built this right from the beginning as a fishing camp. He cut what is now cabin number 5 in two with a handsaw and brought it over to the island; built one cabin at a time and just kept adding on. He lived here in the summertime and opened for business in 1929. Then he sold to a cousin in 1947 because of heart trouble, and my cousin ran it until 1970. My wife and I and my brother and his wife bought it together as a joint venture. My brother originally started here; he helped my father build this place. But after five years we found it was a starving proposition with two couples trying to survive."

Valerie: "So this is our 27th year here. When we started, our children were 7 and 8. Our son worked for us until he was 30."

Horatio: "This place was always a tug at my heartstrings when I came here as a kid and my cousin was running it. When I was 7 years old my father sold it. 'Course 7 years old, it's kind of hard to tear away from a place like this! And so all those years, through school and everything else, we used to spend summers up here on another lake nearby. And as we came through here I always wished I'd been old enough to buy it. In 1970 I got the opportunity to come back. I was an engineer with Florida Power and Light Company, and I said good-bye to that."

Valerie: "Horatio's brother's wife and I had mixed emotions. When we started out, we didn't know anything about running a camp. You're working so long and hard, with little children, and you have no social life with each other because there are people constantly around."

Horatio: "It was the school of hard knocks to get it going. You have to be psychologist, mother, father, and everything to everybody when they come here. This business isn't like a lot of other businesses. I don't know about other sporting camps, but here, where everything is so close, we kind of live with our people. We're here in the evening with them. We greet them, we spend half an hour in orientation with new people to try to make them welcome, and so we feel as though they're a part of our family when they're here.

"One of the things I joke with people about is I don't condone divorce, but it has turned out to be very good for our business because we end up with two families coming here instead of one. I'm serious! I've got about two dozen of these situations where people still come back with their new husbands or wives. The problem is you can't book them at the same time. You make sure they cross somewhere on Route 95! The thing is, the kids make out great because they come with one set of parents and then come back again with another set! Overall, we have about 90 percent repeat business with people coming mostly from New Jersey, Massachusetts, New York, and Connecticut, and the rest from all over."

Castle Island Camps are located at the Narrows. On one side is the more populated shore of Long Pond, including the village of Belgrade; on the other is a section of uninhabited shoreline and marshy area for wildlife. Both areas produce trophy fish. *Horatio:* "This is one of the three best salmon lakes in the State of Maine. We produced more record fish this year than the whole state produced in the last three years. We have just about everything here: landlocked salmon, brook trout, northern pike, large- and smallmouth bass, pickerel, white and yellow perch, shiners, sunfish, everything, even catfish. I was talking to my brother not long ago about the fishing here when he was a kid—he's 19 years older than I am—and he said the fishing is as good, if not better, than it was then, because now the trend is catch-and-release."

The proof of a well-run camp is in the details, and Horatio and Valerie are able to oversee the minutiae of management from their centrally located lodge surrounded by guest cabins. Horatio cooks breakfast and does the grilling, Valerie does the preparing and dessert. She laughs, "Sometimes we'd lose track of what day it was if it wasn't for what we're serving for dinner."

Horatio: "We pride ourselves in the quality of our food, and the quantity—everyone can have as many helpings as they want."

Castle Island Fish Chowder

Horatio's father's recipe for fish chowder is served every Sunday night at the camp.

> 1 large Spanish onion, 4 baking potatoes (size 90), ¼ pound butter,
> 2½ pounds of haddock fillets, 1 quart whole milk

Slice potatoes and onion and add them to a pot with about 1 inch of water (too much water will make chowder too thin). Cook slowly, stirring regularly to prevent burning, and gradually blend in butter with simmering vegetables. Remove from heat when vegetables are well done but not mushy.

While the vegetables are cooking, put the haddock fillets in a second pot and cover with water. Poach slowly (just below a simmer) until the fillets are flaky and fully cooked (will take about half an hour). Remove from heat and drain off all liquid from poached fish.

Flake the fillets into small chunks and add to the pot containing the vegetables. Stir in 1 quart of milk and heat to serving temperature very slowly over a low heat. Do not boil. Add salt and pepper to taste and serve. Serves 6.

4. SADULSKY'S

HK

OWNERS: Walter and Viola Sadulsky
ADDRESS: RR 1, Box 3300, Smithfield, ME 04978; 207-362-2376
SEASON: Memorial Day through Labor Day
ACCOMMODATIONS: 16 cabins (two to three bedrooms; some half-log, some tongue-and-groove redwood siding), with indoor plumbing, shower, electricity, hookup for telephone; bring own linen and towels
RATES: $422 per two-bedroom cabin per week; $450 per three-bedroom cabin per week
ACCESS: I-95 to exit 33. Follow ME 137 west 2 miles into the town of Oakland. Go straight through town. At the four-way stop sign, continue straight, rejoining ME 137. In about 4 miles, turn right at D&L Country Store onto East Pond Road and go 4 miles. The sign and driveway for the camp are on the right. Stop at the white farmhouse on the right. This is the Sadulskys' home, and guests check in at the office here.

Viola and Walter Sadulsky run a low-profile operation. They don't advertise; they don't even have a brochure. But they do have a loyal clientele, and word of mouth has brought them the volume of business that suits this hardworking couple. They have two daughters and a son and nine great-granddaughters. When peers have long retired, they still do most of the work around the place themselves. Walter was mowing a lawn when I toured the camp. As we chatted, he stooped to pick up a cigarette butt, saying, "I hate these things." It was the only one I saw on the immaculately kept premises. Cabins are ranged around a central lawn area with a few chairs, swings, a 40-year-old play gym, and a gently sloping beach. There is a dock and a couple of boats. There is a feeling of airiness (although the long driveway is through the woods and the cabins are surrounded by trees) and of quiet ("no loud parties or hippies," Walter says). They allow cats but no other pets. "This is a family-oriented camp," Viola explains. "We have a lot of season people. They come and stay for a while: A couple from Florida stay 3 months; the ones from Georgia have been coming up for 20 years. Most come from Pennsylvania, New Jersey, and Florida."

Walter and Viola are both native to the area. Walter used to do trucking and road repair. Viola was a nurse. "When Walter was single he used to come in here fishing. Then, in the 1920s, there was just a quarter-mile path down to East Pond. There was an old man who rented boats for 50 cents a day. The farmhouse we're living in was Mrs. Hanninger's home. We bought it in '48 and first rented boats. Then the fishermen wanted to bring their families and we made a beach for the kids. Then people wanted a place to stay, so we started building cabins. Next thing we knew, we had a business! We built the first cabin in '54 and the last in '74."

The camps flourished in the 1970s, when nearby Colby College held a 10-week course for ophthalmologists from around the country, who would come and bring their families. *Viola:* "Now the course is for seven weeks and it's mostly attended by young men in their 20s. But during that earlier time we had four couples from Alabama who wanted to come and we didn't have any room. They wanted to be here so badly they said they'd pay in part to put up a building. So we made two buildings, divided in two, with bedrooms on either side. These were our last cabins. They have electric heating units because the carpenters didn't have time to put in chimneys before the couples were due to arrive."

Walter and Viola have spent all their married lives running the camps and have seen a lot of water go under the dam—or under the docks, to be more precise. "Our biggest challenge," says Viola, "is Mother Nature. When the ice is breaking up, if there is a west wind, it gets under the docks and lifts them up. We've been here over 40 years, and this is the first year we haven't had to deal with damaged docks."

5. SUNSET CAMPS

HK

OWNERS: Mike and Ellie Zarcone
ADDRESS: PO Box 68, Smithfield, ME 04978; 207-362-2611
SEASON: Year-round
ACCOMMODATIONS: 18 cabins (one to three bedrooms) with indoor plumbing, central quarter-metered showers, screened porch, gas for cooking and heating; bring linens, blankets or sleeping bags, towels
RATES: $385 per cabin per week
ACCESS: I-95 to exit 33. Turn left onto ME 137. Go west on ME 137 for 12 miles, through Oakland, to the village of Smithfield. The camps are right in town past the village store, on the left-hand side.

Sunset Camps, a family-oriented cabin community established in 1914, is right in the village of Smithfield. While not remote or made of logs, the camp is the only one listed in this book for the Belgrade area that is open in winter for snowmobilers and ice fishermen. Convenient to supplies and food and easily accessible in winter, it is located on either side of the inlet leading into North Pond. Campers walk from one side to the other by way of a picturesque covered bridge the owners built.

In the summer, fishermen can catch large- and smallmouth bass, white and yellow perch, pickerel, and northern pike from 3-mile-long, 1½-mile-wide, 20-foot-deep North Pond.

In the winter, local snowmobile trails lead directly to the state's extensive International Trail System (ITS). An ITS trail map is available from the Department of Inland Fisheries and Wildlife, Augusta, ME 04330.

6. WOODREST

HK

OWNERS: Tom and Jan Barton
ADDRESS: RR 2, Box 4690, Belgrade, ME 04917; 207-465-2950 (camp); 207-453-7513 (winter)
SEASON: May through September
ACCOMMODATIONS: Nine cabins (one or two bedrooms; one cabin with a loft sleeps five to eight) with woodstove or open fireplace, gas stove, refrigerator; bring sheets and towels; pets (well behaved and on a leash) allowed
RATES: $65 per couple per day; $425–535 per couple per week.
ACCESS: I-95 to exit 33. Go west on ME 137 for 4 miles through Oakland. Turn left at McGrath Pond Road. Proceed 2 miles to the Woodrest sign (with loon) on the left.

As you come down the hill leading into camp, Woodrest's rambling log lodge comes into view on the right. On the left, a line of log cabins veers off to the water's edge. Each cabin sits up on posts and has a screened-in porch and its own picnic table. A swath of lawn sports a big stone barbecue fireplace, two swing sets (according to Jan, "one for the little ones and one for big kids"), a basketball hoop, badminton net, and horseshoe pits. To the right are more log cabins. The cabins have a combined living room, dining and kitchen area, a gas cookstove, bedroom(s), and bathroom with shower.

A dock with boats floats in McGrath Pond, which, together with connecting Salmon Pond, forms Woodrest's waterway. The two lakes together are 5 miles long by up to 1 mile wide. In terms of fishing Jan says, "We have everything but pike."

The camps have been around since the late 1920s (Jan has an advertisement from 1928). Tom and Jan bought the camps in 1982. They had had a cottage "on the other side of Salmon" and were running a 200-site, 500-acre campground. *Jan:* "It was just too much to deal with. It wasn't in the area and it took too much of our time away from raising our family."

Jan is from the area and her father had a hand, back in the 1940s, in constructing her present abode. "My father helped rebuild the main lodge here. Two weeks before opening day the lodge burned down. Well, they hired 40 men who worked around the clock. By the time opening day came, two weeks later, the lodge was done, kitchen and all!"

Jan is president of Belgrade Lakes Region, Inc., a volunteer organization that promotes the accommodation and business facilities in the area. The most visible activity of the group is its information booth on ME 27, open Saturdays 10–5 during the season, as well as some weekdays during the summer. The number for the booth is 207-495-2744. The organization also maintains a Web site: www.mint.net/belgrade.

The Rangeley Lakes Region

Moving inland and upland, we come to the major chain of lakes that makes up this region: Parmachenee, Aziscohos, Umbagog, Lower and Upper Richardson, Mooselookmeguntic, Cupsuptic, Rangeley, and Kennebago. Whereas the Belgrade region is primarily pastoral, the Rangeley area is mountainous. This region is bounded to the west by ME 26 and to the east by ME 27 and contains the headwaters for the Androscoggin River, which flows to the sea. The Appalachian Mountains and Trail run through it, and Maine's major ski areas can also be found here. About 100 lakes and ponds lie within the region, and half a dozen more lie within 10 miles of the village of Rangeley, where a traveler can find cultural offerings and all the basic amenities. For specific information, visit or contact the Rangeley Chamber of Commerce (207-864-5364), located in the heart of downtown Rangeley at the public boat landing and parking area. Moored along the pier in this same complex are floatplanes available for scenic tours or lifts to remote lakes or sporting camps. Once airborne, you will be able to get an overview (literally) of the intersecting lakes and topographical features of this region. Many people prefer to fly to their chosen sporting camp. For those coming from a distance, it is certainly the quickest way to get there. Camp owners can suggest the air service they use.

To get a stunning view of the lakes without going up in a plane, drive on Route 27 to a point called, appropriately, Height O' Land (directions are available from the chamber of commerce). Keep in mind, as you look down, that much of the waterway was originally about 20 feet lower. Logging companies put in a number of dams in the mid-1800s in order to float logs to their mills.

The village of Oquossoc has shops, restaurants, boat and snowmobile services, and a gas station, and is home to the Rangeley Lakes Heritage Trust. Thanks to the efforts of people involved with this land trust, founded in 1991, more than 10,000 acres of land have been preserved, much of it adjacent to land owned by sporting camps in this area. For more information, write to the trust at PO Box 249, Oquossoc, ME 04964; 207-864-7311.

Andover is a stop-off point for Appalachian Trail hikers, who take advantage of the chance to resupply here and perhaps to recharge at one of the restaurants in town. The community is home to Telstar, one of the earliest satellite-tracking stations, which rises out of the landscape like a giant golf ball. The village of Upton sits high on the crest of a hill with gorgeous views leading down to Lake Umbagog. Both Upton and Wilson Mills, farther north, are small, with only very basic facilities for the traveler. To get a good sense of this area, read Louise Dickinson Rich's book, *We Took to the Woods*.

This is primarily trout- and salmon-fishing country. The hiking is plentiful and can be challenging, if so desired. The area is recognized as a fall-foliage destination, and in winter is popular with snow-mobilers for its hundreds of miles of trails.

Getting there: The Rangeley Lakes region can be reached by flying into either Portland or Augusta and then connecting with the local air service, Mountain Air Company (207-864-5307), or by renting a car. Driving time from Portland is 3–4 hours; from Boston, 5–6 hours; from New York City, 9–10 hours.

7. BALD MOUNTAIN CAMPS

AP

OWNER: Stephen Philbrick

ADDRESS: PO Box 332, Oquossoc, ME 04964; 207-864-3671 (camp); 207-864-3788 (winter); e-mail: baldmtcamp@aol.com

SEASON: May through September

ACCOMMODATIONS: 15 log cabins (one to three bedrooms), indoor plumbing, shower, electric lights, woodstove, ice buckets filled daily

RATES: $100 per person per day

ACCESS: Maine Turnpike (I-495) to exit 12 (Auburn). Take ME 4 north to Oquossoc. Continue on ME 4 to the end (just before the boat landing). Turn left onto Bald Mountain Road and go ¾ mile to the camp, on the right. From exit 12 at Auburn, you can also take ME 2 to ME 17 north to Oquossoc.

S*tephen:* "Bald Mountain Camps was established in 1897. This summer we are celebrating our 100th birthday. Governor Angus King came and helped us celebrate, and this is the year we started our horseback riding program. My wife, Fernlyn, and I have wanted to have riding here for a long time and couldn't think of a better time to do it. I'm only the fifth owner in all these years. I bought it from my grandparents, who came up here in the early 1920s and ran it for 50 years. My grandmother's father, Charlie Jacques, worked for the Boston & Maine Railroad and was responsible for putting in the railroad from Oquossoc to Kennebago. You used to be able to get on a train in Baltimore at 7 AM on Friday, have three meals served to you, sleep in a Pullman car, and be here for your summer vacation by 7 AM Saturday. The trains went out in 1889 and it's a shame because it's a sensible and great way to travel.

"My grandfather came up here with his dad as a logger when he was a teenager, became a registered Maine guide, and then worked here as a cabin boy and guide. He met my grandmother, and they settled in and bought the place. My grandparents were Mainers, French Canadian folks. Their daughter was my mother and we were here for vacations, summers. Fernlyn and I have two boys, Tyler and Quinn. We have two other businesses in the area and my wife takes care of those while I mostly take care of this. We live here on the property year-round.

"Ed Wharf, who started this place, decided to build a camp strictly for sportsmen. Back then everybody came down to Haines Landing (around the corner) by the train and dispersed out through the lake

Bald Mountain Camps

on old steamships. We are on Mooselookmeguntic Lake, which is 17 miles long by 5 miles wide and 126 feet deep and has salmon and trout. I encourage catch-and-release. In fact, I'd go a couple of steps further. I believe that the best way to get our lakes back in order is to specifically designate areas in the State of Maine closed completely to any keeping of fish. I could sell my product as a businessman far better if, for instance, when I go to the sportsmen's shows in the wintertime, I'm able to say to prospective guests, 'You can't take any fish home, but you're going to have trophy fishing up here.' I can't do that now.

"Even though I grew up here, I went to college for this—majored in business and hotel administration. Business has increased in a number of ways. We offer fly-in fishing trips to different ponds and streams throughout the region. I have two flying services and three guides and I'm also a registered Maine guide and pilot. So when I have the time, I take them myself. But I don't fish with them, just deposit them and then come back and do my work. I haven't wet a fly in several years. The free time I do have I spend with my boys and my wife. Also, my dinner business has quadrupled. We're getting a lot of outside folks. We do one seating, 16 tables, and then sell all the tables that aren't locked up by our guests. We also do a lot of catering. Our dining room looks out to the west onto 10 miles of protected shoreline and some spectacular sunsets. On Fridays we have a real old-fashioned guide's barbecue with blueberry pancakes for dessert. Our regular menu includes meals like grilled pheasant, trout baked on a cedar plank, lobster scampi, and so forth.

"I've been involved with this business ever since I was a little kid and saw what it was like, at the end of the '50s, when the American Plan was on the decline. Jet travel, the ability to travel all over the world, developed about that time. Now I'm seeing the American Plan coming back. Folks are spending their dollars at places like this throughout the country where they can be served and treated like they want to be treated. It's not just rush in, rush out.

"I've considered winterizing because snowmobiling is a big thing around here. But it's not cost-effective. The low-end cost per cabin to insulate and winterize would be $65,000. Per cabin. Remember these were all built at the turn of the century. Speaking of winter, what we offer here is ice on your porch with fresh springwater twice a day in lieu of a refrigerator. Our lakes are still very clean up here, and in the winter we cut the ice when it's 18 inches thick. We clear it off with a truck plow, shovel it by hand, and then score it so it looks like a big checkerboard. The chain saw cuts down 10 inches and then we cut down the last 8 inches with a handsaw. We chip them off as square blocks, and they come up a mechanized conveyor belt, slide down into a truck, and are hauled off to our icehouse. We'll take out as many as 2,800 cakes of ice. We have this for guests and also use it in our three walk-in coolers, which are lined with sawdust to retain the cold. We cook with gas, so if the power should go out, we have refrigeration and can cook. We just light some candles and keep going.

"I believe families are wanting to be together more. And the things that they're looking for are rustic cabins with fireplaces, which we have; a sandy beach for the kids to play on, which we have; and sailboats and Windsurfers. They're not really into motorboats unless it's to use the water skis. I have games and books for the kids while their folks are finishing dinner. So it's a family focus. It's a nice community, a nice group of people. And as for the regulars, they've watched people come here, grow old here, and die here. It's just a natural progression in places like this."

Grilled Thyme Pheasant

> 4 pheasants (18–20 ounces), 1 cup white wine, ½ cup olive oil, ¼ cup
> lemon juice, 1 T thyme, salt and pepper to taste

Prepare pheasants by removing backbone with a pair of poultry shears. Then re-move wishbone and breastbone with a boning knife. Mix all remaining ingredi-ents in a large bowl. Marinate pheasants in the liquid for 12 hours or overnight. Preheat grill. Cook pheasants on skin side for 6–7 minutes, then finish on the other side for 10–15 minutes or until juices run clear.

8. BOSEBUCK MOUNTAIN CAMPS

AP, SCA

OWNERS: Bob and Diane Schyberg
ADDRESS: PO Box 1213, Rangeley, ME 04970; 207-446-2825 (camp);
207-474-5903 (reservations and information)
SEASON: Year-round
ACCOMMODATIONS: 10 cabins (one or two bedrooms) with woodstove or
gas heater, gas and electric lights, indoor plumbing and shower, screened-in
porch; pets accepted if they are well behaved and kept on a leash
RATES: $85–100 per person per day; boats $35 per day; canoes free
ACCESS: Maine Turnpike (I-495) to exit 12 (Auburn). Take ME 4 to
Rangeley (approximately 88 miles). Continue 9 miles to Oquossoc, then
take ME 16 for 15 miles to Wilsons Mills. Turn right at the sign for the
camps onto a gravel road. Go 13 miles to the camp driveway on your right.

When I drove into Bosebuck, the place was a flurry of activity. The road had just been graded. One man was shoveling ditches, another was chopping wood. Carpenters were working on porches and roofs. But the most dramatic sight was the main lodge, jacked up so you could see through to the lawn and lake beyond. Tom Rideout was over-seeing the face-lift. While clearly elated that the camp was undergoing such an impressive renewal, it was equally clear that he was going to miss the place after 25 years of guiding and owning Bosebuck him-self. Tom assures me the camp will enjoy a graceful transition, since Diane and Bob Schyberg were guests for years before becoming the owners in 1997.

Tom says the camp got its name in the 1920s, when a group from the US Geological Survey got caught in a blizzard one late October, with close to 4 feet of snow. "They started running low on food, and it seems they had a dog named Bow that killed a deer in the deep snow. So when they started naming different places, they called this Bow's Buck Mountain."

Bob: "The camps were originally built in 1909 by Fern Lewhill and his partner and guide, Perley Flint. Perley won fly-casting competitions at the various sportsmen's expos and helped drum up guests. He bought the camps from Lewhill in 1911 for $500 and started building cabins, which were paid for by the more affluent regulars who used them on an annual basis. The camp sits on 25 acres with frontage on Aziscohos Lake. It's strategically located at the confluence of the Big and Little Magalloway Rivers in a 250,000-acre watershed. This is wilderness land protected for a hundred years or more, first by private ownership and by its remoteness, and now by restricted access and conservation regulations by the state, under the Trophy Trout Waters Initiative. To get to the Upper Magalloway we have access to the private gate system under special agreement with the landowners.

"Aziscohos Lake was created for the logging industry in 1914. The dam changed the water level from 28 feet to an average of 45 feet. The lake and watershed support one of the healthiest wild populations of brook trout and landlocked salmon in the State of Maine.

"The area we're in is relatively unexplored by hikers and mountain bikers. We have one trail now, which is about 5 miles long. But we have a huge potential for hiking trails and want to go to the summit of Bosebuck Mountain [3,100 feet] and several other surrounding mountains. We want to encourage diversity in the use of this area beyond just hunting and fishing. We'd like to have a mix of customers, especially in July and August. We have great canoeing and kayaking and we're hoping to have remote wilderness campsites at the Upper Magalloway, accessible only by boat or hiking and only for our guests. It's the totality of the resources that brought us here.

"On the hunting side, the area's been famous for having big deer and moose, but it's also probably the best grouse and woodcock cover I've seen this side of Canada. We allow hunting dogs and help with maps. We actually specialize in guided hunts with our bird dogs, but it's also a good place to train your own young dogs, because the abundance of birds gives them a lot of experience quickly.

"As far as winter goes, we are the only sporting camp in the area open year-round. We're just off ITS 84, halfway between Pittsburg [New Hampshire] and Rangeley. The idea of a remote camp for snowmobilers is good because it provides an emergency phone, shelter, and food. But the most interesting thing is that because we will provide gas, people can now take side trips and explore virgin territory. We'd like to do cross-country skiing, snowshoeing, and I'd like to revive winter hiking—a sport that's harder than people think. We have a 15-mile lake with no ice fishing (there's none in the whole Rangeley area). We're open Thursdays through Sundays and holidays for meals and gas only."

One of the features of Bosebuck is its historic significance as a Native American camping area. Tom relates: "Back in 1980 a guide named Vale was searching for his lost lure and found some Indian artifacts. He showed them to an archaeologist named Dr. Michael Gramly, who explores what's now called the Vale Site every fall when the water's down. You can pick up artifacts on the surface, but you aren't allowed to dig. What we have here is a Paleo-Indian site, 10,500 to 11,000 years old. In the Maine State Museum in Augusta they have an exhibit called 'Twelve Thousand Years in Maine,' and I've contributed a lot of artifacts that Charlie Atkins, the game warden, and I found here. Dr. Gramly found the oldest man-made structure in the New World on this lake. It's a meat cache. The Indians put meat in a rock cairn—sort of a small cellar hole—threw another rock over the top of it, covered it up, and the permafrost would freeze it so when they returned the following year they'd have something to eat until the caribou started coming through again. And that opened the door for 50 years of visitation. You see, when they were here, the glaciers were still receding and this valley was a migration route for caribou. The hunters used this valley to ambush them. They used the natural barriers: a pond, river, or steep banks where the herds would slow down. The Indians stayed on the high banks, on the eastern shore, where the westerly wind kept the bugs off and they could observe the caribou as they migrated. Those high banks are just at water level now. In '81 they drained the lake to resurface the front of the dam, and you could see the original river channel and even the caribou trails in the lake bottom! It's the only documented place that has a habitation site and the kill site related to it. The Indians came here in the summertime. In the winter they lived on what is now the continental shelf.

"The Paleo-Indians were craftsmen at toolmaking. We look for tools like gravers [used to carve designs on wood or bone] made out of stone like obsidian. The next period were the Plano Indians, and they were the master craftsmen. After Plano were the Archaic, and then Woodland Ceramic, who used cheap flint and were so-called throwaway societies. They'd take any type of rock, as long as it had a flat edge to it, scrape the hide, and cast it aside, whereas the Paleo-Indians here revered their tools."

Diane: "It must be the isolation of this place that I love. It's so relaxing to hear the loons calling at night. We counted 17 nesting pairs on the lake. There's a women's group that comes in late July—a spiritual retreat, connecting with nature. And we have writers and artists. There's something about this area that seems to stimulate the creative impulses."

Stuffed Rainbow Trout

Diane says, "We can buy farm-raised trout. It's 2 hours away from us; but that's on the way to the grocery store, so it's not out of the way! Our supplier dips them out of his pond and cleans them while we wait."

Enough cleaned rainbow trout for each person to have one or two (leave heads and tails on), chopped celery, chopped onion, poultry seasoning, salt, butter

Sauté the celery, onion, seasoning, and salt in a little butter for a few minutes until just tender. Fill the cavity of each fish with this mixture. Wrap each fish in a piece of foil. Put the fish packets on a cookie sheet and bake 30–40 minutes at 375 degrees.

9. GRANT'S KENNEBAGO CAMPS

AP, SCA

OWNERS: John and Carolyn Blunt

MANAGERS: James and Beverly Collins

ADDRESS: PO Box 786, Rangeley, ME 04970; 1-800-633-4815; in Maine, 207-864-3608 (summer), 207-282-5264 (winter)

SEASON: May 23 through September

ACCOMMODATIONS: 18 knotty-pine cabins with indoor plumbing and shower, screened-in porch, woodstove or electric heat, electric lights, private dock with 16-foot Rangeley boat

RATES: $105–125 per person per day; boats: $50 per day; canoes: $10 per day

ACCESS: Maine Turnpike (I-495) to exit 12 (Auburn). Take ME 4 north to Rangeley (approximately 88 miles). Go through Rangeley on ME 4/16. At the junction of ME 4 and ME 16, bear right onto ME 16 and go 3 miles to a right-hand turn, where there's a sign for the camps. Check in at the gatehouse (before 6 PM), then drive 9 miles on a dirt road into camp. The road forks uphill to the right just before camp.

When you get to the end of the road, you've reached Grant's Kennebago Camps. The honey-colored pine cabins, each with its own dock, line up along the shore of Kennebago Lake. In the central dining room you'll find red-checked tablecloths, full picture windows, and panoramic views of the surrounding mountains. The main lodge, which houses the office, has a library and sitting area with games, a TV, and a selection of fishing videos.

John: "Grant's was built in 1905 by Ed Grant and was a combination of log cabins and cedar-sided stick-built cabins. Cabins 1 through 4 were used as lumber camps. He developed a sporting camp down on the other end of the lake first, and then migrated up here. Ed Grant was a great storyteller. Ever hear about the man who kept a pet trout in a rain barrel? Well, he'd dip out a little water each day, until finally the fish was at home on dry land. It followed the man around the yard, wore snowshoes in winter, and all went fine until one day it fell in the brook and drowned. That's the kind of tall tale he'd tell his 'sports.'

"In 1977 a fire destroyed about 70 percent of the old buildings. It started in the spring when they came to open up the place. They turned on the gas, checked a few appliances, and went home. There was a tremendous explosion late in the evening and plates, saucers, wood were found halfway across the lake. Thank God no one was living or working here at the time. Nothing was saved from the original lodge except six antique chairs out for repair. Everything was charred right into the ground. Guests were wonderful. They mailed a lot of pictures, so much of the old has been re-created.

"The camps are located on 5-mile Kennebago Lake, the largest fly-fishing-only water east of the Mississippi. The upper river is for brook trout, with several deep pools that have, as one of our guests put it, 'some trout that would scare you.' The lower river has 25 pools with lots of salmon in the 1- to 3-pound range and some up to 6 pounds.

"When Grant's came up for sale, we had been guests here for about six years. I started thinking about all the facets of running a sporting camp, and realized I'd had experience in every avenue. I used to race and build wooden boats when I was a teenager in Saco [Maine], and I'm redoing Rangeley wooden boats and repairing outboard motors now. I'd been in building construction for about 16 years, so nothing about the upkeep of the buildings bothered me at all. I'd been run-

Grant's Kennebago Camps

ning a business, so the record-keeping end of it wasn't a problem. And I'd been fly-fishing for 15 years and had fished right at Grant's Camps. I knew the fishery and the lake and the river. It seemed almost like it was a predestined thing for us to fit right into the business here. So we bought the camps, April 9, 1988.

"Carolyn began fly-fishing at Grant's when we were guests. We were out on a boat one spring, and I was catching a fish with almost every cast. Well, she put her book down and said, 'That looks like fun. Could I try it?' And that was the beginning of it. Now she initiates fly-fishing trips out of state when Maine's fishing season is closed. And both of my children were able to cast a really tight line by age 5. So it's a family thing with us. We evolved from camping in the back of a pickup, to a tent, to a trailer that we'd haul. But it's still a lot of work to camp out. A friend of mine said, 'Have you ever considered going to a sporting camp?' And I said, 'What's a sporting camp?' I had no idea there was a whole industry out there devoted to the outdoor sport. Well, the first place he told us about was Grant's. And fortunately, we had to look no further.

"A guide from Rangeley named Walter Davenport was running Grant's at the time we bought it. The recreational aspect of the place was not being promoted, so we paid for the potential. I kept improving the fishing end of it, but I had to start from the ground up and develop a recreation plan to promote the July and August trade. Coming from southern Maine, seeing what the traffic is like on the southern coast, I knew the potential and demand was there. But people just don't realize there are facilities that exist in the wilderness like this. And you don't have to sacrifice your comfort to take a vacation in northern Maine.

"So I added hiking, sailing, windsurfing, mountain biking, all at no charge to our guests. We put in a small play area for the children, added a few pets. And we have tables on some of the beaches around the lake. Where else can you picnic and possibly be visited by a moose in the backwaters either beside or behind you? A family vacation to some people is driving someplace and then a week later driving back home and you've hardly done a thing together. When you're in our atmosphere, you are hiking together, picnicking, canoeing, fishing together. The kids will come out of the dining hall while their parents are finishing dinner, get a carrot from the kitchen, and go feed the rabbits or play on the swings. Mom and Dad know right where they are and don't have to worry about traffic or safety. We have guides that take families on nature trips, teach the plant ecology associated with the area. There definitely is a need for a real true family vacation. And it's a fun experience.

"We have a floatplane dock for private planes. For a regular flight, we drive out 25 miles to the Rangeley airport, or we have an extra vehicle for people coming into that airport with their own plane. And we have chartered flights out of Grant's all summer."

James: "We have fantastic canoe trips where we take you above Little Kennebago Lake and you can swim, paddle, fish, and picnic your way back. We also have miles and miles of logging roads for mountain biking and have some great hiking trails. For fishing, the lake has a 1A rating, one of the highest in the state. It is 119 feet deep, with catch-and-release only. It's not stocked but it has natural spawning."

The Kennebago Lake fishery was the first in the state to be declared fly-fishing-only by the Inland Fish and Wildlife Department in Augusta. John explains: "Fly-fishing-only means you have to be physically casting the fly, not trolling or dragging it behind the boat. Fly-fishing encompasses fishing with wet line, partial wet line [sink-tip lines], and dry line.

"You really have a sense of history when you're up here in this area," adds John. "The Indians used to live on the shore of Kennebago, which means 'sweet flowing waters,' and they'd migrate back and forth to the ocean. The last caribou seen in Maine was on Kennebago Lake. I think part of the reason the caribou left is that their migratory roads were the rivers: the Magalloway, Androscoggin, the Kennebec. And they've been dammed and flooded so the habitat is gone. But the signs of caribou remain. It's nice there still is a corner of the world like northern Maine. To come to our place and actually live it and bring home pictures is a vacation that makes albums."

Grant's Cream Puffs

Grant's is known for its chocolate chip cookies kept in a jar at the office. Here's another favorite.

½ cup butter, 1 cup water, 1 cup flour, 4 eggs (for pastry shells); 1 box instant vanilla pudding, 1½ cups milk, 1 cup whipped cream (for cream filling)

Bring the butter and water to a boil, then add the flour. Stir well. Remove from heat and add the eggs, one at a time. Mix well until the mixture is glossy and pulls from the sides of the pan. Drop by tablespoonfuls onto a cookie sheet. Bake at 400 degrees for 45 minutes. Remove the puffs from the cookie sheet and cool on a wire rack. When cool, carefully cut off the top of each puff (save the tops), and spoon out the centers. *To make cream filling:* Whip pudding and milk together until thick. Blend in whipped cream. Fill puffs and replace tops.

10. LAKEWOOD CAMPS

AP, SCA
OWNERS: Sue and Stan Milton, Janne Provencher
ADDRESS: Middle Dam, Andover ME 04216; 207-243-2959 (camp); 207-392-1581 or 207-486-3200 (winter)
SEASON: May through November
ACCOMMODATIONS: 12 log cabins with wood heat, gas lights, indoor plumbing and shower, porch; pets welcome
RATES: $92 per person per day
ACCESS: Maine Turnpike (I-495) to exit 11 (Gray), then ME 26 north to ME 232. Proceed north to Rumford Point; turn left onto ME 2; then take your first right, onto ME 5 to Andover. In Andover, turn right onto ME 120, cross a bridge, and at the top of a hill take a left onto a 12-mile dirt road to South Arm Landing. The pickup for Lakewood is beyond the landing to the left (look for the sign).

In order to get to Lakewood Camps, preset a time to have Eric Wight, game warden, author, launch driver, and camp historian, pick you up at Lakewood's private dock. On the 15- to 20-minute boat trip from South Arm to Middle Dam, you progress from sparsely populated to pristine shoreline and learn a bit about the camps from *Eric:* "In 1853 Joshua Rich was living on a point of land off Metallac Island, near the Richardson farmstead that the lake was named after, when a dam was put in. It flooded both Rich and Richardson out, so Richardson went to Bethel and Rich came here to Middle Dam, built a couple of cabins, and began to cater to fishermen. In 1880 another dam raised the water level again by about 20 feet."

The camps come into view. Set in a cove to one side of the dam and on a knoll, the log cabins are dark brown and placed close together in a row to the left of a large main lodge. A few outbuildings and cabins spread out behind and to the right of the lodge.

Author Louise Dickinson Rich lived along the Rapid River from 1934 until the mid-1950s, and her book *We Took to the Woods* is still an accurate description of much of the area.

Sue (reading from historical notes): "Lakewood is one of the oldest traditional sporting camps in Maine and the United States. The main lodge was built in the winter of 1877 by Aldona Brooks and Horatio Godwin of Upton, Maine. Godwin had previously conducted a camp, Anglers Retreat, in buildings that housed the workmen who constructed the original sluice dam. This camp stood on the knoll just south of the present camp. Brooks and Godwin opened their new lodge May 14, 1878, and operated it for one year, when it was taken over by the Androscoggin Lake Transportation Company. The name was changed to Lakewood Camps in 1920. Captain Coburn operated the camps until 1942, when Larry and Alys Parsons took over the operations until 1976. A fire in 1957 burned the original three-story main lodge ('the hotel') and six cabins. Adjacent to Lakewood is the famous Rapid River, which is 5 miles long and holds landlocked salmon and brook trout. Lower and Upper Richardson Lakes are open to general law [meaning you can troll a line or fly-fish] for brook and lake trout and landlocked salmon.

"The dams were built originally to sluice, or transport, logs. The timber company had a boat named the *Alligator* that would haul the logs down the lake. The logs would go from Middle to Lower Dam into Umbagog Lake. From Umbagog they'd float down the

Lakewood, like most camps, keeps plenty of wood on hand.

Androscoggin to the mill in Berlin, New Hampshire.

"Middle Dam has been owned and operated by the Union Water Power Company, a subsidiary of Central Maine Power Company, since 1878. They regulate Upper, Middle, Aziscohos, and Errol Dams. The land around the camps is owned by Seven Islands, a land-management company out of Bangor for the Pingree family. They own lots of land throughout Maine, mostly farther north. So we lease from the

Pingree–Seven Islands Company and the Union Water Company.

"In the fall of 1975, we came up to look at the place. Stan's best friend's uncle was damkeeper here at the time and Stan had been fishing here and knew the place was for sale. We went home and asked Janne if she was interested in going in with us. We're all from the Mechanic Falls–Poland area and went to school together. Janne said yes and we bought it in March of '76. We are only the fifth owners of these camps in the last 125 years!

"There is a damkeeper at the house by this dam—there are five damkeepers in all. One of the stipulations is they have to be married because there have to be two people in here in case someone gets hurt. Bob and Pearl Eliot are the only two people living here all winter. He regulates the water flow, calls in his readings to Union Water Power once a day, and they'll tell him over the CB radio whether to turn the water up or down.

"That first year we moved in I had two little girls, Lori and Jenny, and it was March and we had no running water. We lived with Janne in what we call the guide's house. After that first year the girls stayed with our friends Mary and Phil Learned in Andover. Phil guided here for many years and Mary waitressed. That's how they met. They've been a tremendous help. The girls now like coming back to visit, but neither of them wants to carry on the tradition. Lori was married here on the front lawn by the same minister from Andover she grew up with.

"Alys Parsons helped us out at first. She showed us how she did her bookkeeping, how she managed the cabins, did laundry. We have a laundry room with two washing machines, a dryer, and a mangle iron—a long iron that rolls and you put your sheets and so on through it. Over the years, most of the kids that we've hired have been local. We employ 9 and then there's the 3 of us, so there's 12 in staff.

"At its peak, May and June, we couldn't get any busier. July and August is our slow time. So we offer white-water rafting. Starting at Middle Dam, they raft the whole length of Rapid River, the swiftest river east of the Rockies. It drops 185 feet in 3 miles, with no falls. We then take out at what we call the hop yard, bring the rafts back to Lower Dam, and then raft the fastest part of the river again.

"The biggest thing that attracts people here is the fly-fishing and the remoteness. We're the only sporting camp on this lake." *Stan:* "A lot of sporting camps have been in locations that the general public did not have access to. The access issue was one of the main things that prompted sporting-camp owners to come together and form an association to work with the legislature and the Department of Inland Fisheries and Wildlife. There's a big push by sporting groups to open up all lands, especially paper-company lands, to the general public. A lot of camps have gates and the owners felt that if their land was opened to the public, it would hurt their business and the fishery. Paper companies have made a lot more of their land available to the public. In other words, if there is a brook, river, or lake and there is a logging road, they don't lock the gates.

"There was a lot of pressure in the mid-1980s to take away the tree-growth tax advantage from the paper companies for lands they kept gated. But fortunately that never happened. Certain regulations come up in the legislature that affect us and end up costing money. Like the federal Clean Water Act. Anybody that gives water to the public is affected. A lot of towns are even having a hard time complying, it's so expensive!

"Our phone system is a radio phone from North Anson with relay towers on Sugarloaf Mountain. We have a large antenna and used to have a party line, 20 to 25 people on the same line. The new system's a private line, but you get a real windy day there on the mountain, or lightning, and it doesn't work well, so I hook up the old system and use that."

Janne: "When we bought the place, I had no intentions of ever cooking a meal here. But after a year and a half, I took over from just observing and learning what the other cooks taught me. One of our attractions is that we serve a menu, so people have some choices. We order our groceries once a week from Augusta. They're delivered to a grocery store in Oquossoc. Then we have a man who picks the groceries up, takes them back to my home in Wilsons Mills, and puts them in the freezer. Stan goes out in the morning to Rumford, buys whatever else we need, then goes to my trailer, picks up the order, and brings it back in. Rumford is probably 60 miles from here by road, 14 of it dirt road. It's close to 20 miles to Wilsons Mills, from here driving out is probably 40 miles, from Oquossoc to the freezer is probably 20 miles. Stan does this twice a week, Monday and Thursday, all summer long. He leaves here between 8 and 9 in the morning and gets back around 4 in the afternoon. Nothing's easy here. If something goes wrong and we don't know what to do about it, like the electricity goes, then we have no electricity. That usually happens just before dinner, of course. Our water used to be gravity fed from a spring about a mile up in the woods. So if our electricity was off, we still would have water. But because of the federal water regulations we had to have a well drilled, which means pumps, which means if the generator's off, we have no water. An added complication.

"I lived in here year-round, in the guide's house, for 11 years. My husband got a job plowing roads, so we bought a place in Wilsons Mills for the winter. When I'm here, he comes on Wednesday nights and then Friday night for the weekend. The guide's house used to be a hotel at South Arm in the early 1900s. They brought in the two top stories across the ice on rollers with horses and set it on a foundation here on the hill. People wouldn't bother to do that type of thing anymore!"

Marinated Beef Strips

This recipe is also good made with venison.

> 2 pounds chuck or round steak, ½ cup soy sauce, 2 T sugar, 1 tsp. garlic powder, 2 T olive oil, 1 T minced onion, 1 T sesame seeds

Mix everything, except meat, in a large bowl. Slice meat across grain in thin slices. Place in marinade and mix until well coated. Refrigerate for 1 hour or up to 2 days. When ready to cook, drain off excess marinade. Stir-fry the meat in a very hot frying pan that has been coated with a little oil.

11. NORTH CAMPS

HK/AP

OWNERS: Sonny and Dottie Gibson

ADDRESS: Box 341, Oquossoc, ME 04964; 207-864-2247

SEASON: Mid-May through Columbus Day weekend, reopens in November for hunting

ACCOMMODATIONS: 12 log cabins with screened-in porch, woodstove or oil heater (two cabins have open fireplaces), gas stove, electric refrigerator, electric lights, indoor plumbing, tub and shower; linens, blankets, and towels provided; no pets

RATES: $50 per couple per day; $315 per couple per week

ACCESS: Maine Turnpike (I-495) to exit 13 (Lewiston). From Lewiston, take ME 4 north to Livermore, then ME 10 west to Mexico. Turn left onto ME 17 north. At Oquossoc, take ME 4/16 east (toward Rangeley). Turn right onto Mingo Loop Road (watch for the sign) and go down the hill into camp.

When I arrived at North Camps, Dottie was on the porch of the main lodge working on plastic webbing for some deck chairs. "When you see something that needs fixing, you've just got to be willing to do it. I've done tons of these chairs, could do them in my sleep." Sonny swings by and takes me on a tour: horseshoe pits, badminton court, boat dock, sailing dock, beach, cookout area, and a clay tennis court on a knoll at center stage. The cabins are an eclectic mix of styles and sizes. One is two-storied with a screened-in porch on each floor. "It used to be the main lodge," says Sonny. "The top floor was for the help." He gestures to the water: "The camps look out on Rangeley Lake, which is 10 miles long and 3 across. Good for brook trout and landlocked salmon."

We head back to the porch of the main lodge. As the three of us talk, guests stop by, ducks wander up the stairs, and a parrot named Henry jumps up to perch on Sonny's shoulder. "I had a turtle dove once. He showed up one summer—along with the ducks. We had him seven years. Henry here talks when he's in the mood. Says 'hello, good-bye, good morning, hey come here, whatcha doin?' and if you don't answer him he'll say, 'Huh?!'

"North Camps were built by Mr. North in the 1890s. It started as three cabins and the two-storied main lodge. After North it was run by the Hernbourghs from Norway or Sweden. Not the Maine towns of Norway or Sweden, but over in Europe. Then my dad began running the camps in 1950. My family is the third owner in all that time! My dad was an avid sportsman. In '37 and '38 he was hunting in northern New Hampshire and he happened to come over this way and decided that he wanted to make the Rangeley area his home. At the time he bought the place, we were living in Worcester, Massachusetts, and we owned and operated a dairy business. When they ran this place, my mother did all the cooking. It was straight American Plan. And she did that straight through the '50s. At that point motels and auto touring were hurting the business, and they decided in order to survive they would have to go to housekeeping. So in the early '60s he put in kitchens and we offered housekeeping for the summer, for the family vacationers, and American Plan in the spring and fall.

"In the '60s I helped Dad open and close the place and guided for the fall hunt. I bought North Camps from my father in 1982. And it was just about this time that I was down country, in Massachusetts, and I got in a motorcycle accident. Got banged up pretty good. I stayed at my mother's in Worcester and it was while I was there that I met Dottie. I'd been alone all the years that I was here with Dad."

Dottie: "Sonny and I married in '82. His mother was still running the dairy business, doing the books. She died in '86 and ran it until the day she died. Sonny's first wife had died, and he was hoping for someone to share his life at camp. I was divorced and looking to start a new life. I came up here on a bus and he introduced me to his dad and said, 'This is the woman who's going to run North Camps with me.'"

Sonny: "It takes a certain type of person to run a place like this. If I'm chopping wood, she'll see this and come out and help me. She can make curtains, fix things. Many women don't know the kind of things you need to do, or don't want to learn—just don't want to live out here and do this." *Dottie:* "I love it here. We have 20 acres and you can look out over the lake to the mountains."

Sonny: "We have 850 feet of shore frontage and we own our own land here. It's a way of life. But in this area sporting camps have mostly been bought up and made into private cottages or condos. We're the only camp left on Rangeley Lake that's run as a traditional old camp. The real estate has become so valuable and the taxes so high that a young couple starting off just couldn't do it now. A lot of banks won't even talk to you about loans if you're seasonal. We've had young couples buy camps, would love to live here. They find out it's 15, 16 hours a day, seven days a week. They couldn't make much money; they had to work too much. So they condoed them. It's a shame because it's a good way of life and there should be places like this for people to come to."

As they walk me to my car, Sonny and Dottie point out all the birdhouses. Dottie explains, "One of our guests made most of these and gave them to us. Our people are like that. The swallows were perching on them before we even got them up." *Sonny:* "You should've seen it! They were swarming around trying to be the ones to get into the new improved housing."

12. TIM POND WILDERNESS CAMPS

AP, SCA

OWNERS: Harvey and Betty Calden

CAMP ADDRESS: Box 22-SC, Eustis ME 04936; 207-243-2947

WINTER ADDRESS: Box 89, Jay ME 04239; 207-897-2100

SEASON: May 15 through November (closed August)

ACCOMMODATIONS: 11 log cabins with indoor plumbing and shower, woodstove or fieldstone fireplace, electric or gas lamps, porch

RATES: $105 per person per day, includes Rangeley boat, motor, gas, canoe
ACCESS: Maine Turnpike (I-495) to exit 12A. Follow ME 4 north through
Farmington. Drive another 2.5 miles north to ME 27. Turn right and follow
ME 27 all the way to Eustis. (From I-95, take exit 31B, then follow ME 27
through Farmington as above, to Eustis.) Call into camp from the Texaco
station in Eustis (last supplies) to make sure the gate is open. From here, go
north 3 miles. Cross a bridge and take the next left. Proceed on a dirt road
7 miles and turn left at a gate. Go 1 mile, up a hill, and follow signs into
camp, another mile.

Tim Pond Wilderness Camps has a cozy feel in the midst of a vast
landscape. The body of water truly is a pond: 1 mile long by ¾ mile
wide, snugged up to 2,000-foot Tim Mountain and the East Kennebago Range. And the weathered, homey cabins branch out on either
side of the central lodge, all within view of each other, forming a com-
pact little community.

Betty has traced the camp's history back to the 1860s: "It first started
as a logging camp and then turned into a sporting camp in 1877. Back
then, people would take railroads up to Kingfield, a stage to Eustis
Ridge [named after lumber magnate, Charles Lyman Eustis], and come
the rest of the way by buckboard [open carriage]. Once folks got here,
they usually stayed for the summer." Many of the regulars had cabins
named after them, like Uncle John and so on. "Back then, the cost of
coming here was $2.50 a day. Now, $2.50 was a lot of money at a time
when you figure most people only made $1.00 to $1.50 a day." They
came to relax and fish for trout. Tim Pond has never been stocked, and
its 46-foot-deep waters still offer square-tailed brook trout.

"Our first season was 1982. Harvey and I are both from Maine and
have been involved in hunting and fishing for a long time. Like most
people who run a sporting camp, you start off thinking you're going
to have a lot of time to go hunting and fishing. But sorry!" She laughs.
"Every camp owner will tell you it's an adventure coming into your
land in the springtime and trying to open up camp. If it's going to go
wrong, it's going to go wrong one thing after another. And hopefully
everything's going to go wrong *before* your opening day! Maybe the
water pump dies, or the sewer backs up, or you get every vehicle stuck
in the snow and there's no way out. Which isn't that bad. I mean,
what's wrong with being stranded in a place like this? So one year, on
top of all this, I cut my finger in the new food processor and needed
stitches. I just wrapped it up [fortunately, Betty is an emergency med-

Tim Pond Camps

ical technician], figuring it would heal eventually, and went back to work. You just take these things in stride; that's the attitude you have to have. Whatever comes along, you do what you have to do."

Harvey follows this same philosophy, whether he's piloting people and supplies to and fro in his Cessna 185 or extracting the fishhooks that get stuck in even veteran anglers (a daily event during some weeks). His method: Loop the line through the bend in the hook, press down on the eye of the hook, and jerk the fly straight back and out.

Beside fishing, hiking and mountain biking have become very popular. *Betty:* "For fishing, we provide everything that people would need in one package. That way there are no add-ons. We even have fishing equipment to use—also at no extra cost—and will provide a free fly-fishing lesson. People can bring mountain bikes or we have some to use if folks want to ride around on the back roads.

"I really like my people. We have a 90 percent return rate, so every day it's like old home week. Some of the other 10 percent, though, have never been to a sporting camp before. There's the gentleman who yelled at me one time 'cause we have a generator and I usually turn it off at 10 PM. I flipped the switch and it wasn't long before he came running. 'Young lady, have you ever heard of a computer? You wiped out my whole program.' Then there's another gentleman who was angry because I didn't give him a room with a phone. I told him I didn't play favorites—none of the cabins have phones. I had two boys in here, one was about 9 and the other 11, and it was the first time they had ever picked a raspberry or a blueberry. One little boy from Texas rushed into the kitchen and gushed, 'Mrs. Calden, we've just been looking for moose and we saw one and he turned and ran into the jungle!'" She laughs. "What we see here at Tim Pond," Betty says softly, "we take for granted. But it's different for many people. Here we see stars at night. People from the cities aren't used to that. We find them sitting on their porches at night, midnight sometimes, rocking and watching the stars. We meet really nice people here. And you know, it doesn't matter what they do in life, they're up here just to be themselves."

Traditional Tim Pond Trout Chowder

Betty offers a recipe "from Mr. Husey's day." Husey owned the camp after World War II, and the recipe comes from Mrs. George Hicks, the camp cook at the time: "It's one of those recipes where they just kept a big pot on the back of the stove and added to it each day. As is typical of old recipes, there are no measurements for it."

> Trout (enough for ½ to 1 cup cooked fish per person); potatoes (1 per person); milk (whole or evaporated) or cream (about ½ cup per person); onions (about 1 for every two people); salt pork (same amount as onions); salt and pepper to taste; a small amount of cornmeal; bacon fat for frying; water (1 cup per person)

Clean trout, but leave the heads on. Roll trout in cornmeal; fry in bacon fat (get the fat very hot and then lower the heat to medium as you fry the fish). Remove heads, skin, and bones. Put these in a soup pot. Add water and boil gently for 30 minutes. Remove from heat and strain. This liquid is your stock. Slice the onions and salt pork and fry until golden. Add everything but the trout to the stock. Cook slowly, until the potatoes are almost done. Add trout and heat well through. Serve with biscuits.

The Dead River—Jackman Region

This section is bordered by ME 27 in the west and ME 201 to the east. The Appalachian Trail (AT) skirts Flagstaff Lake and the Carry Ponds (so named because Benedict Arnold's ill-fated band of soldiers carried—or more accurately, dragged—leaking bateaux through here). Both routes are built along scenic river valleys and offer magnificent water and mountain vistas.

ME 27 passes through Kingfield and the Carrabassett Valley, home to Sugarloaf Mountain ski resort. The AT crosses the road between Crocker and Bigelow Mountains, clearly visible along the sweep of road. Beyond Stratton, Flagstaff Lake spreads out, marshy and shallow along the road. North of Eustis the drive parallels the North Branch of the Dead River to the east and Chain of Ponds in the west. Coburn Gore is the last settlement before the Canadian border.

Heading north on ME 201, you parallel the Kennebec River and a bicycle path established on the old railroad bed from Solon to Bingham. In Moscow, the highway passes Wyman Dam (the largest in Maine) with a spectacular view of Wyman Lake and surrounding mountains. In Caratunk, the road goes directly past the wooden Appalachian Trail sign (marked AT, on the right) and heads to The Forks, the confluence of the Dead and Kennebec Rivers. This area is command central for outfitters specializing in white-water rafting. If you wish to catapult through Maine waters prior to your final destination in this region, call the Maine Rafting Association at 1-800-723-8633. The Forks also boasts Moxie Falls, the highest falls in New England.

The section of ME 201 from The Forks to Jackman is noted for moose sightings. In fact, there are so many opportunities for close encounters that the stretch has been dubbed Moose Alley. The important thing for visitors to know is that moose have the right of way, simply because they are large, relatively speedy, and not too bright. An auto collision with a moose can be lethal to humans and moose alike.

In Jackman, the Moose River flowage branches off into many lakes and streams popular with sportsmen and vacationers. Many of the waters in this area are at relatively high elevations (above 1,500 feet) and are spring fed. Once in Jackman you are just down the road from

Canada to the north and the Moosehead Lake region to the east. High elevations also mean good snowfall, and the area is used extensively by snowmobilers. For up-to-date snow conditions around the entire State of Maine, call 1-800-880-SNOW, 24 hours a day.

Getting there: General driving time from Portland is 4 hours; from Boston, 6 hours; from New York City, 10 hours. There is an airport in Jackman and small planes fly in to the Gadabout Gaddis grass airstrip in Bingham. For a chartered floatplane, contact Steve Coleman in Jackman, 207-668-3301.

Guidance: You can get regional information from the Upper Kennebec Valley Chamber of Commerce (207-672-3702). The Jackman–Moose River Chamber of Commerce (PO Box 368, Jackman, ME 04945; 207-668-4171) maintains a Web site at http://www.maineguide.com/jackman/jackcham.html, or can be reached by e-mail: 104251.544@Compuserve.com.

13. ATTEAN LAKE LODGE

AP, SCA

OWNERS: Brad and Andrea Holden

ADDRESS: PO Box 457, Jackman, ME 04945; 207-668-3792

SEASON: Late May through September

ACCOMMODATIONS: 16 log cabins with indoor plumbing and shower, gas lights, woodstove

RATES: $190–225 per couple per day; $1,200–1,400 per couple per week

ACCESS: Exit I-95 in Waterville and take ME 201 north to Jackman. As you come into town, take your first left onto Attean Road (dirt) and go 2 miles to the boat landing. There is a phone at the parking area so you can call the camp for a boat pickup.

There is no way to get to Attean Lodge by foot (except in winter). The lodge is on an island in Attean Lake, and you boat over on the camp launch. Sally Mountain looms up on the right, and pocket-sized islands dot the lake. The dock and beach area leads up the hill to the spacious lodge stained a warm pumpkin tone. The cabins are mostly tucked in a pine grove on a knoll to the right of the lodge. Some are connected by a boardwalk and have built-in benches so you can sit and look out on the peaceful, pristine view.

Brad: "The Coburn family was the original owner of Attean Township [36,000 acres], which they bought in the 1850s. The name comes from the Algonquin Indian tribe. Rumor has it that there was an Algonquin chief named Attean; they pronounced it 'At-tee-in' [now, 'At-é-in']. My grandfather, Reul Holden, was an independent logger and became acquainted with Coburn because he wanted to cut some timber off Coburn's land. In those days there were no set-back [zoning] restrictions. So he bought the land and built a couple of little fishing cottages down on the back side of the island here. There were no other buildings on the lake. The island is called Birch Island and is about 22 acres. Attean Lake is about 5 miles long and 3 wide and is protected in perpetuity. Before Coburn sold it to Lowell Timber Associates, they established conveyances that stated that the land 300 feet back, all around the lake, could not be developed. Beyond 300 feet back are areas that also can't be developed either because of the Canadian Pacific Railroad or 'view sheds.' In other words, you can't look over on the side of the mountains and see any type of cutting. So the views are protected. Forever.

"My father, Langdon Holden, and his two brothers, Lyle and Roland, ran the business until my father bought them out. My mother, Violette, who lives in Jackman, was very, very involved right until we bought the place in '89. Every summer of my life I've been here. My father died in a logging accident in 1973 and I guess you could say I became the man of the family at that point.

"Back in my father and grandfather's day the railroad was the only way to come here. There was no road access to the landing down there or even to Jackman. It was still horse and buggy. The automobile was slow to get here. I remember my father telling stories of how he would row across the lake—this was before outboard motors—to Attean Landing, where the train would stop and let my father's guests off. You can see the tracks from the lake here. There are still trains that go by here. This is the second-longest railroad line in the world. The longest is the Trans-Siberian in Russia. This train goes all the way to Vancouver on the West Coast and to New Brunswick to the east.

"In 1979 there was a fire here. The dining room and kitchen were in one building and the lodge and staff rooms were in another, quite close together. The fire started in the kitchen and spread, and eventually took the lodge, too. I've done most of the carpentry and designing of this new main lodge and we're really pleased with it. We've torn down a lot of the old one- and two-person cabins and replaced them with larger cabins. The oldest cabin now is probably the one I live in, built in 1910.

"I met Andrea because she had written to my mother for a job. I was in Florida that winter. My father was still alive at the time, and my par-

Attean Lake Lodge

ents said, 'Why don't you stop on your way home and interview this girl? She's from the Brunswick area, going to school in Portland.' So I was this big macho guy, you know, been in Florida, come back and interviewed her. Well, she came to work here as a waitress and has been here ever since. Need I say more! Andrea was studying education, and until a few years ago she was the third-grade teacher here in Jackman. But since we've bought this, and our seasons are spilling over into the fall and starting earlier in the spring, the business needs two people running it, really.

"Every school day I get up and boat my son, Barrett, across the lake. A lot of mornings it's through thick fog, so I have to use a compass. I remember my father doing the same thing with me until I got old enough that could take my own boat right through Moose River into Big Wood Lake and I'd go right into Jackman, nearly behind the school. I'd tie my boat up right behind the school, and Barrett will be doing that one day, too. When I graduated from high school, there were seven in my class."

I quip, "So you were in the top 10 of your class."

Brad laughs, "Yes, I was. Barrett's got it tougher—there are 16 in his class."

There are lots of beaches on Attean Lake. "Ours must be 200 feet long, totally natural," Brad says. "It's funny, you go down to the next lake, no beaches, and up the other way, no beaches at all." Fishing in the area is for brook and lake trout and salmon, general law. The region also draws visitors undertaking the Moose River canoe trip called the Bow Trip, which goes around in a loop. "It's a 45-mile trip," Brad explains. "Most people take three days to do it. We have cabins we maintain along the trip. Most people bring their own gear for this. But we also have about a dozen canoes stashed away on other lakes and ponds, and we maintain trails to them for 1-day trips."

Last time I visited the camps there was a couple getting married the day I had to leave. Carol, the bride, had been a waitress at camp 25 years earlier. She told me, "I came back because I had a yearning to be here. Maine does that to you: the attraction, the charm. I was first tuned in to the northern lights and loons here. It's the first place I really felt alive. You have to have a 3-day residency to get married in Maine. So we came into town Tuesday, went directly to Town Hall, signed our marriage certificates. Brad got his notary public's license specifically to marry us. So we'll get married on 2,200-foot Sally Mountain. Basically, how simple can it be? We wrote our vows, for a trousseau we both have new hiking boots! We've been to a lot of places in the States, but we haven't found one yet that matches this. We were out on a canoe trip, a chain of three lakes. Got to the last lake and hadn't seen a soul all day. One loon per lake. Quiet. The only thing you're hearing is the wind through the pines. This is it!"

As Brad deposited me back at the boat landing and my car he said, "Some guests leave here saying, 'Back to civilization.' My father used to say, 'When you leave here you're leaving civilization and heading into the jungle.'"

Apple Chocolate Chip Cake

This recipe comes from Judy I. Mason, Attean Lake Lodge pastry chef.

In one bowl, mix 1 cup sugar, 1 cup oil, 2 eggs slightly beaten, and 2 tsp. vanilla. In another bowl blend 2 cups flour, 1 tsp. baking soda, 1 tsp. cinnamon, and ½ tsp. salt. Combine wet and dry ingredients, and mix well. Fold in 3 cups thinly diced apple, 1 cup chocolate chips, and ½ cup chopped nuts.

Grease and flour a 10-inch tube pan or 9x13-inch pan. Bake at 325 degrees for 1 hour.

14. BULLDOG CAMPS

HK, SCA

OWNERS: Doris and Vlad Vladimiroff

CAMP ADDRESS: HC 64, Box 554, Jackman, ME 04945; 207-243-2853

WINTER ADDRESS: PO Box 1229, Greenville, ME 04441; 207-695-4322

SEASON: Mid-May through mid-October

ACCOMMODATIONS: Six log cabins with indoor plumbing, central shower, gas lights, refrigerator, stove, wood heat; pets welcome

RATES: $18 per person per day; $90 per person per week

ACCESS: Take I-95 to exit 36 (Skowhegan). Follow Route 201 north until you pass Parlin Pond rest area. Turn left onto a logging road 0.2 mile past the rest area. Follow this road for about 9 miles to a parking area and sign where you wait to be picked up.

Fortunately for guests, Vlad Vladimiroff operates an ATV shuttle along the 1.5-mile footpath into camp. The trail is all downhill, but the cabins are housekeeping and people bring in heavy loads of supplies, so the service (a small fee is charged) is welcome. The path emerges from pine woods to pass two cabins on the left. Beyond is a small clearing with a main lodge bracketed by three other cabins. Beyond this, a pond lies sparkling at the base of cliffs. You feel as though you've arrived at a hidden grotto, to a place aptly named Enchanted Pond. I sit and chat with the owners in the main lodge, surrounded by art and books.

Doris: "I was born in Maine and was a fine-arts major in college, first at Berkeley and then on the East Coast. For over 25 years I taught writing and literature in the University of Maine system." She points to a quilt she appliquéd with camp scenes: "I have artwork in all the cabins, and many people do notice it."

Vlad: "I grew up and went to college in New York. In the wintertime I work as a carpenter. When I came to Maine in 1967, I got interested in fishing. Several years later we saw an ad for a set of sporting camps in the Jackman-Eustis area, where I had fished before. So my curiosity was aroused. And we just liked the property. It had the advantage of being a privately owned piece of land rather than on a leased lot. We figured we wanted to have the property whether we would run it as a sporting camp or not. So we ended up buying these camps, with my brother as a partner, in the early spring of 1973 and started running them that first season. We thought we'd just try it for a while and we've been at it all these years! We had a 3-year old son when we came in here." *Doris:* "And he's graduated from college." *Vlad:* "As he got a little older, he would spend summers in here with me while Doris was working. Then Doris would be up here for vacation and weekends. But he seems to have other interests—music and filmmaking. So it's not too likely at this point that he'll want to do anything here. But who knows? I never fished until I was 25 years old, and look what happened to me!

"I think we're about the sixth owners. The camps were built in the 1920s as sporting camps. Before that there was another little settlement here used for loggers. Back at the turn of the century, all the white pines around here I guess were being cut. A big landowner in the Jackman area, Henry McKinney, called it Bulldog Camp, so it had this name before the sporting camps were even built. The natives called Enchanted Pond here Bulldog Pond, because the mountain across the water was supposed to look like a bulldog. Then it became known as Enchanted Pond, because supposedly there were a lot of mysterious things that used to happen here, like, oh, people following a deer out into the middle of the frozen lake to have the tracks disappear all of a sudden. And there are several places around here where streams just go underground, disappear, and then pop up again somewhere else. I know that in one of journalist Gene Letourneau's outdoor columns years ago, about the time we bought this place, he did a write-up about the area. People have written histories of the Moose River valley, and here's a book called *Dud Dean and the Enchanted.* You've probably heard of the author, Arthur R. McDougal Jr. Another book is *The Enchanted: An Incredible Tale,* by Elizabeth Coatsworth. Unfortunately, since we've been here, no mysterious things happen anymore!

"The fishery in the pond is brook trout, general law, with the provision that no live bait be used. And it is very deep, 185 feet. It's basically glacial, and not just one big hole, but more like a big long trough.

"When we first bought the camps, there was a flying service out of Lake Parlin, where you go off at the main road. It was reliable and relatively inexpensive. So for the first four years, that's how people got in here. But then he had to retire. Some people will still fly in, maybe with Steve Coleman in Jackman, or Currier in Greenville, or maybe Steve Bean from Rangeley. Our guests used to be mostly Mainers. Now many are from southern New England.

"I hate to see the intrusion of development in the areas where sporting camps are trying to exist in a wilderness setting. An outfit buys up land to cut the timber and then sells off lots to people who just want to build cabins in the woods. Usually this is something that a small timber company would do. Companies like Boise Cascade, Scott, or International Paper won't do this. But the small guys, they come in, get what they can from the sale of wood, and then, under the old laws, they could subdivide that land as long as the lots were 40 acres or more, to whomever wanted to buy it. We want to stay here, but a lot depends on how invasive of our little area the development becomes."

Doris: "Vlad's devotion to both the environment and fishing is enormous—and mine to the environment and ecological issues. The idea of a camp appealed to me very much. And I like the people who come in here. I like meeting people who are not only professionals and privileged, but also some regular folks."

Vlad: "It's really a mix of people."

Doris: "A very nice mix."

15. CHADBOURNE'S WYMAN LAKE CAMPS

OWNER: Sandra Chadbourne

ADDRESS: HC 65, Box 152, Bingham, ME 04920; 207-672-3771

SEASON: Year-round

ACCOMMODATIONS: 13 cabins (including six log cabins; one or two bedrooms, sleeping two to eight), with heat, electric lights, porch (six screened-in), indoor plumbing and shower (two with tub); pets welcome

RATES: $59–125 per cabin per day; $325–650 per cabin per week

ACCESS: I-95 to exit 36 (Fairfield). Follow US 201 north through Moscow. Camps will be on the left side of the road, 7 miles north of a grass airstrip marked GADABOUT GADDIS AIRPORT.

Sandra: "I have three sons and three daughters, and years ago, when I was divorced, people said, 'You'd better look for an even smaller house and get ready for hard times.' But I told them I'm heading up and on, not down. So I moved into an 18-room home and figured I'd find a way to live there. I didn't graduate from college, but with my father's encouragement I went into real estate and, along with child support, I was able to bring my kids up in that house."

Sandra clearly has this can-do attitude encoded in her genes, for she is the niece of Ardelle "Ida" Allen, a legendary woodswoman of the area. One of 13 children, Ida was born in a logging camp up the road from Chadbourne's. Her book, *Ida: A Happy Life in the Maine*

Backwoods, tells of barefoot races in the snow and how she lived through the early deaths of brothers and her mother because of typhoid and poor doctoring. Ida gave up her education to marry young, worked in the woods sawing trees, was struck by lightning, lived through a house fire, and ran a sporting camp. Ida was the type of person who always had her sleeves rolled up, ready to catch life's challenges.

Sandra: "My daughter and I were the only ones left in the 18-room house. And my dad kept saying, 'You have to sell this,' because a person's always doing work on a big farmhouse. Aunt Ida had died and left her sporting camp to a sister, who asked me if I wanted to buy it. I wanted to, but it was on leased land and needed a lot of repair and it just didn't work out. Meanwhile, Rose and Bill Frigon, the previous owners here, had hired my father, who's a mason, to move a cabin onto a foundation. And my father said, 'Why don't you buy Canadian Trail Cabins? They're for sale.' That was the name of this place. Well, I was not looking for a business. I was going to buy Aunt Ida's place to use for the family. But I got a deposit on my house and I couldn't see anything I wanted. I had horses and needed some land. Three different times I came by to see my aunt, and the kids would say, 'Oh Mom, let's stop and look at the cabins.' And we'd stop and toss the idea around. It was in bad repair, but selling real estate, I thought, well, it's on the water. So it just kind of worked out.

"The earliest cabins are from 1930 or 1931. They had built the dam and then they sold, practically gave away, really, the cabins that the men working on the dam had slept in. And they moved some of those up here. There used to be a big restaurant here when I came, but I had to tear that down.

"When they built the first cabins, the old road used to go in front of them. Now it's all covered with water; they made the reservoir. It comes down from Harris Dam to here, and Wyman Dam is the biggest one in New England, I understand. It generates electricity for Boston. This was all a valley, and the lake now is 193 feet in the deepest part. It's 13½ miles long, half a mile wide, and is good for landlocked salmon and has all five species of trout. In the wintertime it freezes over early and deep, and we have snowmobile races in February, the Wyman Lake 200. It's a big thing and they're making the trails better and better. I'm right by ITS 87.

"Up here there's good white-water rafting, biking—there's a book with all the trails, and many are loops, so you don't have to be shut-tled around—hiking, and also horseback riding. I ride and there are good trails around. For hiking there's Mosquito Mountain and Pleasant Pond Mountain, the Appalachian Trail is only 7 miles up the road, and of course there's Moxie Falls. Everyone who comes here goes to Moxie Falls. It's a hundred-foot waterfall only a six-tenths of a mile walk in from the road. It's called the Niagara of the North—really beautiful. There's another waterfall, Huston Brook Falls, 2 miles down on Wyman Lake. People can boat or walk in, and they can get under the falls and have it cascading over them.

"The water level here fluctuates a little every day. Harris Dam above The Forks has a release, and there's a release for our dam, but it doesn't make much difference because the lake's so deep. At 10 AM there's a two-hour release for power, and that's the time for rafters. We have the Dead River releases in early May. It's wild. And the Kennebec is always good. That's why we're always full for rafting season. In spring there are ice chunks floating around in there. People wear wet suits and just about freeze. But you know what? They'll sign right up the next year and bring friends."

16. COBB'S PIERCE POND CAMPS

AP

OWNERS: Gary and Betty Cobb

ADDRESS: North New Portland, ME 04961; 207-628-2819 (camp); 207-626-3612 (winter)

SEASON: Early May through mid-November

ACCOMMODATIONS: 12 log cabins (one to three bedrooms) with screened-in porch, wood heater, electric lights, indoor plumbing, shower

RATES: $70 per person per day; $136 per couple per day. Weekly rates: $450 per person, $880 per couple.

ACCESS: Lewiston-Auburn is the nearest airport; Bangor and Portland airports are equidistant. To get there by car, take the Maine Turnpike (I-495) to exit 12A (Auburn) and follow ME 4 to Farmington. From Farmington, take ME 27 to New Portland and then ME 146 to North New Portland. At Morton's General Store (last stop for supplies), go north for 23.3 miles on the Long Falls Dam Road. Turn right onto a logging road marked by a sign for the camp. Follow Cobb's signs for 4.5 miles to a gatehouse, where a gatekeeper will call to arrange for you to be picked up by boat at Lindsay Cove.

Pierce Pond Camps sit on a knoll at Lower Pierce Pond, which, together with Upper and Middle Pierce Ponds, makes up a 9½-mile-long waterway surrounded by the Appalachian Mountains. Thanks to the efforts of loyal guests, a trust was created to protect the entire 10,000-acre watershed. The spring-fed waters support square-tailed brook trout and landlocked salmon. There are six outlying small ponds within walking distance of the main lakes, and the Appalachian Trail and other hiking trails are within close range.

The camps were founded in 1902 and can boast of Cobb ownership since 1958. Gary Cobb's parents, Floyd and Maud, brought the family to Pierce Pond. Gary recalls, "One of my most graphic memories is of the magnificent forest and remoteness. There were no roads and very few trails until the mid-1960s. Large areas had never seen an ax." Thanks to the Cobbs' stewardship and protection efforts, the feel is still one of wildness. A booklet in the main lodge, *Birds of Pierce Pond,* states, "Birds are an ecological litmus paper. Many different species are a sign of a healthy ecosystem." The long list available for guest viewing is proof of the area's pristine habitats.

Gary: "Great Northern Paper Company started in Madison and owned land in here, and with the lumbering activity, people could find the ponds. A group of businessmen secretly stocked the pond and almost immediately they were catching these huge trout and salmon. It wasn't too long before word got out and people started coming in to camp. So Great Northern got Charles Spaulding to build a camp to take care of the people rather than have them tenting—they were worried about forest fires—and it's been a sporting camp ever since. My father, Floyd, was a lumberman. But he liked to hunt and fish, so he started guiding at his logging camp. Then he went on and became a bush pilot in the Allagash area. That was wild, wild country in those days, the early 1950s, especially without a radio. The weather might be bad up there and good at home and you'd wonder why he didn't come home. So they decided to settle into a sporting camp. I was 15, and pretty excited, when we moved to Pierce Pond."

Betty: "Gary and I met our freshman year in college and got married in 1964. We then taught school in Millinocket. But every weekend and the whole summer we'd be at Pierce Pond. I was a waitress to begin with." *Gary:* "I started guiding right away but had to wait until I was 18 to be actually licensed. Then in 1969, we decided to give up teaching and go into the woods full time. My folks weren't ready to retire, so we started a wilderness boys' camp here and ran that for 17 years."

Betty: "Our son, Andy, and daughter, Jennifer, grew up at Pierce Pond and it was lucky for them, really. They both work here now.

Old motors at Cobb's Pierce Pond Camps

Jennifer was talking about one Halloween the other day. It was before she started school and we were living in the camps for the winter. We dressed the kids all up and they went from our cottage to Gary's parents' cottage to Robert and Judy's [Gary's sister] and that was it. 'I don't know why you even bothered,' she said to me, laughing."

Gary: "I used to trap beaver. One day Jennifer and our niece,

Katherine, set the beaver carcasses up on their tails around in a circle, gave them each a little cup, and proceeded to have a tea party!" He laughs. "During that time, we started building canoes. They're still being built by our guides—a Pierce Pond version of a Grand Laker–style canoe. Now we start going in to open up camp in late April. That's a real struggle: Wash all the log cabins, all the insides, sweep down the roofs, wash the windows, it goes on and on. There's no water then, of course. You have to dig a hole in the ice, pump it up, lug it up. But it's a very beautiful time of year because you're in total wilderness. You're way in there and there's not another person or human sound."

Betty: "Once things get going, I do the cooking. Each week I usually use 100 pounds of flour, 30 dozen eggs, gallons and gallons of milk."

Gary: "It's a tremendous amount. You're lugging food in here all the time."

Anadama Bread

> 4 cups cold water, 1 cup cornmeal, ¼ cup margaine, 1 cup molasses,
> 1 T salt, 4 packets dry yeast (about 3½ T), 1½ cups warm water,
> 10 cups white flour

Cook the cold water and cornmeal over medium heat, stirring until thickened. Pour the mixture into a large bowl and add the margarine, molasses, and salt. In a small bowl, combine yeast packets with warm water. After 5 minutes, add the yeast mixture to the ingredients in the big bowl and stir in 10 (or so) cups of white flour. Knead on a well-floured board. Let rise in a greased bowl. Punch down. Make into four loaves and place in greased bread pans. Let rise until loaf size. Bake at 350 degrees about 40 minutes.

Oven BBQ Chicken

> Chicken thighs, breasts, and drumsticks (desired amount); 2 quarts
> tomato sauce, 1 pint vinegar, 1 pint brown sugar, 1 pint vegetable oil,
> 2 T onion powder, 2 T dry mustard, 2 T garlic powder, 2 T chili powder,
> 2 T pepper

Cover cookie sheet(s) with aluminum foil. Place washed chicken parts, skin-side up, on top of the foil and smooth some sauce over the top. Bake at 350 degrees for 1 hour or until cooked through. (The chicken turns a little black on top, but people seem to like it that way.)

17. COZY COVE CABINS

HK

OWNERS: Leroy and Dianne Baker

ADDRESS: Box 370, Jackman, ME 04945; 207-668-5931

SEASON: Year-round

ACCOMMODATIONS: Nine cabins (one or two bedrooms; two cabins are handicapped accessible) with electric lights, automatic heat, indoor plumbing, shower, enclosed porch (some cabins have additional outside decks); linens and towels provided; TVs; no pets

RATES: $25 per person per day; $250–300 per cabin per week

ACCESS: I-95 to exit 36 (Fairfield). Take US 201 north to Jackman. Just before town, go over the railroad tracks, take the first left onto Spruce Street, and follow the sign for the camp.

Cozy Cove Cabins are stained a dark golden with green trim. The Bakers long, gray-painted house with satellite disk and second-story, full-length deck is to the left of the driveway. Most of the cabins are on the lawn to the right, which leads to the beach and Big Wood Lake.

Leroy: "The main house was built in '61 and the cabins were here before that. They were always sporting camps. They're all log but some of them I sided over and insulated because we're open year-round. I have two left that show logs on the inside. One is over a hundred years old and used to be the border-patrol cabin and customs office—the former owners brought them down here."

Dianne: "We've been here 10 years now, came to get away from the hectic life in Kennebunkport. I used to own my own restaurant and lobster pound down there. And it's a different kind of living here—real quiet. Busy in the wintertime for hunting and snowmobiling. Come spring and summer, we're sort of slow. It's the right way of living. People fish, spring, summer or winter, at Big Wood Lake or use one of the other lakes nearby. There's trout and salmon and also yellow perch or cusk. My husband's a hunting guide. I had a group here last week that were rabbit hunters. [The season is October 1–March 31.] I don't accept pets and they had beagles—12 of them—but they were for the hunt and they all stayed outside. And they got 21 rabbits."

Leroy: "What the hunters do is they go out walking along the old logging roads in the area and have their dogs run the rabbits. When the dogs get the scent, the guys split up and try to be where the rabbit is when it comes out onto the road. We had an open fire out in the fire pit for them." *Dianne:* "They marinate the rabbits and then cook them." *Leroy:* "The rabbits up here take their dogs for a long run, so in the course of a day these guys cover a lot of territory. Everybody was so tuckered out by the end of the week—dogs and men. Guests we had for deer hunting told them about us, and they said it was the best year they've had since they've been coming to Maine.

"Years ago, a man named Dick Spooner tried to get people involved in having places and events that were handicapped accessible. He was a Vietnam vet from Vermont, and he loved to hunt and fish and wanted other people who had disabilities to be able to have the same benefits of the outdoors he had. We got involved and then they brought the state in. It took almost two years of planning, but a lot of people put together the Disabled Outdoor Adventure program, and now it's a major thing in the community."

18. HARDSCRABBLE LODGE

AP

MANAGERS: Gary and Mary Cota

ADDRESS: PO Box 846, Jackman, ME 04945; 207-243-3020

SEASON: Year-round

ACCOMMODATIONS: Six log cabins with indoor plumbing, shower, 24-hour electricity; main lodge with large-screen TV and living room area; no pets

RATES: $65–75 per person per day

ACCESS: I-95 to exit 36 (Fairfield). From Fairfield, take US 201 north. About 10 miles north of The Forks and 0.2 mile past the Parlin Pond rest area, turn left at the HARDSCRABBLE LODGE sign. Proceed on the logging road 12 miles. Turn left at the sign and go 2.5 miles to the gate. (Make sure you call ahead.) The lodge is just beyond.

At Hardscrabble you emerge from the woods into a visual expanse of lawn, water, and mountains. A two-story, gray-stained lodge dominates the left-hand side of the view, while most of the cabins are ranged off to the right. Beyond is 4½-mile by 1½-mile Spencer Lake. Hardscrabble Mountain, the lodge's namesake, is in back. To the left is Hedgehog Mountain, to the right Bear and Spencer Mountains, and in the distance, dead center, are the Bigelow Mountains. It's easy to see why this area is called the Switzerland of Maine.

Woody and Samantha, Mary and Gary's Great Danes, amble over as the official welcoming committee. The Cotas moved in to manage the camps in February 1995. Prior to that they were employees at

Penobscot Lodge. Before that, according to Gary, they "gave up good-paying jobs in Vermont to come and do what we'd wanted to do for a long time." Gary and the camp's resident Maine guide, Andy Rowe, explain some of the possibilities available to guests. Along with fishing for lake and brook trout and landlocked salmon, there's deer hunting in the fall. In the wintertime, lunch at Hardscrabble via snowmobile (the lodge is open for lunch to snowmobilers 11–3 Friday through Monday) is very popular. There is also cross-country skiing.

The Cotas have raised a family of three themselves, and stress that they are very family-oriented. *Mary:* "It's important to us that we do everything we can to make it affordable for a working family to come here. Children can bike around the yard and our long driveway. We have a volleyball net, horseshoe pits, videotape library, swimming, boating, and a number of hiking trails nearby.

"According to a history compiled about the camps, long ago Spencer Lake was a stopover point for Indians trading south. There was an Indian burial ground on a 2-acre island in the middle of Spencer Lake called Pine Island. When the lumber company moved in, a dam was built at the south end of the lake on Spencer Stream, and Pine Island disappeared underwater. The camps were built back in the 1800s for the logging operation. One of the cabins now in use was originally a post office serving as a central distribution spot for the general area from June 15 to October 15, six days a week.

"Prisoner-of-war camps were located at Spencer Field, about 2 miles north of Spencer Lake. During World War II, most lumber-jacks in the area were called to military service or left to work on defense jobs in the southern part of the state. This left very few to work in the woods. In late 1942 Hollingworth and Whitney Paper Company started constructing the existing 14.5-mile road from Parlin to Spencer. Some areas had never been cut before. They needed men for this huge operation but could not get enough Americans or Canadians. So H&W made arrangements with the US government to use the German prisoners of war living in the barracks nearby. None of them had ever worked in the woods before and they had to be trained to use bucksaws and two-man crosscut saws. When the war ended, some of the men did not want to go back, but the last ones left in February 1946. So if you think the road in is 'backwoodsy' now, imagine building it, or think what things must have been like before it was there!"

Apple Chicken

> 4 boneless chicken breasts, 2 T flour, salt and pepper to taste, 2 T butter,
> 1 onion chopped, 1 cup apple cider (or apple juice concentrate, undiluted),
> 1 clove garlic (peeled and crushed), ½ tsp. fresh (or ⅛ tsp. dried) rosemary,
> 1 T Dijon mustard, 1 Granny Smith apple (cored and sliced), paprika

Flatten chicken breasts slightly. Dredge them in the flour and seasonings. Melt butter in a frying pan. Brown breasts on both sides. Transfer the chicken to a shallow casserole dish. Fry the onion in the frying pan until clear. Stir in any remaining flour mixture from the dredging. Add cider, garlic, rosemary, and mustard. Stir until combined. Pour over the chicken. Cover and place in a 350-degree oven until tender (about 30 minutes). Add sliced apple and bake an additional 15 minutes. Sprinkle with paprika before serving.

19. HARRISON'S PIERCE POND CAMPS

AP, SCA

OWNERS: Fran and Tim Harrison

ADDRESS: PO Box 315, Bingham, ME 04920; 207-672-3625 (radio phone at camp); 603-279-8424 or 603-524-0560 (winter)

SEASON: Mid-May through October

ACCOMMODATIONS: Nine log cabins (five with toilet and sink, four share central shower house and bathroom), gas light, wood heat, porch

RATES: $52–67 per person per day; $335–400 per person per week

ACCESS: I-95 to exit 36. Take US 201 north to Bingham and turn left (west) onto ME 16. As you come off the bridge crossing the Kennebec River, turn right and go 4.5 miles. Turn right at a sign for the camps and follow the signs 11.5 miles to a fork. Go right at the fork, then go 4 miles to the camp driveway (sign).

Harrison's is built on a bluff overlooking Pierce Pond Stream. The final drive in takes you up one side of the bluff, and the camps nestle in an old pine grove going down the other side and into the stream. The long, low log main lodge commands the height-of-land; its wrap-around porch affords views of a picturesque wooden bridge and a cascading waterfall beyond. Inside is a recreation room complete with pool table, library, and fieldstone fireplace. The spacious dining room has picture windows that look out on the falls.

Tim: "The area we're in first sold to William Bingham in 1793 and 'Bingham's Purchase' today is the entire Upper Kennebec Valley.

Harrison's was originally built by Ralph Sterling of Caratunk [which means "rough, rugged country"]. Ralph was a politician, surveyor, did all sorts of things, and received this land as payment for his surveying—about 10 acres in all. He started operating Sterling's Camps in 1934. The cabins were here and what are now our living quarters and the kitchen were the dining camp. The dining and recreation room were added on later. When Ralph was here the dam at Pierce Pond had already been around for almost a hundred years. I think it was 1835 when it was first used for logging. After Ralph died in the early 1950s, the place eventually got passed on to his grandson, Bob Smith, who still owns an acre of the original 10. In 1975 it was sold to Bud and Dorry Williams, of Pennsylvania, and they fixed it up and built a driveway. At the time of the Sterlings, there were no logging roads into here.

"It was Dorry Williams who started the hikers' 12-pancake breakfast, and we simply continue that tradition. The Appalachian Trail is just on the other side of the stream. And there's a blue-blazed trail [the AT has white blazes] that comes from the Pierce Pond lean-to, at the southern end of the pond, straight to our camps. This is about the 2,000-mile mark along the AT here. As a kind of favor, because we like the hikers, we offer the breakfast. It's nothing we make any money on. We ask them at the register that's in the lean-to to come down the evening before and let us know if they want a breakfast. One pancake breakfast is with eggs, another is with sausage, another has both, and the other is just plain pancakes. I put in different types of fruit, make them thin, and sprinkle them with confectioner's sugar because hikers really love sugar. The hikers can come for dinner, but we do require a one-day advance reservation on that. A few hikers have stayed at camp just because it's a real nice spot and a good place to relax for the final push. I built a mini-replica log cabin playhouse for our daughter, Aimey, for her fifth birthday. And she sells lemonade to the hikers for 50 cents a glass.

"Fran and I moved here from Massachusetts. Fran worked for a paper distributor and I was managing an actuarial-calculations department for an insurance company. Office, numbers—boring. I loved the people I worked with and it paid well, but I was unhappy. After 15 years there we wanted our own business. We had no idea what that business would be until one day Fran's sister from Maine told us how she and her husband were thinking of buying a sporting camp. We were all sitting around our pool, and Fran and I just looked at each other with a 'maybe that's it!' look. We ended up with this after almost a year of looking. We

Tucker, Tim, Aimey, and Fran Harrison

were totally obsessed with finding the right one. We looked at American Plan, housekeeping, campgrounds, general stores. We almost bought a housekeeping place, and now we wonder what we'd do with ourselves. I mean, the cooking is what we spend most of our time on here. We saw an awful lot of camps in every part of the state, but if there's a prettier set of sporting camps and setting, we haven't seen it.

Fran's family never did buy a sporting camp, but we did!"

Fran: "When you're a sporting-camp owner, you don't get to be outdoors very often. But you get to be in the woods. I wouldn't do this if I didn't love being here. It's nice to be your own boss and be away from the hustle."

Tim: "With American Plan you have to love cooking, and Fran has always cooked, and cooked really well, since she was a girl. And I have always liked doing breakfast.

"We both like to hike. I've done parts of the AT in New England. Bill Erwin, the blind hiker, came through here several years ago on November 4, and that's really late. Usually once October rolls around, most of the northbound through-hikers—those doing the entire trail in a season—have come by. Bill and his dog, Orient, called themselves the Orient Express. That dog was very special. He was good to Aimey, who was just a year old at the time, just good with all people. The minute Bill got out of a chair, the dog would be right up beside him. He was a long-haired German shepherd, very smart, very surefooted. He went right across our bridge down there that has 2-inch spaces between the slats with no problem at all. Every other dog that goes across it for the first time has real trouble. When Bill came through, the water was up unusually high. At East Carry Pond there weren't any bridges and one particular end was all flooded out. Fran and I knew this because we had hiked it just a week or so before. And we were wondering how he was going to do this. Well, you know what the dog did? The dog bushwhacked him around the flooded area and back to the trail. And this was in the dark! But of course that didn't matter to Bill. He ended up coming in at 10 at night. He had climbed Katahdin first and then come back to do the rest of the trail because it would've been too late in the season otherwise."

Fran: "In the winter we live and work in New Hampshire. Aimey and our son, Tucker, spend a lot of time with Tim's mother, and they seem to learn a lot from each other. At the beginning and end of the school year, we home-school Aimey, and we'll do the same with Tucker."

Tim: "I'm teaching Aimey how to identify wildflowers, and she knows her birds very well, too. She does a loon call and for some reason the loons come to her call. We see a lot of wildlife along the stream, which has lots of pools and wild brook trout. It's general-law fishing until August 15.

"Every year in August we shut down the camps for about a week, except for serving the hiker breakfast, and we spend some of that time up at Mayor's Island in the middle of Pierce Pond. And because we're closed and the Cobbs are closed, we hardly see anybody up there, except all sorts of wildlife. We've seen a couple of golden eagles, and there are very few in Maine. I've counted 28 adult loons as we went up the pond."

Poppy-Seed Salad Dressing

> 1 cup sugar, ½ cup vegetable oil, ½ cup vinegar, 1 tsp. paprika, 2 T poppy seeds

In a small saucepan, combine sugar, oil, vinegar, and paprika. Bring to a boil, stirring constantly. Remove from heat and add poppy seeds. Let cool to room temperature and then refrigerate. Keeps up to 2 weeks. Let stand at room temperature before using.

20. KING AND BARTLETT

AP, SCA

OWNERS: Fred and Matt Thurston
ADDRESS: PO Box 4, Eustis, ME 04936; 207-243-2956
SEASON: Mid-May through November
ACCOMMODATIONS: 14 log cabins with indoor plumbing and shower, wall-to-wall carpeting, gas heat, electric lights, porch; pets welcome
RATES: $140 per person per day; $795 per person per week; boats included
ACCESS: Take I-95 to Portland, then I-495 to Auburn. Get onto ME 4 and follow it through Farmington to ME 27. Take ME 27 to Eustis. Just north of Eustis you'll see a sign for King and Bartlett on the right (east) side of the road. Turn right at the sign and follow the logging road to the camp gate.

King and Bartlett used to be one of the private camps that still dot the Maine woods. Usually a group of private investors join up, or sometimes a timber company uses or builds a camp as a retreat for its employees. King and Bartlett's log camps, stained a dark brown, are ranged around a circular drive on a knoll. A cabin at the base of the knoll serves as a recreation and conference room. The main lodge is nestled by the water's edge. A fireman's bell sits center stage, and there's an open grassy area that was once used as a helicopter landing area for the camp's wealthier members.

Matt: "We're located on King and Bartlett Lake, which is 160 feet deep at its maximum depth. It contains native brook trout and lake trout—some people call those 'togue.' Since this used to be an IT&T [telephone] company getaway, the cabins are all very top-shelf. We have a building that was once a registered post office, which we use as a conference room now. We've had big companies in here for environmental seminars—groups like that. People have referred to it as a kind of Waldorf of the wilderness. IT&T used to fly the old Grumman Goose into here. There used to be an amphibious ramp. And they actually rolled out a red carpet. There were some pretty big-name people who came in here.

"The cabins are around a hundred years old, but this has only been open to the public since 1994. It originally was a logging camp and then it was started as a private sporting camp by the first governor of the State of Maine, Governor King out of Kingfield. Before we opened this up to the public, it was owned by 13 investors. My father and I joined as members and that's how it all came about—it takes a lot of money to run a place like this, and the others wanted out. They were from all over the Northeast—retired generals and such. Two of the men who've been involved here for a long time are still around: Dalbert Sylvester's family owned King and Bartlett for 35 years, and Arkie Rogers used to bring in the paper and mow the lawn. He'd fly out to Eustis every morning and fly back with the paper—did it for eight or nine years.

"We're from New Gloucester, Maine, and originally had a place in the Carrabassett Valley, where we'd fish and hunt. Then we moved to Eustis and my father ran a bear-hunting camp. From that, we got to learn quite a lot about the territory around here. We've got 14 lakes and ponds, we fish 16 miles of stream, and we hunt over 25,000 acres of territory [nearly all of which is leased exclusively by King and Bartlett from International Paper Company]. We own 40 acres right here around the camp and an acre and a half at the gatehouse, which is located on Little Jim Pond. The variety of hunting and fishing opportunities around here is incredible. A lot of people want to fish Big King, because it's close, and because they're just up here to relax and have a good time. So we usually run about eight boats here. But I can almost always find you a spot to fish totally by yourself. During the summertime, I have seven guides here."

Camp rules include a two-fish-per-day limit: one trophy fish and one eating fish. "And we specify where you can catch those fish. We don't want you taking a 2-pound female brook trout out of Big King and eating it, because that's a beautiful breeding fish. Big King is general law, no worms. We have togue, so we sell bait like smelts, and we fish for togue down deep, with a lead-core line. Little King is general law as well and has brook and lake trout and salmon. Everything else that's on our lease, all the streams, lakes, and ponds, are fly-fishing-only. And we have canoes on every one of those ponds.

"For moose hunting, we have the southwestern zone. Moose flourish in this area. As a matter of fact, I just saw two come into camp when I was dropping off my deer hunters. The deer get big really quickly around here, so we figure they're eating like kings. It's rugged territory, but we're in kind of a valley with some nice lowland and a lot of under-growth, so the feeding's good. You can get a deer going in this terri-tory and he can take you 5 miles before you even know it.

"The last week of hunting season we're not open to the public. That's for the locals only. Whenever we have a big project to do in here, like pulling out docks, doing boat detail, putting up tree stands, my father or I bring in friends to help. Some weekends we have up to 20 people in here just helping us out. You've got to have help from friends to run a place like this. So that last week is a kind of thank-you from us.

"With deer hunting, we do it right. Since we hunt so much territory, I go out with my father and scout out areas. And we put up roughly 30 tree stands. I put our hunters in those stands and tell them if they put the time in at their stand, they're going to get a chance at a buck. And it works out well, because that's what happens. The network of logging roads has chunked this territory into parcels of land that are fairly easy to control. I can put a person in a piece of woods that I know has roads on all sides, and that gives him boundaries. Usually the hunters have a hand-held radio, so if they get into trouble, they can call me. Right now, as we're sitting here, it doesn't look like we've got any-thing going on. But when it comes about 3:30, 4 o'clock, hopefully the radio will come alive. Guys will be calling in—'I got one down.' It's fantastic."

Cranberry Butterscotch Bars

> 1 cup chopped cranberries, 1 pound dark brown sugar, ⅓ cup raisins, ¼ cup rum or water, ½ cup butter, 2 large beaten eggs, 1 tsp. vanilla, 1¾ cups flour, ½ tsp. baking powder, ⅔ cup toasted walnuts

Boil raisins and rum (or water) together for 5 minutes, or until liquid is absorbed. Let cool. Add 2 T sugar to chopped cranberries. Let sit until ready to use. In a saucepan, melt the butter and add the remaining sugar. Cook until bubbly. Let cool 15 minutes. Transfer to a bowl and add remaining ingredients. Fold in berries, walnuts, and raisins. Spread in a 9x13-inch greased pan. Bake at 350 degrees for 35–40 minutes.

21. LAKE PARLIN RESORT

HK/AP

OWNER: Jay Schurman
ADDRESS: HC 64, Box 564, Lake Parlin, ME 04945; 1-800-864-2676; fax: 207-668-7627; e-mail: rafting@maine.com
SEASON: Year-round
ACCOMMODATIONS: Nine log cabins (one or two bedrooms) with indoor plumbing, shower, automatic heat, woodstove, electric light, screened-in porch; no pets
RATES: $35 per person per day, $85–175 per cabin per day; boats included
ACCESS: I-95 to exit 36. Take US 201 north for 75 miles (14 miles north of West Forks). Camps are on the right side of the road.

A couple of other camps have profiles similar to Lake Parlin Resort—the Birches Resort on Moosehead and Bald Mountain Camps in Rangeley come to mind. All have a set of classic log cabins, modernized to include electricity, that form a compound a driveway-length from a paved road. The lodges have a TV room–sitting area, and the places hum with a variety of activities organized for guests, in addition to hunting and fishing. In other words, they have the look of a traditional sporting camp with the feel of a resort. Lake Parlin Resort, for example, offers a number of "family adventure" packages geared around white-water rafting.

Jay: "In 1997 we opened the place up to snowmobiling, and it was a huge success. So we're winterizing more cabins and upgrading our grooming. We groom 30 miles connecting to ITS 86, 87, and 89. Snowmobiling is as popular as rafting. We thought people would come here as a destination spot and travel from here. But now that I'm in snowmobiling, I think about 30 to 40 percent of the business is in meals, because people ride someplace to eat. We're applying to the state to be open to the public for food. [Snowmobilers around here travel] for lunch to Eustis, Rangeley, Greenville, Jackman, Pittston Farms. Pittston Farms serves around 3,000 people on the weekend during winter. Snowmobilers stay longer than the rafting clientele.

They're more like the families that come in the summer. They stay for a weekend, or even for four days, and they come with five sleds and a $30,000 car and trailer. They're coming from Maine, New Hampshire, Massachusetts, some as far away as New Jersey.

"We had to separate our rafting from the sporting camp because according to the state, it's not a permitted use. So we run our rafting out of a base camp across the street and have the main lodge and cabins on this side of the road." The new main lodge, with cathedral ceiling, large windows, and massive fieldstone fireplace, looks out on 2-mile by ½-mile Lake Parlin and Parlin Mountain beyond. "The lake is deep—180 feet at its deepest—so it has trout and salmon. But it got over-fished in the 1950s, so now it's fly-fishing-only and we encourage catch-and-release. We have sailboats and paddleboats for people, along with boats and canoes.

"I have four sons, Jack, Bobby, Luke, and Daniel, and I live with them down in Brunswick so they can go to school there. We come up here as often as we can, though. I grew up in Washington, D.C., and used to come up to Sunset Camps in the summers. I always loved sporting camps. We used to have family reunions there, 50 of us or so getting together every few years. Then, when I was in college, I answered a want ad for rafting guides. That was in 1976. I started Unicorn Outdoor Adventures in 1979, my senior year in college. I named it Unicorn because I thought it would be easy to remember and it had a good connotation. By 1986 business was so good that I was short of lodging, and I bought this place.

"This has been a sporting camp since 1947. There used to be an old hotel here, the Lake Parlin House. It was four stories with 90 rooms—huge—but it burned down and the owners didn't have insurance. The place did really well until the Depression, like most things. In the 1970s a group of nine families bought it. I got it and built this main lodge in 1993 and have been building and upgrading ever since. This is much harder as a business than rafting, a lot more work-intensive. But it's steadier work in ways. For rafting, you go from three employees to a hundred and then back to three again and it's hard to keep training new people every year. With the camps and the snowmobiling, you have year-round work. Families and snowmobiling are our fastest-growing business."

22. THE LAST RESORT

HK

OWNERS: Tim and Ellen Casey
ADDRESS: PO Box 777, Jackman, ME 04945; 207-668-5091
SEASON: Early May through late November
ACCOMMODATIONS: Eight log cabins, each with outhouse, gas lights, evening electricity, porch, central shower, wood or gas heater; dogs not allowed during July and August
RATES: July and August, $275–$400 per cabin per week; otherwise, $18 per adult per night
ACCESS: I-95 to exit 36. Follow US 201 north to Jackman. Turn right at a sign for the camp and drive 6 miles on a dirt road to the camp gate.

Making the turn into Tim and Ellen Casey's long "driveway," you begin to get a sense of the good times ahead, as upbeat signs start emerging along the way. By the final dip into camp, the day's drive begins to blur and you enter camp chuckling and ready to devote full attention to the matter at hand: rest and fun. The main lodge sits at the base of a "bowl" with cabins, a garden, a chicken coop, and outbuildings encircling it, and with a long body of water beyond.

Ellen: "How did you like the drive in? When we first got here, our road was really bad. I mean, we're talking big boulders, huge puddles that you'd have to tell people, 'Don't worry, you're not going to disappear!' We worked on that road in our spare time. I remember making a contraption with an old bedspring, weighing it down, so when you drag it the gravel gets turned up and hopefully it will get dragged into some of the holes. Then our neighbor had a 'york rake' with big tines and so we pulled that behind our truck once a week. The better you make the road, the more people use it, and the more people use it, the more they make the holes! You've got people who fuss, 'Boy, that's some road you got there!' But then you have little old ladies who come out joyriding, so you think, well, it can't be all that bad. So I put signs in the shape of a fish up along the way for encouragement. Things like: SO FAR SO GOOD, at the beginning, NICE AND EASY DOES IT for a particularly bad stretch. Another is YOU'RE ALMOST THERE. I wanted to put one a little farther that said, OK, SO I LIED, but my husband didn't think that was too good so I had to put OH FISH TALES! ONLY 1.1 MILES. REALLY!

"When we first came here we wanted a place as far out in never-never land as possible, because I've always loved animals and being out in the woods. We didn't name it the Last Resort, but the funny thing is we own some land in Massachusetts and I had called it the Last Resort. So it was right. We came over to see the place the day after Christmas in '86. I'd never been on a snowmobile before, and the realtor met us halfway down the lake. I got on the back of his snowmobile and away we came. Soon he gets off and says, 'You want to stop here a minute?' and I say, 'No! Keep going!' because I was afraid we'd fall in! There was about 3 feet of snow on the ground, and there were some bunnies around the camp from the previous owner. So we fed them and I videotaped the place. I had graduated as an elementary school teacher, our youngest had just graduated from high school, and Tim had just finished as a director at a computer company, so it seemed like the perfect time to do something else. That night we thought it over and said, well, we've gotta try it because we'll be kicking ourselves if we don't. And if we leave after 2 years, at least we know we've tried. So we bought it.

"We were very lonely the first year and actually put the place up for sale because it was getting to be a very expensive 'vacation.' But then business picked up and we took it off the market. So now we've found our niche and we're doing just fine. Our niche is moose-watching. In mid-June every year I try to count the maximum number of moose I see at one exact moment. The most I counted was 18. They come to the mouth of the river because all the silt builds up there, and once the pond weeds start growing they just go out there and graze. During the summer they may be out there all day long and you can go out in a canoe or boat and just mingle with the moose. They go back in the woods in the fall. Often in the summer, if you're on your porch, you can hear them out there sloshing around in the closer coves. In the spring they're all over like crazy, eating the young buds off the trees. They won't bite the branches, they'll just 'lip' all the leaves off. Moose are good swimmers. They can swim up to 6 miles an hour for up to 2 hours at a time. And they can run at speeds of up to 35 miles an hour through the woods. In the fall, the males are out looking for mates. Gestation is about 8 months and the babies are light chocolate brown. The mother usually doesn't bring them out to the lake until the leaves have come out.

"We're on Long Pond here. It's 12 miles long and connects, by Moose River, to other lakes. The fishery is salmon, trout, perch, and chub. You never get bored out there, that's for sure. I know logs used to come down Moose River because you can still see the boom piles. And the big white rock over there used to be called Eel Rock, because people used to catch eels over there and then smoke them. The eels can go from salt to fresh water, and they used to migrate up here to do their spawning. They don't come up here anymore because of the dams at Brassua Lake, one on the Kennebec River, and then Wyman Dam.

"The original owner of this place was back in 1902, a man named Henry Hughey. He used to do guiding, deer hunting mostly. When Jackman was in its heyday, families would take the whole summer off and come in here by boat or carriage trail. Then in 1958 there was a big forest fire that started from the dump and came this way. I guess everyone in camp at the time headed out in the lake in boats. At the last minute the fire turned and went up from the lake. But the original lodge burned down, and then they built this lodge. Around that point they sold to Lyn Tanner and his wife. Tanner built some cabins and did a lot of nice wood-burning of birds and animals in the cabins for decoration. There have been two or three owners since then, but the place is still basically the same. We bought it in 1987 and have been loving it ever since.

"Sometimes we have lived in here year-round, not at the camps here, but over at our cabins on Route 15 heading into Jackman. Or we go wherever there's work. But we love getting back in here. We love the moose, and we also have a lot of hummingbirds around here, plus loons. It's calm, and peaceful, and quiet."

23. RED BUCK CAMPS

HK

OWNERS: Sandy and Tom Doughty
ADDRESS: PO Box 114, Jackman, ME 04945; 207-668-5361
SEASON: Year-round
ACCOMMODATIONS: Eight log or stick-built cabins (one or two bedrooms), with indoor plumbing, shower, electric light, automatic heat, TV, some with screened-in porch; pets allowed
RATES: $25–46 per person per day; $170–275 per person per week
ACCESS: I-95 to exit 36 (Fairfield). Take US 201 north toward Jackman. Red Buck is 13 miles north of The Forks (12 miles south of Jackman) on the right side (east) of US 201.

Red Buck has basic amenities and is located right off US 201 within relatively easy access to Lake Parlin. The camp is perched on top of Parlin Mountain at 1,650 feet above sea level and receives snow earlier and longer than surrounding areas.

Tom: "It's usually about 10 degrees colder here than in Jackman [7 miles away], so we have great snowmobiling because of our elevation. We're near three ITS trails—86, 87, and 89—and we groom our own connector trails. In fact, we've got people who've rented one of our cabins for the whole winter, three months, so they can come up here to snowmobile. Another cabin we've got rented for an entire year. Besides the ITS, there are over a thousand miles of unplowed logging roads. Snowmobiling is a big thing around this area. We're so close to the Canadian border our trail systems connect in with the trans-Québec trail."

Sandy: "We bought this place in 1985, came up from Portland. I was working as a waitress and Tom was with S.D. Warren [a logging company]. This was originally a logging camp in the 1920s. Tom got his guide's license and leads hunters."

Tom: "This western mountain region has thousands of acres of softwood forests with hardwood ridges, and logging has left huge areas of blueberries and raspberries. So there's a lot of food for bears. In the '70s, Maine eliminated the spring season for bear hunting, which has meant that the population has doubled to something over 20,000. We hunt from baited tree stands or blinds. We also have really big deer here, a lot over 200 pounds. We kind of cater to bow hunters, and we allow hunting dogs in season."

While we talked, a serious game of horseshoes was in progress in the backyard, and I noticed a side table covered with trophies. *Tom:* "We have tournaments in town all the time. We play for fun. Everyone goes individually and you get teamed up with someone by drawing numbers. People come in from all over—downstate, and a lot from Canada. We play from 1 to 7 or so, and players pay 6 dollars. Everyone gets trophies, and then they split the pot up for the winners. It's at Northland, in Jackman, a place with a bar, motel, and in back it's got big horseshoe pits. The whole town plays there. We start in June and play once every month until October. The first week in February, they go and shovel the pits out for a game. It could be 20 below, 30 below . . ."

Sandy: "That's why he's got two trophies over there with a horse's ass. That's what they call the February tournament. They figure that if there's anyone crazy enough to be out there in the freezing cold playing horseshoes, that's what they should get!"

24. SALLY MOUNTAIN CABINS

HK

OWNERS: Corey and Sally Hegarty

ADDRESS: HCR 64, Box 50, Jackman, ME 04945; 207-668-5621 or 1-800-644-5621

SEASON: Year-round

ACCOMMODATIONS: Eight log cabins (sleep two to ten people) with automatic heat, indoor plumbing, shower and tub; three condo-style modern lodgings; TV

RATES: $19 per person per day; $125 per person per week.

ACCESS: I-95 to exit 36 (Fairfield). Take US 201 north to Jackman. After the railroad tracks, take the first left onto Spruce Street and follow the signs to camp.

Sally Mountain Cabins feature something I have not seen at any other sporting camp: three-tiered containers (visualize a green-plastic file cabinet), in each cabin, for recycling. Each log cabin has a wooden nameplate over the door with a date, such as SUNSET, 1955. A few of the interiors are painted white. The newest cabin has wood paneling with a spiral wooden staircase leading to a loft. Although the decor is an eclectic mix (as in most camps), the place has a continuity of color (dark stain and with red window frames) and feel. The Hegartys and their preschool daughters live across the street in one of the condominium units they also own and manage.

Sally: "We've been here six years, but my husband grew up in Jackman. His parents bought the place in '74, I think it was. Then it was called Gay's Cabins, and his parents changed the name to Sally Mountain Cabins because we're right across from the [2,221-foot] mountain. My in-laws run the Jackman Trading Post."

The trading post, at the height-of-land as you head down into town, provides a few visual chuckles along with supplies. In fact, what with several other roadside spoofs in the area, you get the impression that there are a number of individuals around here with a good-natured, if not quirky, sense of humor.

Sally: "My husband's parents owned this place as he was growing up. I know that the Gilbert and Dreamland cabins and the main lodge were all personal homes. In the very beginning there were two cabins that were dragged from farther down the lake. I'm not sure if it was the Gays, or someone before them, who turned it into a cabin rental. Dreamland was built in 1936. They originally put down a beautiful

The view from the dining-room window

wood floor and over the years covered it with newspaper and then layers and layers of linoleum. We have some of the old newspaper articles framed in the cabin to show people.

"My husband left here to go to college in southern Maine and I'm from Auburn. We met there. When we had the opportunity to buy this place from his parents, we jumped at the offer. And it's been great. Jackman's not very big [the population is 900] but it has everything: a bank and post office, a medical center, restaurants, churches, and an airport for people who want to come in that way.

"Big Wood Lake is 6½ miles long by 2½ wide and 72 feet deep at its maximum, with salmon, brook and lake trout, splake, smelt, and cusk. In the winter we rent out ice shacks, and have the only live-bait shop in town. We say, 'Our bait is guaranteed to catch fish . . . or die trying!' We get a lot of fishermen. Actually, it's about half fishermen and half snowmobilers. Which is good, because if the snowmobiling's bad, we still do well.

"When I go on vacation, I want a clean place. And I like my cabins to be very clean. It's a big deal, because a cabin can be very old and crooked, maybe in need of repairs, but if it's clean, it makes a big difference. The hardest thing is finding help because no one cleans as well as, you know, you do. So my husband and I work right along with the chambermaids because the last little finishing touches count. The first two years we had no children and the 'go get 'em' was really there. Now it's more challenging because the kids really hold me back, and I need even more help with laundry. With the condominium we have 11 places to take care of. So we're looking for more employees.

"Our biggest challenge is having what the customers want. They expect more than people did years ago. Like they'll say, 'Oh, you have coffee pots'—the smallest thing can make a difference. And we really want to please them. They want the rustic atmosphere but with all the supplies, and they love the low rates. It's hard to do both, but in this business I find the repeat customer is what it's all about. On the other hand, in the summer we get drive-ins from all over because we're so close to the Canadian border—just 16 miles. We get a lot of people from Europe driving to Québec. There's a lot of history to the old 201. [Around 1833, Captain James Jackman, for whom the town is named, built the Canada Road from The Forks to the Canadian border, and thereby linked the area up to civilization.] We're 100 miles from Québec, a couple of hours. And people from abroad are usually doing New England. They fly into Boston and go to the White Mountains, Vermont, Québec, Niagara Falls. We even had someone from Australia a few years ago. That's what's great about the summertime—the world comes to your door!"

25. TUCKAWAY SHORES

HK

OWNERS: Phil and Paulette Thomas
ADDRESS: HCR 64, Box 44, Jackman, ME 04945; 207-668-3351
SEASON: Year-round
ACCOMMODATIONS: Seven cabins with one to three rooms, indoor plumbing, shower (one cabin has a tub), automatic heat, electric light, porch, TV; advance permission for pets
RATES: $25 per person per day; $150 per person per week
ACCESS: I-95 to exit 36 (Fairfield). Take US 201 north to Jackman. After the railroad tracks, turn left onto Spruce Street and follow the signs.

Tuckaway Shores, Cozy Cove Cabins, and Sally Mountain Cabins are all ranged along the shore of Big Wood Lake and within walking distance of one another and Jackman's Main Street. Of the three, Tuckaway Shores is perhaps the most basic camp in terms of its facilities and cabins. The cabins and log main lodge facing the street are stained dark brown with red window frames. The Thomases live in a tan frame house they built.

Paulette: "The place started in the '20s, and we were the third owners when we purchased it in 1987. We moved here from New Hampshire. I'm a naturopathic physician and an R.N. and a P.A. There aren't that many holistic practitioners, but it's becoming more popular. The National Institutes of Health now have an office of alternative medicine. And last year they advised all medical and nursing schools to start teaching integrative medicine: meditation, homeopathy, acupuncture, reflexology, that type of thing. As it is now, 50 out of 135 medical schools have integrative medicine. I have a small client base around here."

Phil: "What intrigued us about the area was that Big Wood Lake is the third lake in a chain of six and Moose River runs through it and goes down to Moosehead Lake. It was the water, basically, that got to us. We like to fish catch-and-release ourselves, and we just enjoy boating around, looking at the mountains. These are the boundary mountains between the States and Canada. Our side of the lake is settled and the rest is basically pristine.

"Snowmobiling and ice fishing is our busiest season. Jackman itself has 200 miles of trails with three groomers going 24 hours a day, flattening and widening trails. If we have a group or a prior reservation, I will cook for people. I have a culinary degree and do consulting for some places around here. I was planning on getting into art. The fine-arts classes were full, but the culinary-arts classes were open, so I got that degree instead. I have my doctorate in parapsychic sciences, the study of the unknown: apparitions, magnetic fields, past-life memories. I've always been fascinated with ghost stories, miracles. It's amazing how many people have experienced a psychic phenomenon they can't explain. When we first came in and looked at this place, we just sat for a couple of hours looking out at the lake. There's good energy in this area."

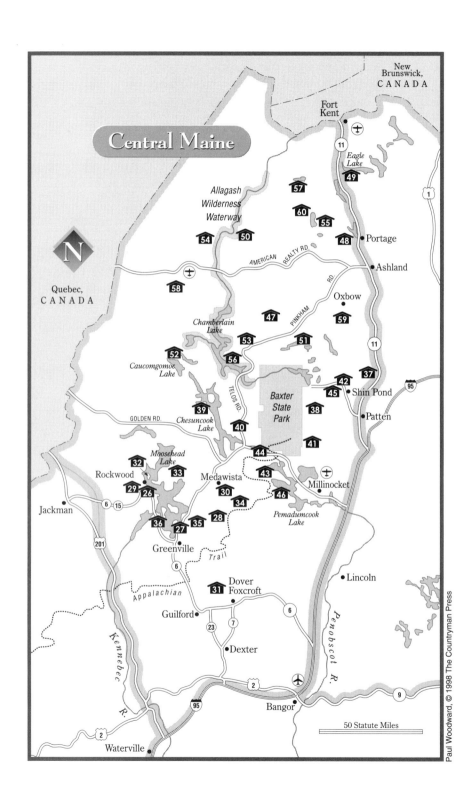

Central Maine

Quebec, CANADA

New Brunswick, CANADA

Fort Kent

Eagle Lake

Allagash Wilderness Waterway

Portage

Ashland

Oxbow

Chamberlain Lake

Caucomgomoc Lake

Baxter State Park

Shin Pond

Patten

Golden Rd.

Chesuncook Lake

Telos Rd.

Moosehead Lake

Rockwood

Jackman

Medawista

Millinocket

Pemadumcook Lake

Greenville

Lincoln

Appalachian Trail

Dover Foxcroft

Guilford

Dexter

Kennebec R.

Penobscot R.

Bangor

Waterville

50 Statute Miles

Paul Woodward, © 1998 The Countryman Press

PART TWO
CENTRAL MAINE

This section is bounded by US 201 to the west, ME 6/16 in the south, I-95 and ME 11 to the east, and the Canadian boundary in the north. The major areas include the Moosehead Lake region, the Baxter State Park region, and the North Maine Woods. Most of the land in this region is privately owned by pulp and paper companies but is accessible to the public. Moose outnumber people in some areas. Logging roads outnumber paved. Be prepared to answer questions about your travel plans and pay tolls at the various gatehouses within this vast area. For further information, write North Maine Woods, PO Box 421, Ashland, ME 04732. Camps will send driving directions, but the DeLorme *Maine Atlas and Gazetteer* showing the network of logging roads is almost a must (DeLorme Mapping, PO Box 298, Yarmouth, ME 04096, 800-452-5931). Many camp owners in this region strongly suggest flying into their spots by floatplane. If you drive, be aware that you need to leave ample time for the slower rate of travel, and don't expect to run into any gas stations once you're on logging roads. The driving times noted in the various regions are averages only, since some camps are farther off in the "willy wack" than others and some have rougher access roads than others.

The Moosehead Lake Region

The Moosehead Lake region, although in the "southern" portion of this central section, is nearly level with the most northern area of our previous section. The camps here are in the general vicinity of 40-mile-long, up-to-20-mile-wide Moosehead Lake, the largest lake in the Northeast. The Golden Road (so named because of the expense involved in hacking out every mile of this dirt throughway for pulp trucks) forms the region's northern boundary. Another logging road, Church Pond Road, forms its eastern boundary.

Moosehead Lake drains an area of about 1,226 square miles and serves as the headwaters of the Kennebec River. Nearby are an additional 175,000 acres of water in lakes, ponds, streams, and rivers, including the Moose River and the headwaters of the Penobscot River. The town of Greenville, at the base of the lake, is the unofficial capital of the region, and can meet most provisioning, medical, and banking needs. From here, outfitters offer spring and summer white-water rafting, and the 110-foot steamboat *Katahdin*—a last remnant of an earlier form of transportation—plies Moosehead's waters. Greenville is also home to the largest seaplane base in New England and hosts an international seaplane fly-in each fall. In the winter, a 100-mile snowmobiling trail encircles the lake and there is ice fishing and skiing at 3,196-foot Squaw Mountain.

The Appalachian Trail winds its way through this area. Among other hiking destinations, Gulf Hagas, nicknamed the Grand Canyon of Maine, is a 4-mile-long gorge along the west branch of the Pleasant River, with 400-foot vertical slate walls and numerous waterfalls. Moose are plentiful in this region; the area sponsors the annual Moosemainea, a monthlong series of events during the spring.

Getting there: Bangor International Airport is the nearest airport (with rental cars available). Driving time from Portland is 3–4 hours; from Boston, 6–7 hours; from New York City, 9–11 hours. Float-plane services are available in Greenville: Folsom's Air Service, 207-695-2821 (Folsom's also serves as the phone link to some of the camps listed here); Currier's Flying Service, 207-695-2778; Jack's Air Service, 207-695-3020.

Guidance: For a visitor's guide or a listing of summer events, contact the Moosehead Lake Chamber of Commerce, PO Box 581, Greenville, ME 04441; 207-695-2702 or 207-695-2026; fax: 207-695-3440; e-mail: moose@moosehead.net; Web site: http/www.moosehead.net/moose/chamber. html

26. THE BIRCHES RESORT

AP/HK, SCA

OWNERS: John and Bill Willard
ADDRESS: Box 81-SC, Rockwood, ME 04478; 207-534-7305, 1-800-825-9453; e-mail: wwld@aol.com; Web site: http://webcom.com/birches
SEASON: Year-round
ACCOMMODATIONS: 15 log cabins with indoor plumbing, showers (central

bathhouse for winter), electric and gas light, woodstove or fireplace; 12 "cabin tents" with outdoor fire pits; central lodge with TV, bar, and living-room area

RATES: $40–115 per cabin (HK); $80–125 per person per day (AP); $525–795 per person per week (AP)

ACCESS: I-95 to exit 39. Go north on ME 7 to Dexter, ME 23 to Guilford, and ME 6/15 to Greenville. Continue on ME 6/15 to Rockwood. After the Village Store, turn right across a bridge and then right again at the camp sign. The Birches driveway is several hundred yards farther on the right.

The Birches Resort is located about halfway up the west side of Moosehead Lake and looks across to Mount Kineo. It has the look of a traditional sporting camp, but at the main lodge, which quietly bustles with staff and activities, it has the feel of a resort. The State of Maine has purchased Mount Kineo and 21 miles of shorefront beyond the mountain, "so," John Willard smiles, "the pristine view you see is what will be there in the years to come.

John: "The Birches was built in the 1930s by a man named Oz Fahey, a logging contractor up in this area. When the Depression came along, the logging industry fell off but he had crews still willing to work, basically for room and board. So he made his house the main lodge, built cabins on either side, and went into the sporting-camp business. Each year he would build another cabin. The last one, as far as we can tell, was built in 1945–1946. We did some new roofing and found boards from shipping crates that said FAHEY, ROCKWOOD, MAINE on them from when they were rationing lumber. He had wealthy guests that would come here for the summer—spin-offs from the Kineo Resort. Some of the guests liked it here so much he would let them design their own cabin.

"Fahey ran the place during its heyday in the '40s and early '50s. A man named Telford Allen, the president of a cosmetics company, bought it in 1960 and sold in '64. He had a Spanish manager because he lived in Central or South America somewhere. He built a swimming pool, a marina, a new lounge—spent a lot of money and then went broke. So from '64 to '69 the camps were closed. And then my dad was looking around for a place for a kids camp. He was in the construction business and decided he wanted a change. Well, he found the Birches, and he and I and my brother were going to run it. We decided not to open for kids but to try it as a sporting camp. We opened in 1970 and we've run it ever since.

The Birches: John Willard and kids Joel and Jamie

"The summer of '78 my father had a heart attack. It rained just about every day that summer. Even the customers left early; it was pathetic. So there was nothing for him to do really. So he picked names for our cabins from a Henry Mancini album, found pieces of driftwood, dried them out, and painted the names on the driftwood. We've got Ramblin Rose, In the Mood, Days of Wine and Roses, and so on. A lot of people will call back and say, 'I want September in the Rain,' or something. Most of us who've been here a long time will automatically know which number cabin that is.

"When my brother Bill and I bought Dad out, we had to change the whole marketing scheme because I felt there was no way I could make a living here just renting out cabins. So that's how we ended up doing canoe trips and white-water rafting, which grew into our Wilderness Expeditions outdoor-adventure programs. We now have Moose Cruises twice a day, flat-water and white-water kayaking, mountain biking, challenge courses, sailing lessons, interpretive hiking, ski trails, and snowmobiling. We're dedicated to offering the largest activity-based resort in the country: 11,000 acres of pristine, private wilderness.

"There's a pattern to our year. March is the end of ice fishing. April we'll do our spring cleaning. First part of May fishing season starts up for lake and brook trout and salmon. There's been a pattern to the fishing, too. When we first came here it was lousy. Then in the '80s it was great and got fished out. Usually the best year of fishing is just before the worst, because it's fished out. We're on the upswing again now. The pressure on the fishery is 40 percent what it used to be because there's more catch-and-release. Also in May the white-water rafting season comes in. We've got a base camp at The Forks on the Kennebec River and one on the Penobscot near Baxter State Park. People stay at the base camp or we have a shuttle from here. It's about a 50-minute drive. A lot of people that started rafting with us are now bringing their families and staying here.

"The end of school starts our summer season. Summertime we're maxed. Sometimes we'll have a hundred people in the lodge for dinner. We then have about 10 full-time staff here. In the summer we also have what we call cabin tents. They're sort of between a cabin and camping: four beds in each one, lights, a door, windows. They're cheap to build and great for weekenders. Fall season is September and October. We get weekend types, a lot of them from southern Maine, for the fall foliage. And then the hunting is in November. Most of our winter business comes from snowmobilers, cross-country skiers, and ice fishermen. In the lodge we've got four bed & breakfast rooms, plus the 15 cabins. In the wintertime people come mostly on the weekends. In the winter it's probably 70 percent Maine residents, and in the summer it's just the other way around. The spring people are the hearty-type fishermen and the heartier white-water rafters. In the summer we get the families.

"My brother's a real backhoe-type of person, always fixing and building. Several years ago he built a large float in front of the main lodge with some octagon tables out there so people can eat right on the water. I do all the marketing. What I've always thought in my business is to market to myself, to offer folks what I'd like to do. I knew I would have a hard time providing a decent living standard for my kids, Jamie and Joel, and myself if I didn't put in these extra things like the skiing and rafting. When I first came up here I went to the University of Maine and did forestry. Then I lived in here in a trailer and one of the smaller cabins. I lived two or three winters with no running water and dug holes in the ice just to get my water out. I know what it's like to live hard. Some people come up here and say, 'Geez, you got it made.' And I say, 'Hey, if you stick with the same job for 27 years, you'll have it made, too!' This is the accumulation of a lot of plain old hard work."

Baked Stuffed Onions

4 big sweet onions, peeled, cut in half, ends cut flat to sit up; 4 slices Muenster cheese

Stuffing: ⅓ cup Parmesan cheese, 2 cups bread crumbs, 1 cup chopped mushrooms, ½ cup chopped onions, ½ cup chopped celery, ½ cup melted butter, 1 tsp. chicken base, salt and pepper to taste

Sauté vegetables in butter, chicken base, salt and pepper. Mix with the Parmesan cheese and bread crumbs. Place a handful of the stuffing on each onion half. Cover with Muenster cheese slices. Place in pan, loosely covered. Bake at 375 degrees for 20 minutes.

27. FOSTER'S MAINE BUSH SPORTING CAMPS

HK

OWNERS: Chip and Laurie Foster

ADDRESS: PO Box 1230, Greenville, ME 04441; 207-695-2845

SEASON: Year-round

ACCOMMODATIONS: Seven cabins (sleep one to ten people) with indoor plumbing, shower, wood or gas heat, gas stove, refrigerator, electric lights; linen supplied; pets allowed for a fee

RATES: July and August, $390–1,000 per cabin per week; otherwise $55–150 per cabin per day

ACCESS: I-95 to exit 39 (Newport). Take ME 7 north to Dexter, ME 23 to Guilford, and ME 6/15 to Greenville. At the blinking yellow light, continue straight and go 3.5 miles on Lily Bay Road to the camp sign. Turn left and go 0.5 mile on a dirt road to the camps.

Chip: "Our camps have been around since the early 1900s. And we've got a thousand feet of shoreline here at Sandy Bay, on the eastern side of Moosehead Lake. Moosehead is New England's largest lake: 40 miles long, 10 miles wide. It's only 60 miles from the ocean, as the crow flies, but we're 1,100 feet above sea level here. As you look out you can see Big Squaw Mountain, Katahdin 40 miles to the east, and Mount Kineo out in the middle of the lake. We're running this camp and are also involved in developing the resort at the base of Mount Kineo's cliffs. It's on a peninsula that's 2 miles long, with a 1-mile water shuttle from Rockwood. The Mount Kineo Hotel used to be world famous.

"The Indians came up to this area from all over because of Mount Kineo. It's a solid mass of flint, which they needed for arrowheads. *Kineo* means "flint" in Abenaki. They thought the shape looked like a moose's head. The story goes that an Indian chief was once chasing two moose. He killed them, and one became Mount Kineo and the other turned into Little Spencer or Kokadjo Mountain. That's how Moosehead got its name."

Old brochures give a glimpse into the early 1900s, Moosehead's golden era. One features the area's "absolute freedom from hay fever" and extols its scenic beauty: "Back from the coast, hidden among mountains and in forests seven times larger than the Black Forest in Germany, is a spring-fed water system of vast extent and unequaled purity. Maine has one lake to each 20 square miles of territory, over 1600 square miles in all. More lake surface than a million square miles of the United States." The brochures continue with information regarding transportation. There were trains to Greenville, Maine, from Michigan, Boston, Albany, Baltimore, the White Mountains, New Haven, Hartford, and Providence. From New York City, you could leave Grand Central Station on a daily 8 PM overnight sleeper, eat breakfast in the dining car, and arrive at Greenville or Rockwood in time for lunch.

Chip: "This is a four-season playground, with good hunting, skiing, and snowmobiling. The fishing was going downhill, but I pulled together a coalition to work on the resources around here and hopefully it will help. My wife, Laurie, and I see a lot of potential for this area. It's interesting. You get some people who come here and they start out thinking there's nothing to do. All of a sudden the artificial over-stimulation comes to a crashing halt. Then slowly—or quickly, depending on the person—it's replaced by natural stimulation from the real world. That's what these places are all about."

28. LITTLE LYFORD POND CAMPS
AP, SCA

OWNERS: Bud and Kate Fackelman recently sold the camp to Arlene and Bob LeRoy

ADDRESS: PO Box 1269, Greenville, ME 04441; 207-695-2821 (radio/camp); 207-534-2284 (office)

SEASON: Year-round

ACCOMMODATIONS: Eight log cabins (each sleeps one to six people) with

gas lights, woodstove, running spring-fed water, outhouse, camp sauna, and
open-air shower

RATES: $85 per person per day, includes use of boats

ACCESS: I-95 to exit 39 (Newport). Go north on ME 7 to Dexter, then take
ME 23 to Guilford, then ME 6/15 to Greenville. In downtown Greenville,
turn east onto Pleasant Street (uphill) toward the airport, past Moosehead
Farms, past Rum Ridge, and follow the camp's blue-and-white signs
12 miles to North Maine Woods Gate (fee). Proceed another 5 miles
to the Little Lyford Pond Camps driveway.

You drive into Little Lyford down a gently sloping hill, past lawns and
the owners' home, to the low log main lodge and its covey of honey-
colored log cabins. (Many guests have never been this route but enter
by way of the extensive network of cross-country ski paths.) Under a
conifer canopy, lined up behind each cabin are log outhouses. The
Fackelmans say they once contemplated modernizing the plumbing,
but guests set up such a hue and cry that they dropped the idea.

Kate: "I read an article in 'House for Sale' in *Yankee Magazine* and
thought, 'Doesn't this sound great!' My husband, Bud, said, 'Cut the
kidding,' and—here we are! We were living in Grafton, Massachusetts,
at the time. Bud had been in academics [as department head of surgery
at Tufts School of Veterinary Medicine] for 25 years or so and was a
little bit tired of the folderol that goes along with academic life, and
was not doing what he really likes to do, which is surgery. He's a large-
animal orthopedic surgeon. So we decided to come to Little Lyford
in the fall of 1987. The whole family moved there, which was six dogs,
three cats, two parrots, a variety of finches and canaries, and a goat.

"Then things evolved and ongoing international research projects
that he had, particularly with a group in Switzerland, developed. And
he became involved in revising a medical text he'd done 10 years ago
and working on a CD-ROM project for L.L. Bean. So we had all these
things going which require more communication sophistication than
we've got at Little Lyford. We're surrounded by small mountains
[Indian, Elephant, Baker, and White Cap]—the camps are basically in
a small alpine valley—so our communications are terrible. That's the
plus and minus. Then, although we're technically open 365 days a year,
there are definite patterns of business. So in 1992 we decided we'd set
aside blocks of time to be at Little Lyford, and the rest of the time we
would have to base ourselves elsewhere.

"I think the most important thing we learned about running a

Little Lyford offers cabins such as this one for cross-country skiers.

sporting camp right off is 'The buck stops here.' You can talk about calling the fire department, the police, the plumber, the electrician, but there isn't anybody to come out there. Although that's not entirely true. The wardens are there, and they're great. We had a wonderful rescue recently. These people went off for a lovely day of cross-country skiing along Gulf Hagas nearby, near the Appalachian Trail. And we had discussed the route and timing, the fact that they should not go on the

Rim Trail. And what happened was, they crossed the river and then crossed back again, but in the process of making that triangle they missed the fact that the sign for the trail is on a stretch that they didn't cover. The Rim Trail's very, very tough going.

"They found themselves out of time, but felt they could not make it back physically. They didn't know how far they had to go to get out. Night came, and it was 20 below. And the man had gotten wet. So we had a very serious situation on our hands. We require that guests be back in camp by 4 PM in winter. When they weren't in, Bud went out to look for them. Fortunately, we had a very good idea where they were. So he took the snowmobile as far as he could, and then he skied. He saw what happened. He did not pursue them on the Rim Trail because by then he was out of daylight. He radioed back to me and said, 'I'm going around to see if they came out the other end, but I think you'd better call the wardens.' The wardens got to them at midnight and got them out at 4:30 AM. The man's feet were in pretty bad shape when they found him. He was hypothermic, and his feet were encased in ice, but when they thawed him out, no damage had been done. He was very lucky. I wrote a personal letter to all the guys who were out there: five wardens and two EMTs from 7 at night until 4:30 in the morning, plus the two of us.

"We immediately wrote to the governor about the warden service. There's talk about cutbacks. But if you're going to promote the tourist industry, which is the second-largest moneymaker in Maine—in fact, in real terms maybe its largest, since if you look at the timber industry, most of the money goes out of state, they are not Maine corporations—then you must have infrastructure to support bringing urban or suburban people into what is more wilderness than many of them have ever seen before. And you can talk yourself blue in the face about rules and regulations, but it's the human element that's going to screw you up every time. We had a nice gal in her early 60s. She'd done a fair amount of hiking and we sent her out with a very good trail map. Well, she was finally escorted back to camp by a forest ranger. And she told me that I was mistaken, that on this map the river was running the wrong direction. Now, sorry, if the river is on your left when you go, it's only logical that when you come back it will be on your right. It was as basic as that.

"I've learned a tremendous amount running Little Lyford, from basic plumbing, and believe me, we don't have much, to all kinds of cooking. I love to cook and at camp you have a captive audience. What you see is what you get, and your nearest fast-food joint is at least

3 hours away. There's been a definite evolution in eating habits; we get a lot of 'no red meat' people. So we ask about eating preferences.

"Running this business has been a big growing experience for both of us. I think you need a pretty strong relationship for starters because it can be a tight little island. I'm far more tolerant of all kinds of things than I used to be—with the possible exception of people! Initially I felt that Bud was being too kind to me. I needed to know how to change a spark plug in a snowmobile or generator. I needed to know how to do everything in case I needed to be able to do it myself sometime. There are a great many people in the world, probably more in the United States proportionately than in any other country, who are unable to cope with day-to-day living. I've listened to my husband's parents, who went through Hurricane Andrew, say, 'You can't imagine what it was like.' Well, I've lived for two years in West Africa; I've been all over the world. I do know what it was like. You have to learn to think and plan ahead. If you don't have a hose clamp, you make one. Or you by-pass the whole problem. If you run out of propane for your gas lamps and don't have any kerosene around for the kerosene lamps, then you don't read past 6 o'clock at night, or whatever. You have to learn to be creative and to cope."

Black Bean Salad

> 1 cup raw long-grain white rice, 2 cups water, 2 cans (16 ounces each) black beans, 1 can (14½ ounces) stewed tomatoes, 1 can (4 ounces) chopped green chilies, 1 can corn or 1 package frozen corn, 2 T barbecue sauce or catsup, 1 T ground cumin (or to taste), freshly ground black pepper

Cook rice until tender (about 18 minutes). Add the drained beans and the remaining ingredients. Heat thoroughly. Serve hot or cold. Leftovers can be thinned with broth and served as hot soup. Makes 4–6 servings.

29. MAYNARD'S-IN-MAINE

AP

OWNERS: Gail and Bill Maynard
ADDRESS: PO Box 220, Rockwood, ME 04478; 207-534-7703
SEASON: May 1 through December 1
ACCOMMODATIONS: 12 cabins (each sleeps one to six people) with wood-stoves or automatic heat, indoor plumbing and showers, electricity; pets accepted

RATES: $50 per person per day

ACCESS: I-95 to exit 38 (Newport). Go north on ME 7/11 to Dexter. Continue north on ME 23 and then take 6/15 through Greenville to Rockwood. After the Village Store, turn right across a bridge and then take the first left (sign) to Maynard's on the right.

Maynard's is on the north side of the Moose River right past the village of Rockwood's general store. A circular drive leads up to a lodge and cabins along an expanse of lawn. Set back high and far enough from the road, the camps have the feel of an enclave. It's pretty hard to miss Maynard's. Taking up much of the roof area, a huge white wooden sign sits atop a classic main lodge. Morning glories twine around porch posts, weathered rocking chairs face lakeward in a long row. Inside, old fishing paraphernalia and photos, stuffed animals, and exotic African artifacts grace the office and living room area. One group of cabins is within a grove of trees, the other set makes a gentle arc down along the lawn.

Gail: "I married into this business. I married Bill in the late '60s, and with him came this. We started a family early, so I was waitressing and carrying a baby on my hip day after day at first. The good thing was we weren't open all year round so I had a little bit of time. When I married Bill, my father-in-law, Roger, was doing the cooking. Previous to that my mother-in-law did it, but she had a stroke and Roger had to learn in a hurry. He was doing the books and we were sharing the cooking. Then Roger had a bad heart attack in 1990 and after that, I was doing everything."

I had interviewed Roger in 1994, before he died, and Gail asked that his comments be included here. *Roger:* "Well, my father, Walter, was born in Massachusetts, and as a kid he heard Mr. Wilson, of Wilson's Camps here at East Outlet, talk about running camps and decided that's what he wanted to do. When he bought this place, nothing was here. This was just an old farm, but it had burned down. One of the cabins here was built, painted, and occupied by guests in a day and a half! By 1919 it was a real sporting camp. The main lodge was built in 1932. I remember there were a lot of guides here. We had as high as 42 guides at one time; one for each person, basically. I figure around the mid-1930s were the golden years for this place. My father was running it then, and my mother, Vivian, did all the cooking. As for me, I remember running around as a kid mostly steppin' on nails!

"We had seven or eight governors together here at one time. We had

Maynard's-in-Maine

the leading contralto of the Metropolitan Opera with us for three seasons and the leading cellist. And the manager of the *I Love Lucy* show. Chet Huntley was here. When I was growing up, this side of the river was all farms and cleared land, with very few houses. My father died in his '70s, so I started running the place in the 1940s. When we first started running the camp we was getting $2.50 a day, including meals. But in the early 1900s you were making money. You didn't pay over a dollar for a loaf of bread. Loins of beef were 15 to 18 cents at that time. It was easier getting fresh produce then, because the Maine Central train was running in here daily from Portland, coming out on the wharf down to Rockwood. The Mount Kineo Hotel [a huge resort hotel at the base of Mount Kineo in the middle of Moosehead Lake] was operating then. We had a garden here and two cows and 67 chickens, so all our milk and eggs were taken care of. Plus we had homemade ice cream. We'd think nothing of taking 3 quarts of cream and making ice cream so rich that when you ate it, it stuck to the roof of your mouth. We put up the ice ourselves, cut it in the cove, and put it in the icehouse."

Gail handed me Walter Maynard's typed memoir. It starts: "The Autobiography of Walter Maynard: Maine Guide, Trapper, River Driver, Game Warden, Deputy Sheriff, Camp Owner and Builder, Big

Game Hunter, commercial fisherman, Captain of Commodore's Yacht at Moosehead, collector for American and British museums in the jungles of South America, agent for public schools, Harbor Master." And it goes on to relate just how one man did, in fact, do all these things! Walter Maynard was born in Rutland, Massachusetts, in 1885. His mother died when he was 8, and he was sent to an orphanage. He then became a "bound-out boy," from which servitude he shortly escaped on a passing train. In March 1911, after an incredible number of jobs and escapades, he "bought fifty acres of land from Harry Johnston on the north bank of Moose River about one mile from its mouth. The natives called it 'a pile of brush.'" His son, Roger, "was born premature, only weighing 3¾ pounds, but turned into a healthy boy." Healthy enough, indeed, to carry on the Maynard tradition into future generations.

Gail: "We have three children—Bill, Missy, and Kristy—and they all help a lot—shovel roofs in the winter, cut wood, help my husband plow, whatever else has to be done. In the wintertime, I usually work somewhere and Bill plows 80-some-odd driveways. Off-season we pray for snow, 'cause if there's no snow, there's no plowing, and if there's no plowing, there's no money. We try to budget ourselves in the summertime to carry us through the winter.

"We own 99.9 acres here, and we've been lucky in one respect that this whole place is grandfathered—been in the same family generation after generation. So much in this town depends on our type of business. There are no factories around. If the camps go under, what are people going to do? Nothing. You can't collect unemployment forever, and if you're in this kind of business, you can't collect unemployment anyway. We're seasonal, so my crew work for four months, or whatever, and then they have to look for work somewhere else. And insurance, forget it! I let that go long ago. I've got insurance for the place, and workmen's comp, but as far as medical insurance for my family, I haven't had it in years.

"Every Labor Day weekend for years we've had a pig roast as a fund-raiser for cystic fibrosis. We've raised about $5,000 each year, which is really pretty good for a little town like Rockwood. Something else is that the fishing around here has improved. We have a lake coalition trying to help things, and I've never seen so many salmon brought in as I have this year. Not only the stocking helps, but also a lot of people are doing catch-and-release, so there's more for everyone. It's a good sign, and I hope it keeps up."

Frozen Pumpkin Dessert

> 20 crushed gingersnaps, 1 cup canned or fresh pureed pumpkin, ½ cup
> sugar, ½ cup chopped pecans or walnuts, 1¼ tsp. pumpkin-pie spice,
> ¼ tsp. salt, 1 quart rich vanilla ice cream

Butter a 1½-quart oblong glass baking dish. Sprinkle with half the gingersnaps.
In a medium-sized bowl, stir ice cream until softened, but not melted. Blend in
the remaining ingredients. Pour into a baking dish. Sprinkle with the remaining
crumbs. Cover with foil. Freeze for 3 hours or until firm. Cut with a sharp knife.
Serve with whipped cream and chopped nuts.

30. MEDAWISLA ON SECOND ROACH POND

HK (AP IN WINTER), SCA

OWNERS: Shannon and Larry LeRoy

ADDRESS: Route 76, Box 592, Greenville, ME 04441; 207-695-2690 (radio
phone) or 207-695-2821 (Folsom's Air Service)

SEASON: Year-round (closed December and April)

ACCOMMODATIONS: Seven log cabins (one to three bedrooms) with indoor
plumbing and shower (no running water in winter), gas lights (electricity in
the evenings), woodstove

RATES: $30–90 per cabin per day; $300–450 per cabin per week

ACCESS: I-95 to exit 39 (Newport). Take ME 7 to Dexter, then ME 23 to
Guilford, then ME 6/15 to Greenville. Go straight on Lily Bay Road,
20 miles to Kokadjo. At Kokadjo Trading Post (last supplies), keep left on
Baxter State Park Road and go 1.25 miles to the big camp sign on the right.
Turn right and go 5.75 miles. Cross the wooden bridge. Turn left. The camp
is within 1,500 feet.

S*hannon:* "The camp was built in 1953 by Ray and Louise O'Donnell.
He was a bush pilot and had his own flying service. Ray died in the
mid-'60s and Louise married Freddy Rogers, then they ran the camps.
Freddy's still around."

Larry: "He's been a real help. We bought the place in 1992 from
our friends Russ and Mimi Whitten. In the early 1900s, they backed
up the waters of Second Roach Pond to run pulp. The flow starts at
Moosehead Lake, then up to Spencer Bay, which is the outlet of the
Roach River. Then at 7 miles you run northeast up Roach River, which
is famous for salmon fishing, to First Roach, a lake 7 miles long. Then

the run from First to Second Roach is about 1½ miles, to Second Roach, a lake 3½ miles long. We're the only camp on it. It's 48 feet deep with salmon and square-tail trout, no togue, and lots of smelt. It's a great breeding ground, so the entire Roach River drainage is closed to ice fishing. Beside fishing, we offer some guided canoe trips. They go down the West Branch [of the Penobscot] to Chesuncook. It can be done in one 7-hour day or they can stay in the village and Maggie McBurnie will feed and put them up for the night. Folsom's Air Service then flies them back here afterwards."

Shannon: "We're 8 miles from the Appalachian Trail. The hike up Whitecap Mountain is a wonderful hike with great views. We also have a couple of hiking trails right out of camp."

Larry: "During the summer we're booked mostly with moose watchers. You see, we have a unique setting in that we have both a lake and a river environment here. The dead water out front is a fabulous habitat for wildlife." *Shannon:* "We've had as many as 12 moose at one time out there." *Larry:* "Occasionally we have to change the energizer batteries in one of them!" *Shannon:* "But seriously, we get a tremendous number of loons and eagles. They recorded the loon sounds for the movie *On Golden Pond* here. We get some pretty interesting wildlife questions from our guests, like, 'How old does a deer have to be before it turns into a moose?' To which I replied, 'I haven't seen it happen yet!'

"We raised three children here: Stoney, Lacey, and Skylar. We home-schooled them until high school, and they're off now to continue their education." *Larry:* "I'm pleased with the home-schooling and how well they've adapted. Stoney has a full scholarship to the University of Arizona, which I see as a success story for all of us."

Shannon: "Larry and I got married in the church in Chesuncook. Flew the minister in by bush pilot. And I fell in love with Maine. I never realized there was a place with water and trees like this. I was born and raised in the deserts of Wyoming, which is where we met. Larry was born in South America." *Larry:* "Dad worked for Mobil and Texaco on an overseas oil project. I lived there until I was 13—actually spoke Spanish better than I did English at an early age. In 1960 my folks, Frank and Jean, came to Maine and traveled by canoe and plane up Moosehead, across and down the West Branch into the Eagle Lake area. My dad said he wanted to go to the most remote spots in Maine. So they had an old Indian guide and picked out a spot near Caucomgomoc Lake, just north of Chesuncook Lake, and explored all around that area. And when they got to Chesuncook Village they just fell in love with it. Dad ended up buying one of the camps and then building his own place. We spent all our summers there as kids. I was up there for the first time in 1961. We were on a canoe trip, and it took my older brother, Tom, my dad, and myself three days in a 20-foot canoe to get down Chesuncook Lake in a bad storm. I worked for Bert McBurnie in Chesuncook, and then at Pray's cottages back when Charlie Pray was in his first year as senator. But I was not making a living in the woods. I didn't want to become a lumberjack and run skidders. At that point we lived in the mountains in Wyoming, and it was a 13-mile drive to town and snow lasted seven months of the year. It was a survival environment, and we've always enjoyed that. Dad raised us like that, and Shannon's father raised her that way. So we figured the sporting camp was probably the best way for us to go."

Shannon: "Our neighbors have been wonderful. There are only four full-time residents in Kokadjo, but they welcomed us with open arms and have been a tremendous help. Carol Sterling and her father, Cliff Kelliher, over at West Branch Pond sporting camps have been like family." *Larry:* "Actually, Shannon's got her own business because of Cliff. It got started when I made myself an ultralight fly rod and Shannon asked me to build her one. I said, 'I'll teach you how to build one yourself.' Then she made one for Cliff, a 9-foot, 5-weight, and gave it to him for his 80th birthday. He shed a tear—we all did. His was number 1, and he was so proud of it he showed it off all over town and people started asking her to build rods. So now she has the Roach River Fly Company and makes her rods right here at camp." *Shannon:* "I've built 21 to date, all numbered and with names on each. They've gone to people all over the country—Alaska, Colorado, North Carolina.

"A lot of our people are coming up here primarily to relax. With the pressures of modern-day city life, people need a place to escape and unwind. They hear about wildlife in the cities, but they don't get a chance to touch that in their lives. I tell our guests that wristwatches aren't allowed in here. Eat when you're hungry, sleep when you're tired. And I'll tell you when it's time to go home."

31. PACKARD'S CAMPS

HK, SCA

OWNERS: Jerry and Amanda Packard
ADDRESS: RFD 2, Box 176, Guilford, ME 04443; 207-997-3300
SEASON: May through November
ACCOMMODATIONS: 20 log cabins (one to three bedrooms) with electric range and lights, heat, refrigerator, screened-in porch, indoor plumbing, shower; a few full hookup campsites available; post office and tackle shop during summer; no pets, no jet skis
RATES: $15 per day for the campground; $25 per person per day in the cabins, $315–470 per cabin per week
ACCESS: Maine Turnpike (I-495) to Augusta, then I-95 to exit 39. Follow ME 7 north to Dexter, then ME Route 23 to Guilford. Take ME 150 north out of Guilford 13 miles to Sebec Lake (the road ends at the camp).

J*erry:* "In 1894, my great-grandfather started this place. The family were shipbuilders in Searsport. Marlborough Packard, my great-great-grandfather, helped build a lot of those big schooners. His son was kind of a rebel—didn't want to build ships. He liked to fish and hunt, so he came to this area and that's how it all started. This was an old farmhouse, and he started taking in a few log drivers and fishermen in the spring. One thing led to another and within two or three years he began building cabins. My grandfather took over from him, then my father, then me, and my children are the fifth generation. In 1900 they started a post office here, and it's been here ever since, open June 1 through September 15. This is the end of the road, so people around the lake come by boat or on foot to get their mail. Years ago you'd get to the camps by train. There was a narrow-gauge that went through Monson and then everything—the mail, the passengers—would come up Sebec Lake by steamboat. And people bought all their things locally. Until about the late 1960s, this was the old store right here. I used to tend store when I was a kid, cut ice for the soda. All the people in town walked down to get vinegar for pickling. That's the old molasses barrel, still half full of molasses. There's the old kerosene pump—turn the handle five times and you had a gallon of kerosene for lights and things. We keep everything.

"My grandfather was born right in this room [now the dining area], my father was born in one of the cabins, and my grandfather's sister was born in another one of the cabins. My mother came up here to work, just for the summer, met my father, and never went home. Same

Bert Packard, Packard's Camps

thing with my grandmother." *Amanda:* "And I came to waitress here, met Jerry, and here I am. Must be something about this place!"

Jerry: "Sebec Lake is really unique. We're an excellent cold-water fishery, which means salmon and trout, but we're also an excellent warm-water bass fishery. Very few lakes are good at both. It's a very deep lake, 165 feet at its deepest, but it's also got some large bodies of shallow water. It's 12 miles long by 4 miles wide, a natural lake.

"When this was an American Plan camp, we'd have a hundred people for supper sometimes because we ran it kind of like a restaurant. We had 10 or 11 employees just in that part of it. But costs went up and it became hard with all the government regulations, so we started going to housekeeping back in the late '50s, when people with families just couldn't afford to do American Plan. My grandfather rented our first housekeeping cabin in 1917, and the guy who ran the steamboat up here told him he was crazy, no one would pay to rent a housekeeping cabin. At that time he got $14 a week for it, which was a lot of money. He settled on that because he said, 'My dog's 14 and that's what I'm gonna charge.' And when we started our campground everyone said, 'You're crazy—you're gonna ruin your place.' Well, that campground pays the taxes and the hired man's salary. Now if you wanted to build it, they wouldn't let you. So we've been kind of ahead of our time. Here at the main camp I've taken five cabins out so I could build kitchens on and have better spacing. We also have some outpost cabins: four on Lobster Lake, two on First Buttermilk Pond, and three others. I've got to get around so much I have a floatplane. I don't take people because of insurance requirements, but I've been flying 25 or 30 years now. My father wanted to fly, but my mother told him he'd have to get a new wife if he took it up. I was fortunate in that I got flying before I got married—I beat the system!

"Our camp at Lobster we use mostly for hunting—deer, and the moose hunt in October. We guide the people and feed them. We have 48 acres and the state owns about 4 miles of frontage. There's a lottery for hunting moose—2,000 permits in 1998. Ten percent of those go to nonresidents, and about 20,000 are applying. About 60,000 residents apply. Then the Fish and Wildlife Department sells five permits to the highest bidders and 100 percent of that goes to scholarships for the Maine Conservation School. Seven zones are open to moose hunting and they manage the harvest by issuing a different number of permits for each zone. The south-central zone at Lobster is a big one. It goes from the Golden Road south to around Milo. It's consistently been one of the most successful zones. It's legal to shoot with a bow and arrow, a handgun, and a rifle. You can't use any bird shot, but you can use a slug in a shotgun. Bow hunting is getting to be a real big thing now. Which is good, I think, because it's a lower-profile-type hunting. You don't see or hear any of the hunters. And it's probably the safest kind of hunting there is. No accidental discharges. There have been no bow fatalities that I've been aware of.

"The moose population is on the rise in Maine generally, because of the clear-cutting. All the new hardwood sprouts are perfect for moose at least 10 years after the cut. When I was a kid, if you saw one moose a year, it was a big thing. Nowadays you don't even slow down to look, it's so commonplace. Bull moose are usually pretty reclusive. You don't see them a lot in July, August. September and October, at the 'rut,' they're out searching for females, and their whole personality changes. Hunters kill more bulls than cows. That's generally by design and is a good thing. A cow might have one or two calves, although I've seen as many as three. They don't mate for life. The average adult moose will go from 550 to 850 pounds or so. Hunters kill a lot in the 600- to 700-pound range. By the end of the rut in October, their diet starts to change. They start to come out of the water where they've been feeding on aquatic plants, and they move up into the clear-cuts.

"Many Mainers hunt by driving the logging roads and get moose from clear-cuts or bogs. To pull them out we use chainsaw motors with winches and about 175 feet of cable. Those setups cost $700 apiece. Most people only go moose hunting once in their life, if ever. But we do it every year, so we have four of them. We can then hunt by canoe or boat, and by foot.

"The hide on moose is a real good insulator. The whole trick on preserving meat is to cool it down quickly, to get the insides out. If you don't do that, the blood stays in the meat and it tastes forever. And then you get the hide off as quickly as possible. We go right into Greenville. They have a couple of refrigeration trucks right there at the tagging station. I like to guide for moose, it's my favorite thing. Number one, it's a nice time of year—there's a lot of foliage. And two, you typically see a lot of animals. For deer, I'm a nervous wreck, you see so many people careless with guns. But on a moose hunt you're always there with the person. And then we always get a moose, so everyone goes home happy. Our success rate is 100 percent since 1980, and the state's is 80 percent. Very high. Maine and Alaska are the two greatest opportunities for moose in the United States."

Amanda: "We're lucky, first of all because we deal with a very nice clientele. The second thing is, we are closed during the wintertime so we can replenish. We have two daughters, Laura and Jessica, and that's the time we do things with them. We're the only constant at this northern end of the lake, so people come to us for a wide range of things. Their boat breaks down, how do they get a telephone put in, where do they go for a doctor. It's been helpful, my being a nurse. At some point nearly everyone comes in and gets patched up. It's not just hunting and fishing questions, it's everything.

"One thing we have working for us, and a lot of camps do, is that people come back for the atmosphere. And when they come back, they'll be remembered. We will remember if they caught fish, if their daughter got married, or whatever. So they come in and right away they can just relax and feel at home. It's not just Jerry or me, it's all the people who are here at the same time they're here. It's an instant little community. And when things happen, good or bad, the community shares in it. About five years ago, I looked out and there was a man walking around in the front lawn. And I went out and said, 'Can I help you?' thinking he was lost. He said, 'I don't believe it. The place hasn't changed!' And I'm thinking, yeah, it has. We've painted, put on new roofs. Well, he was here 50 years ago! He was 14 at the time, stayed for two weeks. That's the only time he ever came. So we called to Marlborough, Jerry's uncle, and those two men sat on the porch and talked for two hours about the fishing, the waitresses, it was a riot! He remembered all this from two weeks when he was 14, it made such an indelible impression. We have all the bookkeeping records from before 1900. So if I knew your name, I could tell you what cabin you stayed in, what guide you had, how much money you spent and everything. Well, we found his record and copied it and he was tickled silly."

Jerry: "That's why you have repeat business. When people leave, they know that when they come back everything will be the same. We'll be here and the kid their kid played with in the next cabin will be here. Certain weeks each year, until someone dies, we don't have many openings."

32. SIM'S SPORTSMAN'S HIDEAWAY
HK

OWNERS: Emile (Sim) and Marie Simoneau
ADDRESS: PO Box 340, Rockwood, ME 04478; 207-534-7370
SEASON: Year-round
ACCOMMODATIONS: Five cabins (three log) with indoor plumbing and shower, electric or gas lights, woodstove, gas stove, gas refrigerator, porch; bring your own linens; pets accepted
RATES: $20 per person per day; $295 per couple per week
ACCESS: I-95 to exit 39. Go north on ME 7 to Dexter, take ME 23 to Guilford, then ME 6/15 to Greenville. Go straight at the blinking light onto Lily Bay Road, and go 20 miles to Kokadjo. One and a half miles after Kokadjo's Trading Post, take the first left and follow Sim's signs (red on white) 20 miles on dirt roads.

Sim's is in a secluded bay on Moosehead Lake. In fact, as you get out of the car to unlock the gate, you can hear the gentle lapping of the water a few feet away. The camps are snugly clustered at the end of the driveway, which also serves a few private cottages. The main lodge, which is also the Simoneaus' home and the camp office, is in the middle of camp within easy reach of the self-contained cabins.

Sim: "We're located on the east shore of North Bay right within view of Mount Kineo. Farm Island is in front there and Mount Kineo's to the left. It's within walking distance from camp and we have three different hiking trails for people to use. The cabins we have were brought over here from the Mount Kineo Resort and the Deerhead Farm [which provided food for the resort]. This was in 1945, when the place had pretty much gone under. A man named Myron Macomber used to be a guide out of Kineo, and he's the one who started this over here."

Marie: "We're both from Maine, from Livermore Falls, where we worked in the paper mill. We just got tired of that way of life and wanted to get back to the basics. So we bought the camps in 1983 and started living here year-round in 1986." *Sim:* "There was enough going on year-round to justify it." *Marie:* "There's good deer hunting." Sim: "And snowmobiling's a big thing. Route 66 goes around the whole lake. It doesn't go through our land, but it's only 2 miles away. People come across from Rockwood, or we can pick them up if they don't have a machine."

Marie: "We have journals in each of the cabins and one thing people always write about is the fact that there are no through roads here, no traffic. They love the peace and quiet. So do we."

33. SPENCER POND CAMPS

HK, SCA

OWNERS: Bob Croce and Jill Martel

CAMP ADDRESS: Star Route 76, Box 580, Greenville, ME 04441; 207-843-5456 (camp) or 207-695-2821 (Folsom's Air Service)

WINTER ADDRESS: PO Box 580, Holden, ME 04429; 207-843-5456

SEASON: May through November

ACCOMMODATIONS: Six log cabins (one to three bedrooms) with gas stove, gas lights, gas refrigerator, woodstove, hand-pumped water, outhouse

RATES: $17–50 per person per day

ACCESS: I-95 to exit 39 (Newport). Take ME 7 north to Dexter, then ME 23 to Guilford, then ME 6/15 to Greenville. At the blinking yellow light, continue straight on Lily Bay Road, 20 miles to Kokadjo Village. At Kokadjo Trading Post (last supplies), keep left on Baxter Park Road. Go 1 mile and at the sign turn left onto a dirt road. Follow signs 12 miles to camp.

Spencer Pond Camps looks like a family compound (a few of the cabins are out of sight in the woods). There are vegetable and flower gardens, a small wire-mesh enclosure for poultry, and a cozy, lived-in main lodge. Spencer Mountain rises up behind the lodge. Guests drop off supplies upon arrival and then deposit vehicles in the parking area by the gate. With this, the sense of having stepped back in time is complete.

Jill: "We've been coming to the Moosehead Lake region for 31 years. We visited the camps for the first time in 1983 and bought Spencer Pond Camps in 1994 from Anne and Chick Howe. Anne was just in here the other day looking after things while we were off briefly visiting family. We see ourselves as stewards of the Spencer Pond traditions that they, and others before them, started."

Not surprisingly, Bob and Jill asked that I use Anne's account of the history of the camps, from my first edition of *In the Maine Woods*.

Anne: "The original cabin was built in 1901 by Mose Duty, a guide who was born on one of those 200-acre homestead farms on Moosehead Lake. He guided for a Mr. Stetson, who owned this entire township. Mose told Mr. Stetson that he always wanted to have a cabin on this lake. So Mr. Stetson said, 'Go pick out your land, son.' He picked out this spot and started building the big cabin in the center of camp. He called it Sabotowan, the Abenaki Indian name for Big Spencer Mountain. The name for Little Spencer, the one that's right handy here, is Kokadjoweemgwasebemsis, so it's understandable he didn't use that!

"Well, in 1944 he became ill. His wife, Lillian, put a sheet out on the side lawn so that the next plane that went overhead would see it. This was their only means of communication. And Ray O'Donald, who was the third bush pilot in the State of Maine, and was stationed out of Greenville, flew over and saw the sheet, landed, picked up Mose, and took him to Greenville hospital. Meanwhile, Lillian had to contend with the cow and horse. She let the horse go loose. But the cow had to be milked. Well, there was the added problem that Lillian was blind. So she hung on to the cow's tail, attached a little bucket to her own waist, and away they went down the blazed trail to Kokadjo. And every time she was hungry, she'd milk the cow. I don't know how long it took her to get there. It's 12 miles now, and the way she went was considerably longer, with several brooks to go across, rivers actually. There were no logging roads, of course, no roads at all. She left the cow at Kokadjo, hooked a ride with the mail carrier into Greenville, and got to the hospital in time for Mose to die. Well, of course she couldn't come back in here. So Lillian sold the camp to George and Louise Dulac [Louise was from the next-door 200-acre parcel]. And it wasn't until 1948 that the lumber company [the Stetson lands had sold out to Oxford Paper Company] permitted them to open it as a sporting camp. And we then bought from them in 1970.

Gulf Hagas, one of many good hiking destinations in the area

"Little Spencer Mountain was a volcano. It erupted three times that we know of. It was formed before there was any life on earth. The ocean was halfway up it, right where the cliffs are. The lake itself is very shallow, about 10 feet on average, and is a hundred million years older than Moosehead Lake, which was formed by a fissure, a breaking away of rocks. This has a beautiful, smooth bottom, but it also has at least 2 to 3 feet of silt over the bottom because it's in the last stages of natural eutrophication [filling in].

"We have a high moose population around here, and I may be the only person in the United States that has raised a moose from birth. What happened is, some dogs chased the mother away. The people walking the dogs mistakenly attended to the newborn. Eventually, realizing they had a problem on their hands, they called the local wildlife biologist, who asked me if I would take him. And so we did. We raised him with no information at all except for a small text from the University of Alaska, which I later grew to disagree with. Also, what we didn't know was that a moose, if you get him in the first three days of his life, imprints on humans. So he never becomes a moose; he stays a 'people.' And we got him within the first three days. It was an amazing experience. Amazing. This was in 1983, and it has deeply affected our lives. He wasn't able to live in the wild, and so we were forced to have him put down. Chick still needs to talk about it. For me, putting together my book, *Bully*, was a real catharsis. It took seven rewritings to get it out of my system."

Bob: "The first year we came here we met Bully. Right outside our cabin. It really was an amazing thing, part of the 'magic of Spencer' we talk about."

Jill: "Previous to becoming caretakers of Spencer, we looked at other sporting camps. We wanted to work and live in the outdoors, rather than just visit. When this became available it was a 'Eureka!' experience, something I've wanted all my life."

Bob: "We have a desire to preserve what we've loved here over the years and help others have the same enjoyment. That's an important part of our personal satisfaction, seeing the enjoyment our guests feel being here. The rewards are intangible more than financial in a place like this.

"We've added a few of our own traditions since we've been here. Every Saturday we bake up a batch of Maine-style yellow-eyed baked beans. When supper time comes, the guests bring over what they'd like and we have a potluck meal."

Jill: "I also maintain a small flock of laying hens for the children to gather fresh eggs. It's very popular and it gets back to our home-steading legacy. Also, I have animal-shaped cookies I give to the guests when they leave that they can eat while they're on the road. Each year it's a different theme: So far we've made moose, bear, loon, and trout. Now I'm looking for a deer, fox, or eagle cookie cutter. One thing we have continued is the tradition that our guests can come right into the vegetable garden and get whatever they like to eat for their meals."

Bob: "We continue to offer excellent self-maintained hiking trails from around camp, and now we also have mountain biking. Our range of hiking is from easy to difficult, like Little Spencer, and we have bird walks, canoeing. The moose-watching is incredible." *Jill:* "We're on their feeding route, and we don't have a generator, so it's quiet. The other night we had the coyotes and owls yipping and hooting back and forth to each other. Then a moose came along, feeding on the water grasses by camp in the full moon. What a special night that was!"

Bob: "Since the Howes have been here, the forests have begun to grow back and there are more boreal birds: spruce grouse, black-backed three-toed woodpeckers, boreal chickadees, and wildlife that's more common in the deeper woods, like martins, which are a bellwether for healthy old-growth forests. We also have fishers, coyotes, and bob-cats, and guests have reported seeing wolves." *Jill:* "If people show even a hint of interest in the outdoors, we have reference books we show them." *Bob:* "We want to promote guests discovering the magic on their own, like we did. With our encouragement. We can help by sharing our knowledge and experience, but we want them to have the self-satisfaction of active involvement. There's too much already that's passive: TV, theme parks, guided tours. We like to promote the re-wards and learning that come from self-sufficiency."

Jill: "The magic of Spencer really does get down to our spiritual side. It's a real connection to our heritage, our natures, which feeds the soul. We have journals in each cabin for guests to share their thoughts with other guests. And we hope people walk away with a better under-standing of our place in the real world. As Anne always said, and it's true, 'We don't deal with people's pocketbooks here; we deal with their souls.'"

34. WEST BRANCH POND CAMPS

AP, SCA
OWNER: Carol and A.T. Stirling
ADDRESS: PO Box 1153, Kokadjo, Greenville, ME 04441; 207-695-2561
SEASON: May through September
ACCOMMODATIONS: Eight log cabins (one or two bedrooms) with indoor plumbing and shower, woodstove, electric lights (until 10:30 PM), porch; pets accepted
RATES: $58 per person per day, includes boat or canoe
ACCESS: I-95 to exit 39. Take ME 7 to Dexter, ME 23 to Guilford, and ME 6/15 to Greenville. At the blinking light, go straight on Lily Bay Road 19 miles. Take a right onto Frenchtown Road (at a sign for the camps) and go 10 miles on the gravel road. "Follow the telephone lines to the end of the road."

C*arol:* "The camps were started in the mid- to late 1880s as a logging camp. Then Charles Randall sold to my great-uncle, Lewis Chadwick, in 1910 and it's been in our family ever since then. When my grandparents were ready to sell, they first offered it to their oldest child. But he was in the Marines and wanted to make a career out of that. So they offered it to my mother and it wasn't a matter of 'Well, maybe we'll give it a try.' It was just expected that that's what you do. So my parents took over in the spring of 1950 when I was 2½ years old. And then I took it over, so it's been through two generations in the female line. One way or the other, the family's been running it a long, long time.

"West Branch Pond here is the source of the West Branch of the Pleasant River. The West and East Branches converge just north of Brownville [Junction] and eventually drain into the Piscataquis River, which flows past Milo, where my parents are from. At Howland it reaches the Penobscot River, which flows to the sea. This is a different watershed from Moosehead Lake. We're a summertime camp for vacationing and fishing. The pond is fly-fishing, with nice pan-sized brook trout.

"Each generation in my family has handled education for their children differently. My grandparents sent their children back to Milo to live with relatives when school was in session and they were working here. My folks wanted us all together, so my father built a house in Greenville, and my sister and I started there in kindergarten, worked our way through high school, and went off to college. Our three boys,

Jack, Nathan and Eric, were home-schooled. Two went on to college and graduated summa cum laude. People come in here and marvel that children from out here in the 'backwoods' can do so well out in the world. Our oldest went to Montana and became a wildlife journalist. He had an injury, and I lost him in the fall of '95. It's something, I imagine, that you never get over. But these camps have helped in a way. I talk to friends, and relationships come and go, people move, bad and good things happen, but the camps are the one constant in my life. They are a precious thing to me, and to our guests. I think one of the boys may take over eventually. It's too much of a family heritage, too unique to let it go. These places generate quite a story."

Graham Muffins

"This is a recipe from my grandmother's cookbook," Carol says. "It's basic, but everybody loves it. I think good, home-cooked food is getting harder and harder to find. People sure appreciate it here."

> 1 cup graham (or whole-wheat) flour, 1 cup all-purpose white flour, ⅓ cup sugar, pinch of salt, 1 T baking powder, 1 egg, 1 cup milk, 2 T melted butter/margarine or oil

Sift the dry ingredients together. Make a well in the dry ingredients and add the egg, milk, and melted butter. Stir until moistened (if you mix it too much, the muffins will be tough). Cook at 400 degrees for 20–25 minutes.

35. WILSON POND CAMPS

HK

OWNERS: Bob and Martine Young
ADDRESS: PO Box 1354, Greenville, ME 04441; 207-695-2860
SEASON: May 1 through November
ACCOMMODATIONS: Seven cabins (one to three bedrooms) with woodstove or automatic heat, electric lights, stove and refrigerator, indoor plumbing and shower; pets accepted
RATES: $60 per couple per day; $395 per cabin per week
ACCESS: I-95 to exit 39. Go north on ME 7 to Dexter, take ME 23 to Guilford, then ME 6/15 to Greenville. In Greenville, turn right opposite the cruise ship *Katahdin* onto Pleasant Street and go 3.5 miles to camp.

The Youngs' camps are the only housekeeping cottages on Lower Wilson Pond. Four cabins are right on the water, the other three are a short walk away. The Youngs have owned the camps since 1995 and are currently living in the largest cabin.

Martine: "My husband and I are from Maine originally and have always loved camping and being in the outdoors. We spent a lot of time with our children in the Moosehead area and at Fish Creek Pond in the Adirondacks. These experiences made such an impression on us all—no TV or phones, learning how to water-ski and do outdoor things. My husband was helping his brother, who was living in Texas at the time, try to find a cottage to buy in the area. They had been looking around when the realtor told them there was a sporting camp for sale. Well, I could just see his ears go 'ding!' Now, we had just built our dream house. From scratch. It had taken us two years. My husband came home and said, 'Martine, you've got to hear what happened!' and I knew, somehow, just by looking at him that we'd be losing our beautiful new home.

"Bob at the time was head of the maintenance department at the Hathaway Shirt Company, and he'd heard all the rumors about the company closing up. So he knew he might be losing his job and he said this might be our opportunity to go into a business that was a lifestyle as well. We could live our dream. I asked him how we could possibly afford it, and he said we'd have to sell our brand-new home. I knew we'd be able to operate a camp because my husband holds all the licenses—electrician, plumber, boiler operator—and we'd both had a lot of camping experience. The other thing is that between the two of us we had lost three parents in three consecutive years. We knew how short life is and how important it is to try to follow your dreams. So we put our house on the market one Friday and on Saturday it was sold! I'm a strong believer that there's a reason for everything. So we built another little home in Winslow for the off-season and are now building our home at Little Wilson, so we can eventually be here and run the place full time. Meanwhile, Bob has a job at Kennebec Valley Technical College to help tide us over.

"Wilson Pond is almost 7 miles long and over 100 feet deep, with lake and brown trout, salmon, and some white perch. The fishing is good because we have a lot of people who catch-and-release. We have fixed the place up considerably since we've been here. All the former guests comment on it. One woman used to come in with her son and his family. And she'd get a motel room in town and visit them on the pond. She was just floored at how clean and neat everything was and said, 'I think I've died and gone to heaven.' We stayed in each cabin at first and every time I needed something I'd get seven. So they're fully equipped. We have an editor from *Sports Illustrated* who comes for what he calls 'total mental relaxation.' As we say, 'Come once and you'll come again and again.'"

36. WILSON'S ON MOOSEHEAD

OWNERS: Wayne and Shan Snell
ADDRESS: Greenville Junction, ME 04442; 207-695-2549
SEASON: Year-round
ACCOMMODATIONS: 15 log cabins (one to five bedrooms) with indoor plumbing and shower (some with tubs), electric lights, automatic and wood heat (one cabin has a fireplace), electric refrigerator, gas stove, screened-in porch, TV hookup; pets (leashed) accepted
RATES: $65–$250 per cabin per day; $425–$1,500 per cabin per week
ACCESS: I-95 to exit 39. Go north on ME 7 to Dexter, take ME 23 to Guilford, then ME 6/15 to Greenville. Wilson's is 6 miles past Squaw Mountain on Rockwood Road (ME 15).

Wilson's is about halfway between Rockwood and Greenville, within walking distance and view of the East Outlet Dam at the headwaters of the Kennebec River. The half-mile driveway passes over railroad tracks that brought guests to the camps in the latter part of the 1800s and into the 1900s. One can tell that this was once a thriving hub. An ocher-colored building with maroon trim looms large and somewhat Victorian. Hotel-sized, with a square tower, the structure is sagging and may not be long for this world. The cabins spread out on the lawns under gracious old trees and span the outlet into the Kennebec and its entrance cove in Moosehead. At the white-clapboard main lodge (which houses the tackle shop and office, but does not have a common lounge area), a goat comes bounding to the car to greet and escort you to the door. Walk in and a parrot calls out a startling, "Hello!" You have definitely arrived.

Shan: "Wilson's started in 1865 and is the oldest continuously running sporting camp on Moosehead Lake—and probably about the oldest in Maine. [It shares this distinction with Lakewood in Rangeley and Tim Pond in Eustis.] We are on the widest part of the lake, and from here you can get a 120-mile view out across the lake and islands to Big and Little Spencer Mountains, Squaw Mountain, and even

Katahdin. Moosehead is 40 miles long by 20 wide and from here you can see 20 miles across, the widest view of Spencer Bay. Each of our cabins has a great view.

"The East Outlet is fly-fishing-only. You can get salmon or square-tail trout in one of the eddies below the dam or cast into the big pool above the dam, just in front of the sucking water of the spillway. We've got great hunting and fall foliage. In the winter Squaw Mountain, for downhill skiing, is just down the road, cross-country skiing is out the back, and we have a thousand-foot frontage on the lake out front for ice fishing. There's a 152-mile snowmobile trail around Moosehead that you can get onto right here at our entrance.

"My husband and I have been here since 1983. He was a school principal down in southern Maine and we just wanted to get away from it all. But we're still working hard, harder than ever, up here! It's a big place to take care of, there are a lot of rules and regulations and expenses, and there's always something that needs fixing in an old camp. We've seen a lot of changes over the years. At the end of the '80s we were losing some of our families because of the economy. In the '90s we're getting more couples. And it used to be that 90 percent of our guests didn't want TV. Now I'd say it's about 50 percent. But these camps have a long history, and hopefully they'll be here a whole lot longer."

The Baxter State Park Region

This region includes the land and waters surrounding 250,000-acre Baxter State Park, a forever-wild wilderness area left to Maine by former Governor Percival Baxter. The Golden Road and Church Pond Road form the southern boundary, with ME 11 to the east and the Canadian border to the west. The northern boundary of the park serves as the northern boundary of this region as well. Looking at this area in terms of physical features, you find Chesuncook Lake to the west, Shin Pond area to the east, Grand Lake Matagamon to the north, and the town of Millinocket in the south. Millinocket is the major city and gateway to most of the camps in this region, and has most of the facilities a traveler might require. East Millinocket is home to Bowater Paper Company, one of the country's largest paper manufacturers. Farther north, the town of Patten serves as the focal point for the village of Shin Pond and its group of camps. It is also a center for lumbering operations. You might want to visit the Lumberman's Museum (207-528-2650), which features the history of Maine's lumbering industry.

Within the park, the northern terminus of the Appalachian Trail is atop "mile-high" Mount Katahdin—at 5,267 feet, Maine's highest peak. About 45 other peaks and ridges provide additional hiking opportunities. There is a perimeter road (narrow, windy, and dirt) around the park leading to public camping sites (reservations required). The park does not allow motorcycles or pets.

Getting there: The closest airports are Bangor International Airport and Presque Isle (rental cars available). Driving time from Portland is 4–6 hours; from Boston, 7–8 hours; from New York City, 10–12 hours. Floatplanes are available through Scotty's Flying Service, Shin Pond, 207-528-2626; Katahdin Air Service, Millinocket, 207-723-8378; Folsom's Air Service, Greenville, 207-695-2821; and Currier's Flying Service, Greenville, 207-695-2778.

Guidance: For further information, contact Baxter State Park Headquarters, 64 Balsam Drive, Millinocket, ME 04462 (207-723-5140).

37. BEAR MOUNTAIN LODGE

HK/MAP/AP, SCA

OWNERS: Carroll and Deanna Gerow

ADDRESS: Moro Plantation, RD 1, Box 1969, Smyrna Mills, ME 04780; 207-528-2124

SEASON: Year-round

ACCOMMODATIONS: Five cabins (each sleeps two to eight people) with indoor plumbing and shower, electric lights, oil or gas heat; two outpost cabins have outhouse, woodstove, gas lights and gas cookstove

RATES: $18–30 per person per day, $120–175 per cabin per week (HK). $250 per person per week (MAP). $50 per person per day, $350 per person per week (AP).

ACCESS: I-95 to exit 58 (Patten-Sherman). Take ME 11 north through Patten. Bear Mountain Lodge is 12 miles beyond Patten on the left (east) side of ME 11.

Deanna: "These camps were built prior to 1955. Carroll and I used to run it in the summers during the 1960s for a man named Ray Lorentz. Then we bought the place in 1970. I'm from Patten, 12 miles away, and Carroll is from Knowles Corner, only 4 miles away, so we joke that we didn't go far in life! Since Carroll's from right here and he was trained as a forester, he knows where to guide people. November is our busiest time, when the trophy-size deer around here are in rut. Rifle season in November is bucks-only with doe by permit only, and we have application forms. In fact, our place is the local game-inspection station. The season for natural-feed areas [not baiting] for bears is the same as the rifle season for deer, so it gives people a chance to hunt bear along with deer, which is why we're so busy. During that time most guests eat their meals in the lodge.

"We're not on a lake or stream, but there are a lot of fishing options in the area. We're right on Route 11, which is very scenic during fall-foliage time. For a two-lane highway, it's a pretty important road. I read the other day that the North Maine Development Commission figured out that $7 million worth of commodities go by on this road. Daily!

"After hunting season is over, we get snowmobilers. Clubs and individuals make reservations to stay with us, or just eat a meal at the lodge. To reach us by snow-sled you go on ITS 75—which is groomed—from Patten, Island Falls, and Oakfield [20 miles south], or north to ITS 85 and Oxbow [30 miles] or west to ITS 85 and Shin Pond [20 miles]. And from these areas there are trails heading out in all directions."

38. BOWLIN CAMPS

AP/HK, SCA

OWNERS: Jon and Betty Smallwood

ADDRESS: PO Box 251, Patten, ME 04765; 207-528-2022

SEASON: Year-round

ACCOMMODATIONS: Nine log cabins (one to three bedrooms), three with kitchenette, gas range, and indoor plumbing and shower; six use central shower and bathroom, have wood heat, gas and electric lights; for HK bring linen (available for an additional fee) and cooler(s)

RATES: $65 per person per day; $385 per person per week (AP); $50 per family or couple per day (HK)

ACCESS: I-95 to exit 58 (Patten-Sherman). Turn left onto ME 158, then right onto ME 11 and go north to Patten. From Patten, take 159 west to Hay Lake. Turn left at the sign, just beyond the ranger station. Follow the dirt road and signs 8 miles to camp.

As you pull into camp, you see the East Branch of the Penobscot River to your right and a small pond on a knoll to your left. The driveway leads up a hill past the log main lodge nestled in the hollow surrounded by maples and pines. To your left, on the top of the knoll, a cluster of honey-colored log cabins spreads out toward the woods. A large garden and cleared field stretch out behind the cabins. As we look down the slope toward the river, Jon points to the pond: "I stocked that with trout for the kids. There's a coffee can full of feed; go give it a try if you want. Everyone gets a kick out of it." I threw some pellets and half a dozen healthy trout jumped out of the suddenly boiling water.

Jon: "This was always a sporting camp. It started in 1895 and we have two of the original cabins. The rest pretty much all burned down in 1948. The camp was started by Charles McDonald. The artist Jake—Maurice, but nobody called him that—Day did a picture of the camps." *Betty:* "There's a museum in Damariscotta of his works. This one is from 1935 and is in watercolor, but he did oils too. He had a cottage on Matagamon Lake and got to know Mr. and Mrs. Chapman, the second owners. He's the person who created Bambi for Walt Disney Studios. Our Fish and Wildlife people captured two baby whitetail deer, fawns, from here along the East Branch and sent them to California. This was in the '40s. And the people there kept watching them and taking pictures the whole time they were growing up. And Jake Day drew them. We have a copy of the original Thumper."

Jon: "So after the Chapmans, we came. There have been only three owners in almost 100 years! We came in June 1968. I'm from Patten and she's from St. Francis." *Betty:* "Which is way up north, next to the Allagash. We went to school together, Patten Academy. Then we got married and came over here." *Jon:* "Tons of work had to be done." *Betty:* "He's learned to be a carpenter, mechanic, small-engine repairman, electrician, everything!" *Jon:* "This building [main lodge] had no running water and we really used only kerosene lights when we came. I guess it was five years before we had running water."

Betty: "We have four boys who were brought up here. We did some home-schooling. Then they were, I believe, the first and only kids in the State of Maine who ever flew in a floatplane to school each day."

Jon: "They would walk 2 miles to Bowlin Pond in the morning. There were no roads then. The plane would come in, pick them up, fly them to Shin Pond, where they'd catch the bus to the Patten school, and then the reverse at night. We had a team of horses and a buckboard; that's how we got in and out. We've only had the road in here since '86.

"Baxter Park is very close on our western side. In fact, I have one camp 50 yards from the park border. So from the dooryard you're looking at Traveler Mountain and Katahdin. There was a huge fire in the park, in 1912, I believe, and families who were in the woods near Grand Lake Matagamon all moved out. But the fire never jumped the lake. Most of Baxter burned. It started sometime in the fall, and it was still smoldering in the spring. Some places it burned 10 to 12 feet deep in the ground. This whole area is full of great huge blackened stumps of those big pines that burned. In fact, I know where there's one stump that's so big and burned so deep that one of the roots comes up and then down into a boggy place and you can walk, standing straight up, under that root.

"We use the river here mostly for fishing, but we do offer canoe trips. From here down 16 miles is a great place for beginners. And from the Matagamon Road there are a lot of falls. There's a 30-foot drop in the river—Grand Pitch, and the Hulling Machine behind that, which is a very nasty piece of water. You can do each piece to here in a day. And from here down to Wetstone Falls in a day, where there are camping sites. We can pick people up when they're done canoeing."

Betty: "We have beavers just above the pond and sometimes they come down and we end up swimming with them. They'll slap their tails and splash us!" *Jon:* "The Atlantic salmon used to come up the river, before they dammed it years ago. There's a natural crossing right here, and the owner's wife, Mrs. McDonald, would shoot—actually shoot—an Atlantic salmon in the shallows to eat." *Betty:* "There were so many, she could choose the size she wanted for her frying pan!"

Jon: "Winter is our busiest season, with the snowmobilers and cross-country skiers. We have different trails for each. We have about 8,000 to 10,000 snowmobiles here in a season. Sometimes we'll feed 200 people for lunch. We're 30 miles from Millinocket, and ITS 85 goes right by us. We also have something I don't think you'll see at any other sporting camp. We built a suspension bridge to get people over the river. It's 122 feet long, all on cable. It looks sort of like the Golden Gate Bridge. I just built a log cabin, kind of a honeymoon cabin, away from the main camp, and it looks out over this bridge.

Jon and Betty Smallwood made this suspension bridge for their many snowmobilers.

"In the fall we have good bear and deer hunting, and we have a group in here now hunting ruffed grouse—'partridge.' There are two kinds of grouse, ruffed and spruce. Ruffed is a little bigger than spruce with a red mark over the eye, and the tail is darker. Spruce is almost tame and isn't hunted. The season on ruffed is from October 1 to November 30."

The partridge hunters are happy to share with me what their yearly visit is like. It includes a great deal of banter, some practical jokes, close camaraderie, and, oh yes, some hunting. *Tim Murphy:* "I like bird hunting. When you go deer hunting you have to get up very early; hunting partridge you can talk to each other. It helps flush them up. They have to be in full flight before you shoot them. The average gun used is a 20-gauge with 7½s for a shell size. They weigh about a pound and they're good eating. We have a cookout in the woods each year [see recipe on page 134]."

Linda Lambert: "When we leave to go home, each person can only have two days' catch, which is four birds a day, eight birds max. Only eight in your possession at one time."

Tim: "If you decide you want to take a bird and have it mounted, you have to clean it, put it in a nylon sock, and keep it on ice. And when you take it that way to a taxidermist, it comes out looking beautiful. The purpose of the nylon sock is to keep the feathers from getting mussed up. With bird hunting, the weather is beautiful up here this time of year. You get a lot of exercise walking around and everything. One time I came back here around 2:30. It was beautiful. The sun was shining, the trees were in full color, and I said, 'Ah to heck with it. I'm not going to hunt anymore.' And I just sat there. It gives you a chance to really think. You don't think about work, but about things you maybe take for granted every day. Like your wife, your family members, whatever it may be. It's so peaceful. I went inside the cabin and got a bottle of Opal Sambuca and I sat on that porch and had two little glasses. And I fell right to sleep and spent about two hours in the rocking chair. And it's just something I'll remember."

Ruffed Grouse Cookout

This is Tim Murphy's recipe for "partridge."

You take each bird and skin it while it's fresh by standing on the wings, holding onto the legs, and just pulling up. You take out the breast and fillet it into pieces. Then we have a little olive oil in a pan, some Dash, cut up an onion really fine. Fry the bird first—just get it light brown. Meanwhile we have baked beans in an 8-inch-round cooking pan. When the bird turns white, we put it in with the beans and let it simmer. And then we have brown bread in a can. And we sit out in the woods and eat that.

39. CHESUNCOOK LAKE HOUSE

AP/HK, SCA

OWNER: Maggie McBurnie

ADDRESS: Star Route 76, Box 656, Chesuncook Village, Greenville, ME 04441; 207-745-5330 (camp) or 207-695-2821 (Folsom's Air Service)

SEASON: Year-round

ACCOMMODATIONS: Inn (spring through fall) sleeps 11; has electric lights, indoor plumbing, shower and tub, automatic heat or woodstove. Lodge and log cabins (year-round) sleep 12–15; have wood heat, gas lights, gas stove, and gas refrigerator; indoor plumbing and shower in summer, outhouse in winter

RATES: Inn $85 per person per day (3-day minimum); HK cabins $38–40 per person per day; AP cabins $53–78 per person per day

ACCESS: I-95 to exit 56 (Medway). Take ME 11/157 northwest to Millinocket. From Millinocket, follow signs for the West Branch Region.

One mile past Millinocket Lake, stop at the gate ($4). Drive on the Golden Road (33 miles from Millinocket) to the Allagash Gateway Campsite, where there is a sign for Chesuncook Lake House. Leave your car in the security parking area here and take the boat to the camps from the boat landing. (Call ahead.)

Inaccessible by car, Chesuncook Lake House is located 18 miles and a 35-minute boat trip from Chesuncook Dam on the northwest end of the lake. Chesuncook Village can also be reached by Folsom's Air Service out of Greenville or by hitching a ride on the fire-patrol flight. It is a 5-mile overland cross-country ski or hike in to the white-clapboard Lake House, which sits on a sweep of lawn within walking distance of the West Branch of the Penobscot River. The Mount Katahdin range is visible in the distance. Bert McBurnie, a larger-than-life fixture of the sporting-camp business, died in 1997, but his wife Maggie says, "I'm continuing on here. It's the life I've known and loved." She asked that I use Bert's quotes from the first edition of this book because, "He said it all the way I would want it."

Bert: "The real history of Chesuncook starts back in the early 1800s. It was a little village that the Penobscot Log Drive Corporation used. They had water communication into it, they had storehouses, it was sort of the hub of a wheel. They had a dam at the foot of the lake, probably around 1820 to 1845. Thoreau came through here in 1845, and it was a thriving community. It later became taken over in a sense by the paper companies. In the early 1900s they started buying up all the land around here. This was for the second growth—they'd already cut the first growth off. They'd take it to Bangor, which, up until at least 1864, was the busiest seaport exporting lumber in the United States. Up until Fulton invented the propeller and steel ships came in, all the ships were wooden. And the only place in the world they could get the re-sources to build these ships was in New England—this is what we had all our wars over, ships' masts and lumber to build homes. I have a book here someplace by the Fin and Paddle Club of Harvard and it says they took a trip here prior to the Civil War. They complained about the fact that the tall pines no longer dominated the horizon, that there were rotting wooden dams. And this was before the Civil War!

"If you go to Bangor and take Route 15 to Greenville, every 12 miles or so you'll find a village. That was the distance a yoke of oxen went in a day. And they'd stop and make a farm, clear the land, raise hay and oats. When horses came along I guess they could double that distance.

Chesuncook Lake House

But that's how these farms grew. If you follow that increment of about 10 or 12 miles, you'll come to Chesuncook Village. Chesuncook was the end of it. People came here and settled permanently, because they would service the lumbermen, who needed immense amounts of hay and oats to feed the horses and oxen they used.

"During the War of 1812—and I think the Civil War too—soldiers' bonuses were paid in land. And you didn't even have to prove it up. You'd get your senator to make some land bond and then contact your lawyer to send the papers to a soldier who signs the land over for your check. I mean, he's never even seen it. And then of course the land was controlled by a few timber barons who'd form corporations. You cut your logs on this watershed and you paid a fee to have them transported to a sawmill. But I don't believe it was a big-profit operation. The Great Northern Paper Company bought out Penobscot Log I guess around the turn of the century. In 1917 they built Ripogenus Dam, which flooded this whole area. And I believe it was at this point a new method, either sulfite or sulfate, had been discovered in making paper. Before, it cost you, even in those days, $50 million to build a mill. With this new process you could build the same mill for $5 million. They were cutting the wood with a bow saw, which is a Swedish invention. We referred to it as the 'misery whip' when I was a kid, 'cause it was a misery to run it. You cut the wood in 4-foot pieces. The original lumbermen were 'long loggers'—used crosscut saws and axes, and they cut logs. They refused to cut this pulpwood, were furious with that. They moved out. And if you drive from here clear to Michigan, Wisconsin, Oregon, you'll find Maine names all through there.

"The crooked knife, the drawknife, and the ax, and probably the spokeshave, were tools that everybody had to have all through this time. You had to make paddles, ax handles, wiffletrees for your horses. The original crooked knife goes way back—God, I don't know how old it is. They had a gouge at the end of it so you could make a bowl or a spoon, whatever. Later they were made out of straight razor blades. My father could go out and make anything he wanted out of wood.

"My family was from Presque Isle, the potato fields. My father came here in 1935. According to Mother, he was born a hundred years too late—should've been a mountain man. He came from a farming family. His two brothers were farmers, but he was sort of a wanderer. We lived here and he trapped and then worked on the river drive in the summer. I was 4 years old when we came here and I went to the Chesuncook school, which is now the church. It seems as though it was full of kids—17 or 18 probably. But then, as the years went by, and the Second World War started, around '39, '40, people began moving out of here. You see, you could live here during the Depression years. You could work for Great Northern all summer and trap and hunt around a bit. Wasn't anything great, but you could survive. The school was closed down the spring of '41 and I'm the only one that came back. Maggie and I came back in '57 and started running a sporting camp, kind of low-keyed, strictly hunting and fishing. I got by with contracting to cut pulp and was foreman on the river drives. When the drives got through in '72, we said we'd stay and really go full at it. The place was built in 1864 and we leased from Great Northern before we bought it."

Maggie: "We met in Paris in the early '50s when Bert was in the service. Back then, in France, they were looking for people with a little knowledge of the English language. I had just come back from England, and there was an opening for what they called then the European Exchange System. It was a liaison-type of work between the American and French governments. A lot of bases were installed in France and you had to have a contact between the French contractors and the American troops for construction and so on. So it was my job. I enjoyed it. Bert was the officer in charge of the base where I was, and we started talking about Maine and then, the next thing we knew, six months later we were married! We stayed one year in France and then we came back to the States. My first encounter with Maine, the day we arrived, was in November 1957, and I loved it."

Bert: "I consider myself a conservationist, not a preservationist. I believe in utilizing properly. But corporate America has taken over and they don't care about the long-term affect of clear-cutting. Just gotta make X number of dollars. They're shocked at the power some of the environmentalists have. We're in this transition period now of who controls what, and where we're going.

"The recreation business, in my opinion, is on the upswing. But it's a different kind of business, not the same old hunting and fishing per se. Like on this lake, we still have probably the same harvest of salmon and trout we've had for the past 20 years. But now, instead of two people harvesting, it's seven or eight. So the pie is getting smaller all the time. There are more and more people coming up here just for the aesthetic value, or to relax. It's a different world. I tell my people I'm not after hunters anymore, I'm after sportsmen. We're more and more from an urban society, and people don't get the outdoor training that kids used to have. They don't know what to expect. They feel wilderness means you're free—free from regulations, free to be alone, to do what you want. But more and more you can't do what you want. The freer you are, the more responsible you have to be or you'll lose it! It's starting to turn around. I see the younger people having much more appreciation of the wilderness and responsibility towards it than the older people. It's as though a door closed on this past era, and I heard the slam of it, but I can't tell you where. It's a new time we're into."

Maggie's Normandy Apple Squares

Piecrust: 2 cups flour, ¾ cup shortening, 1 tsp. salt, 1 T sugar, cold water

Mix the first four ingredients and add enough cold water so dough forms a ball. Roll out half the dough and place on a cookie sheet, or the desired pan.

Filling: 4 cups homemade or canned applesauce; 2 T Calvados, Cognac, or brandy, if desired; 4 T apricot jam or currant jelly

Spread the filling on the piecrust. With the remaining dough, roll out and make strips and lattice over the filling on the diagonal. Pinch the edges of the lattice underneath the crust. Cook at 400 degrees for 10 minutes. Meanwhile, on the stove, mix several tablespoons of apricot jam or currant jelly with some Calvados (or orange juice) and brush on the lattice. Put back in the oven until crust is golden brown.

40. FROST POND CAMPS

HK, SCA

OWNERS: Rick and Judy Givens

CAMP ADDRESS: Star Route 76, Box 620, Greenville, ME 04441; 207-695-2821 (radio phone)

WINTER ADDRESS: 36 Minuteman Drive, Millinocket, ME 04462; 207-723-6622

SEASON: May through November

ACCOMMODATIONS: Five log cabins and three frame cabins (each sleeps two to eight); seven cabins have outdoor water tap, outhouse, coin-operated shower house; one has indoor plumbing and shower, gas lights, gas stove, gas refrigerator, woodstove, porch; 10 campsites, no electric or water hookup

RATES: Cabins $20–26 per person per day; campsite $13 per person per day, $78 per person per week

ACCESS: I-95 to exit 56 (Medway). Take ME 11/157 northwest to Millinocket. Follow Baxter State Park Road for 9 miles, past Northwoods Trading Post, which is the last source for supplies. Go 1 mile to a camp sign, bear left at a gate (you pay a toll here), and drive to Ripogenus Dam. Cross the dam and continue on a dirt road for 3 miles along Chesuncook Lake to the camp (distance from Millinocket to the camp is 35 miles).

Getting to sporting camps is part of the adventure, and the Frost Pond Camps access offers a drive over a dam and along a meandering road within several feet of Chesuncook Lake. The well-graded entrance drive has a long allée of shade trees. The main lodge and camps to the left of the road lead down to Frost Pond, 1 mile long by 1 mile wide and 40 feet deep.

Rick: "We're the only place on the pond except for a secluded private cottage. People fish here for square-tails [brook trout] and on the West Branch of the Penobscot for world-class landlocked salmon. We also have a canoe at Little Frost Pond and are right by Harrington and Chesuncook Lakes. For guests who like to hike, we have a couple of trails. One goes along Rip [Ripogenus] Dam through the gorge along the river. In November we gear up for deer hunting, and for moose we're in the central zone, which has an excellent success rate.

Judy and Rick Givens at their camp

"Most of what we know about the history of the camps has been handed down by word of mouth, and I don't know whether it's gospel or not. But Ripogenus Dam was completed in 1916, and as soon as it was done they pushed in a road 3 miles to Frost Pond, where there was a lumber camp for about 10 years. Eventually they pushed the road in about 3 miles farther and built what was called Duck Pond Storehouse. A lot of the lumber camps were portable and they'd move them around on skids. So Frost Pond was discontinued as a lumber camp. Harry Bowe and, supposedly, Al Nugent took it over and ran it as a sporting camp. They built four cabins, but it wasn't too long before Al Nugent realized there wasn't enough money there for two of them to make a living. So the story is that he migrated north and started Nugent's Camps. This took place around the late '20s. Then Flossie and [A.E.] Boot Levensellar owned it. Boot worked on the telephone lines for Great Northern Paper Company and he built canoes and traded horses for the logging operations. One of the stories about Boot is that this pond at the time was fly-fishing-only and Boot would go out and 'clean worms.' If he was out there and Flossie saw a game warden coming, she'd go down to the dock and yell, 'Boot, telephone!' and he'd know that he'd have to dump his worms overboard. That was their code! Boot built a log cabin, three frame cabins, a workshop, woodshed, and garage. In the frame buildings, no two studs are the same distance apart.

I put a floor in one of them and the floor's not square. One building he just shoveled an area for the sill logs out in the snow, set them down, and built up from that. And the cabin's still there!

"We're from Pittsburgh, Pennsylvania. When we graduated from college, I had it in my mind that I wanted to work in a remote area. So I looked for a job in Montana, Idaho, and Maine. I graduated as a mechanical engineer and I was able to get a job at a paper mill in Rumford, Maine, and Judy got a job teaching school at Andover. We were there almost two years, but it didn't take me long to figure out that I wasn't going to be happy behind a desk the rest of my life. So in '67 we started a canoe-trip-outfitting business for the Allagash River. Usually when someone starts a business he's had some experience or worked for someone for years and says, 'I think I can do that.' Well, we just skipped those steps and said, 'I think we can do that!' We'd had canoeing experience in Minnesota and Canada. Our Canadian trips had all been loop trips, connected by short portages, where you'd end up at the same spot. The problem here was getting back to the beginning, because all the rivers go one way. We were the first outfitting business to start in Maine—1967 was the first year the Allagash Wilderness Waterway was in existence, and we figured the Rip Dam area would be a good central location. So we went to Great Northern officials and asked if we could get a lease and eventually we got a lot on Frost Pond and began building a log cabin. During the winter we got to know Hazel and Henry Hanson, who owned these camps after Boot, and they were upset because they thought we would be infringing on their business. At the time, Great Northern owned and operated a campground at Sourdnahunk Lake on the western side of Baxter State Park. So we started our outfitting business there and ran the campground. It was six years after we started our outfitting business that the camps here became available, and we bought them in the fall of 1972."

Judy: "We have two daughters, Kimberley and Heather, who've graduated from college and are on their own now." *Rick:* "Kimberley was born in the middle of an 18-inch snowstorm and we couldn't get back in to camp because the road wasn't plowed. I had to put chains on, come in, get the plow on, and plow out the road. And I think it was like 17 degrees below zero. Just in the time it took to get Judy and the baby and the few odds and ends in the cabin, the flowers she'd gotten in the hospital had frozen. It was that cold." *Judy:* "It was more or less the same craziness when Heather was born." *Rick:* "We lived in the log cabin we'd built and then eventually moved into camp." *Judy:* "We use that cabin for guests now. It has its own driveway and when people are there they don't know there's anything else in the world. And the cabins here aren't lined up close to each other, they're spaced far enough apart so you don't know what your neighbor is doing. Our guests tell us how delighted they are by how clean the cabins are, and how everything is so quiet."

41. KATAHDIN LAKE WILDERNESS CAMPS

AP/MAP/HK, SCA

OWNERS: Al and Suzan Cooper

ADDRESS: Box 398, Millinocket, ME 04462; 207-723-4050

SEASON: Year-round

ACCOMMODATIONS: 10 log cabins (one or two bedrooms) with outhouse, gas lights, woodstove

RATES: $100 per person per day (AP); $75 per person per day (MAP); $40 per person per day (HK)

ACCESS: I-95 to exit 56 (Medway). Take ME 157 north through Millinocket and follow signs to Baxter State Park. Just after the Togue Pond (Park) gatehouse, take the right-hand fork (Roaring Brook Road) to Avalanche Field. Park your car and walk 3.5 miles in to camp, or call ahead to reserve packhorses to bring you and your gear in.

By the time you leave your car and walk, cross-country ski, fly, or ride a horse in to Katahdin Lake Wilderness Camps, the buzz of a plugged-in world are far behind. Log cabins and outbuildings form a thin oval around a clearing (think of an open exclamation point with the lodge as the dot). Down the embankment is 3-mile-long by 1½-mile-wide Katahdin Lake. Turner Mountain and Katahdin are so close they are reflected in the spring-fed waters, which hold square-tailed trout. Sandy beaches ring most of the shoreline. The camp has 200,000-acre Baxter State Park as its next-door neighbor, and there are no other public camps within 11 miles in any direction.

Suzan: "Oliver and Della Cobb were the previous owners. They owned it from the late '20s to the early '60s—44 years. I had the honor of knowing Della before she died in 1977. She had a diary for every year she was here, and that woman could keep you right at the edge of your chair with stories about the camps. Oliver Cobb Jr. remembers coming in here by buckboard when he was a child. And he said you could drive a buckboard through the woods anywhere because all the trees were such massive virgin trees they blocked the sun, and there was no understory. Back in the 1800s, before Baxter Park became a park [in 1930], people would come by train to Stacyville and then walk and ride the buckboard 11 miles to camp. Millinocket wasn't even on the map until 1903. They call it the magic city because, with the pulp mill, it popped up overnight.

"We've been here since 1975. My dad was originally from Maine, but was 25 years a dairy farmer in Massachusetts. And when I was in college in '69 my folks, Embert and Josephine Stevens, bought these camps and moved away. It was empty-nest syndrome in reverse. I mean, your parents aren't supposed to up and leave after you've lived in the same house 20 years! They lived here five years, but then Dad was thrown from a horse—he fell 13 or 15 feet and broke his back on the rocks. So Al decided he'd like to try to buy the camps, and we did. And it was pretty miraculous, really. The paper company had never given a 10-year lease before and we had to have that in order to get a mortgage from the bank. So we prayed and said, 'Lord, if you want us to have these camps, You're going to have to do this.' And, lo and behold, we got the lease! So we knew it was right.

"When we came here we were newlyweds. Our son, Alfie, was just a year old, and we didn't have much of anything. I was a schoolteacher, Al had no experience running a business. But Mom and Dad said, 'Work here with us for one year. We'll put all the wages you make toward a down payment.' So we went back to Massachusetts, had a big yard sale, and sold everything except our bed, a bureau, and Alfie's crib.

"These camps have been here since about 1885. Always sporting camps. They say that Teddy Roosevelt hunted caribou around Katahdin from right here. The original owner, to the best of my knowledge, was John Cushman. And his great-great-great-grandson sometimes guides for us! Al is a registered guide, so we hire only one other guide. Dana and Ruth Cushman came in to Sandy Stream Pond the other day. They're in their '80s and she had to use two canes. She said it took them two hours and it's about a 15-minute walk. I see that determination in the generation that came before us. Like my mom and dad starting a new adventure in their 60s. And here my mom is, she's just drawn her second moose permit for the hunt, she's 90 years old—and she's going! Now that's motivation. I've got a quote up in the kitchen we found at a flea market that pretty much says it: 'A wishbone ain't as likely to get ya someplace as a backbone.'

Left to right: Sam, Al, Suzan, and Chris Cooper, Katahdin Lake Wilderness Camps

"Katahdin is the northern terminus of the Appalachian Trail and Alfie went to college in Georgia, just a very short distance from the southern terminus. So I joked if he didn't like college, he could walk home! Our sons have all been home-schooled. Alfie went to high school at Lee Academy, east of Lincoln, because they had a five-day dormitory. He had to leave at 4:30 on Monday morning to get to school."

Al and the Coopers' second son, Sam, come into the kitchen from a provisioning trip with the horses. It is pitch-black outside. Suzan introduces us. *Suzan:* "Our boys have all learned how to tie flies, and they sell them to our guests. It's a way for them to learn about business and money. They can't have a paper route."

Sam: "I really like to tie nymphs. Now, a nymph would be like any kind of larva that would hatch out before it changed into whatever it was going to be. I also like to tie dry flies, but they're a little harder. On a dry fly you have a hackle. And hackle is usually dyed or natural-colored rooster-neck feathers. And you also have saddle hackles, the hackles on the back. They should be stiff, long, and not fuzzy. You tie it onto the hook. Then you take your hackle pliers and you wrap it around the hook so it sticks out and makes a wing—it looks like a wing to a fish, anyway. And then you tie on the body for that particular fly.

You follow a pattern. All my flies are $1.25 apiece, but you have to sell quite a few to make up for your supplies, plus I'm saving for a bike."

Al: "We used to have a nice hovel here to keep the horses in, all handmade with logs, a beautiful thing, but it fell in. And to get that back is going to be almost impossible. Just one log weighs eight, nine hundred pounds! You're not talking about a two-by-four. It's an arm-wrestling match between humans and Mother Nature. Some people think humans have conquered nature, but that's a joke. Just look at the abandoned blacktop roads with the cracks in them and you'll see delicate flowers growing out of the blacktop."

Suzan: "Della Cobb spoke of a time when they got 8 feet of snow. In one storm. They climbed out of the upstairs window, and it took them two days to get down to the horse hovel to feed the horses." *Al:* "There's always been horses here. We used to have Belgians, now we have Appaloosas, and we'll be getting mules again. Yesterday was my birthday and I have a headlamp my wife gave me. It really helps when you're hauling in the dark."

As we eat birthday cake, I ask about the taste. It's sourdough. *Suzan:* "When you tell people it's been sitting on the counter for 2 years, un-refrigerated, and it still works, some people don't understand. It came to me from Delaware, but it's kinda fun to think it could have come from our forefathers." *Al:* "Sweets are a big thing in fall and winter because you're working like crazy." *Sam:* "You're hungry all the time." *Al:* "We went through 60 pounds of honey in a year and a half!" *Sam:* "I smear about half an inch of peanut butter on crackers or bread and then the honey on top. It's the best." *Suzan:* "We don't have beehives. You'd have to put them on telescoping poles out of reach of the bears."

Al: "The good thing about our getting mules is they're not balkish of bears. We had a bear in 1990 that was 265 pounds. Dressed. There were four of us out in the wilderness trying to put it on the mule, and the mule took it back to camp about 10 miles away. For bear, if they don't get a 'mast crop' of either beechnuts or acorns, it triggers their systems to go into their dens early. If they didn't get enough food, they'll die. Females den first in a situation like this. Some of the boars will stay out. The boars and females never den together. The reason for that is the females have their babies in January. They breed in June, but the egg doesn't implant until she goes into the den, because her condition when she goes in determines how many eggs will implant. And she doesn't want the male in the den because he would kill the babies. And for the whole six months they don't defecate or urinate in the den at all. As soon as they're into the den, the urine that would ordinarily have been expelled is automatically transferred to a special system where all the urine changes over into protein and is reused to make them survive the winter. This system has put the scientists in great awe. They cannot figure it out, and they cannot duplicate it. And another thing, when a bear goes into a den, he or she will defecate around the den so every bit of its intestines is emptied. And then he goes over and wolfs down a great big mouthful of leaves and stuffs his gullet so it's plugged solid. And it will stay that way all winter until he eats again and forces it out." *Suzan:* "In the spring they can't digest meat right away. They eat pussy willows and grass shoots, young greens, which would have a laxative effect, to clean their system. And then they can eat meat."

Al: "You know what saved this place? The difficulty of getting here. People have access to Maine wilderness now more than any other time in history. They never had logging roads, ATVs, or snowmobiles."

Suzan: "If there's a quiet and secluded wilderness, it ought to be preserved. Because there's not going to be that many left. What's that Maine motto? 'Maine—The Way Life Should Be.' Well, the sporting camps are 'Maine—The Way Life Used To Be.'"

Bear Roast

> 4–6 pounds bear roast (from hindquarter), 4 strips bacon, 1 onion (sliced into rounds), 3 garlic cloves (sliced), pepper

Remove all fat from the bear and bone it out. Roll and prick the meat and insert slivered garlic. Tie with cotton string if necessary. Sprinkle with pepper. Arrange onion rounds and raw bacon strips on top, securing with toothpicks as necessary. Roast, uncovered, in a slow oven (325 degrees) for 35 minutes per pound, or until internal temperature is 185 degrees. Internal temperature is very important, as with pork. Remove from oven and serve.

42. MOUNT CHASE LODGE

AP/HK, SCA

OWNERS: Sara and Rick Hill
ADDRESS: Mount Chase Lodge, RR 1, Box 281, Patten, ME 04765; 207-528-2183; fax: 207-528-2479
SEASON: Year-round

ACCOMMODATIONS: Five log cabins (one to three bedrooms), with indoor plumbing, shower, wood and propane heat, electric lights, porch (one enclosed), three cabins are fully HK, two have coffeepot and refrigerator; main lodge has eight guest rooms, fireplace, TV

RATES: Cabins $65–75 per couple per day; $375–450 per cabin per week. Main lodge, $48–55 per couple per day.

ACCESS: I-95 to exit 58 (Patten). Take ME 159 10 miles west to Shin Pond Village. Pass the store and campground and head up the hill, to the camp sign and driveway, which will be on your right.

The Hills' camp compound is focused on the white main lodge; the cabins are off to either side among the trees. The main lodge has a big central living room with a fireplace and a music area. A glassed-in room serves as a dining area with tables pushed together into one long seating arrangement. The windows look out to what appears to be a river; it is actually the thoroughfare leading into Upper Shin Pond.

Rick: "The pond is 2 miles long by a mile and a half wide and 70 feet at its deepest [45–50 feet average], with landlocked salmon and brook trout. It's at the base of Mount Chase, which got its name because of an American-Canadian skirmish back in the 1800s, maybe the 1820s or '30s. The town of Patten wasn't settled yet. A man by the name of Jim Chase, I believe, affiliated with a Bangor logging enterprise— although this is hearsay—came up from Bangor. He was supposed to burn the hayfields where the Canadians were staying, since hay was the prime feed source for the horses they used in logging. This was so the Canadians would move out back across the border and relinquish cutting. The Canadians may have come down via the waterway out of Houlton. We're pretty much centrally located here from New Brunswick. Anyway, he was sent to burn the hayfields, and the day he came here was a brisk August day with the prevailing wind out of the west. Windy day. And the fire got out of control. It forced him into the highest area, and, as I'm told, he subsisted on berries on top of the mountain [Mount Chase] for three weeks. The fire burned many thousands of acres encompassing as many as seven townships, each of which is 6 square miles! After the fire, the woods grew back to hardwoods and softwoods, which is what it is today. And, as the story goes, Shin Pond gets its name from this same Jim Chase, who thought the lower pond had the shape of a foot or ankle as he was sitting looking down on it from up on the mountain.

"This lodge was built in 1959 by Henry and Mary Schmidt. At one point there were three places in Shin Pond owned by Schmidts, none of them related. Henry and Mary built three cabins and owned the place from '59 to the spring of '76 when we took over. My family had roots in the Patten area, my grandmother and her family—her father was a sheriff there in the early 1900s. This great-grandfather came over here and built a cabin on Lower Shin Pond as a summer place. The camp still remains in the family. My mother and father brought us up here summers.

"Prior to buying the lodge, I worked as a computer-parts designer for Digital Equipment in Massachusetts, which is where I grew up, on a farm. Sara was a corporate buyer there, bought office supplies. We had originally looked at another place, but as luck would have it, the previous owners asked if we were interested in the place and we knew it was what we had in mind. When we got it, it was primarily a bear-hunting and fishing camp. But that changed in 1981 when the state eliminated the spring season on black bears. Our business had to transition to a recreational base and we are a year-round operation now. More people are getting involved in winter recreation than ever before. We have snowmobile rentals, tour packages, guide service on the trails, as well as the traditional hunting and fishing. We're right on ITS 85A at Shin Pond. There's ice fishing and downhill skiing at May Mountain, Island Falls, and also Mars Hill.

"I've been a registered Maine guide since '76 and an active member of the Professional Maine Guides Association, holding the office of president and vice president, and now I'm chairman of the board of directors. I oversee the legislative-action committee. There's a structured procedure for becoming a Maine guide now. The Department of Inland Fisheries and Wildlife gives a comprehensive written test and there's an oral exam administered by a registered guide and two members of the warden service. Our association was formed in 1978 for the purpose of educating legislators about the issues and concerns affecting the guiding industry. There are approximately twelve to fourteen hundred registered guides on the books. Most are 'patch holders' and don't guide for a living. About four or five hundred are people who derive at least 50 percent of their income from guiding services. The rule of thumb for guides is $100 to $250 a day, depending on the services. The high end is the striped-bass guide, who provides the fishing boat, motor, lunch, equipment, versus someone who might do a half-day canoe trip. There are several different categories of guides: hunting, fishing, white-water rafting, and recreational (which includes hiking, cross-country skiing, snowmobiling, naturalists).

"The most important thing for today's Maine guide is that they be a good communicator. You need to be an educator about the woods and waters, be a good businessman, but most of all be good with people. It's extremely important when you're taking people into situations out of their comfort zone that they can trust the guide's ability to take them safely through their experience. People should not question a guide in a safety situation. People who haven't done much hiking should really consider getting a guide if they're planning to do Katahdin. More people get in trouble there, and become problems to the park service, because they aren't properly equipped. The old, scruffy guy with a plaid jacket is no longer the image or the case. Today's guide is a professional, safely and effectively working with people for their own benefit—1997 was the 100th anniversary of registered Maine guides. And the first registered guide in Maine was a woman, 'Fly Rod Crosby,' out of the Rangeley area."

The address for the Maine Professional Guides Association is PO Box 847, Augusta, ME 04332; 207-785-2061.

Sara's Heavenly Cloud Biscuits

> 2 cups flour, 4 tsp. baking powder, 2 T sugar, 1 stick margarine, ⅛ tsp. salt, 1 egg, ⅔ cup milk

Mix dry ingredients together. Add margarine until crumbly. Beat egg and add to milk. Blend with the dry ingredients. Knead 10 times only! Roll out ¾ inch thick and cut into biscuits. Bake at 450 degrees for 15 minutes.

43. NAHMAKANTA LAKE CAMPS

AP/MAP/HK

OWNERS: Don and Angel Hibbs

ADDRESS: PO Box 544, Millinocket, ME 04462; 207-746-7356

SEASON: Year-round

ACCOMMODATIONS: Seven log cabins (sleep two to eight) with screened-in porch, woodstove, gas lights, gas range, gas refrigerator, spring-fed water spigot in front of each cabin, outhouse; camp has two shower houses with toilets; bring towel and washcloth; (November through April) bring a sleeping bag

RATES: $75 per person per day (AP); $55 per person per day (MAP);

$35 per person per day (HK)

ACCESS: I-95 to exit 39 (Newport). Take ME 7 north to Dexter, then
ME 23 to Guilford, then ME 6/15 to Greenville. Go 20 miles on Lily Bay
Road to Kokadjo. At Kokadjo Trading Post (last supplies), keep left on
Baxter State Park Road 1.25 miles. Turn right and go 5 miles (NLC sign).
Turn left, go 7 miles, and at the sign for the camps turn left again. Go
12 miles (pass Penobscot Pond, visible from the road) and cross a bridge.
Turn right and go 1 mile in on the camp driveway.

As you cross Pollywog Stream just prior to the camp driveway, you
notice white markings on the trees at either side of the road and a
path leading into the woods. You are that close to the Appalachian
Trail at Nahmakanta. The drive in takes you past a doghouse village—
the Hibbses use sled dogs for winter transportation into camp. Some
discrete yellow trail blazes a little farther on mark the location of a
1½-mile nature trail complete with educational "stations" or plaques.
An informational booklet describes such concepts as "geotropism"—
an organism's response to gravity, as with tree roots—and "phototro-
pism"—a response to light, as with tree shoots—and helps with bird
and tree identification.

The camp is set amid a swath of lawn with spring-fed, 4-mile-long
Nahmakanta Lake beyond. On either side of the compound are trout
streams. And near the main lodge, a low outbuilding sports a sled on
its roof, a harbinger of the winter to come. The Hibbses' two young
sons toddle up to greet you, hugging close to your heels and popping
questions: "Where are you from? What's your name?"

Nahmakanta has been a sporting camp since the 1870s. In 1990 the
Land for Maine's Future program spent $11.7 million to purchase the
29,692-acre parcel that encompasses Nahmakanta Lake. The Bureau of
Public Lands manages the property, which includes within its boundaries 24 lakes and ponds as well as numerous streams, many of which
are accessible only by walking. A walk up nearby 1,560-foot Nesunta-
bunt Mountain looks out on a pristine panorama. The AT traverses 9
miles of public lands in this neck of the woods, and future management
plans provide for the land to remain as wild and natural as possible.

A conservation easement prevents personal boats from being
launched from camp, and the camp boats themselves are limited to
6-horsepower motors. The camp maintains canoes at eight to ten hike-
in-only brook trout ponds. At Nahmakanta Lake there are shallows
near camp conducive to moose-watching, and nearby stream deltas

Plumbing "out back" at Nahmakanta

attract wildlife of all sorts. The Hibbses say, "We try to live close to nature here, and offer a backwoods atmosphere and experience."

44. PLEASANT POINT CAMPS

HK

OWNER: Jean Sargeant

ADDRESS: PO Box 929, Millinocket, ME 04462; 207-746-7464 (call between 7 and 9 PM)

SEASON: Year-round

ACCOMMODATIONS: Four log cabins (each sleeps two to four) with outhouse, inside hand pump for water, kerosene lamps, woodstove, porch, gas stove; no refrigerator

RATES: $20 per person per day

ACCESS: I-95 to exit 56 (Medway). Take ME 11 west to the JoMary gatehouse at the southern end of South Twin Lake; turn right and drive 14 miles to the Nahmakanta Unit Preserve gatehouse (pay only once). Go 6 miles, then turn right at the sign for the camps. Go 2 miles, cross Nahmakanta Stream, and continue 1.5 miles on very rough road (or walk) to the boat launch. Use a boat or hike in the rest of the way.

The rustic, maroon-brown log cabins of Pleasant Point Camps are built along a peninsula on Fourth Debsconeag Lake at the base of a 1,400-foot cliff. Two young men are at camp. One is a warden, checking in and helping out, the other is an intern who, with his partner, is raising falcons for Maine Inland Fisheries and Wildlife. *Jean:* "The cliffs are a peregrine falcon 'hacking site,' where they release the birds and feed them until they're old enough to fend for themselves. They feed them through a long tube and stay out of sight behind the cliff so the birds don't become dependent on humans.

"The story of how I'm here is pretty simple, really. My husband died in 1985. We had been married 32 years and were very close. He was a carpenter and part of the job was to cut asbestos. He became allergic to fiberglass and died when he was only 53 years old. I went to work at real estate for eight years. But I found after my husband died that all my friends were disappearing, and I had to look around and make new friends. I retired and was pining away. I knew I had to do something, so I decided since I was having to start all over, I might as well really start over. So I did a complete flip and sold my beautiful saltbox house in North Conway, my antiques, my crystal, and came here.

"I always used to go fishing with my husband. While he fished, I'd do my bookwork—he had three businesses and I kept his books. We used to go to Camp Phoenix, in Baxter, which is now private. We had four children and my husband and I would have loved to run Camp Phoenix, but it wasn't feasible. When I was looking around for what to do, I figured I could run housekeeping camps, live on the water, and supplement my Social Security income a little. Plus I could meet people. I didn't come here to make money—it won't happen—but I have met some wonderful people. Friends thought I was crazy—at my age, not being terribly mobile, out in the wilderness running a sporting camp that needed a lot of work, thinking I'll meet people! I looked at the camps in '93 and bought them October 1, 1994, and lived in here that first winter. My children's reactions went from support to complete rejection. But they're all coming around now. That first winter I came in with a gentleman friend, but he couldn't manage it. So my son, Dan, came in to help. And no matter what we did, there were always two more jobs needing to be done before we could do what had to be accomplished. We threw out all the mattresses and put in all new chimneys. Only one motorboat worked, so we had to bring in boats and motors. We had to buy a snow machine to go any-

Pleasant Point Camps

where, and a generator. It was just a totally new way of living, and it took awhile to get used to the systems."

Dan: "Everything you do is weather-related. You start out and then realize plowing on would be foolish, so you turn around. Common sense goes a lot farther out here than intelligence."

Jean: "A fellow came in early on, took one look at me, and said I'd never get on a snow machine. When Dan came in and heard that he said, 'You'll learn.' And I did.

"The upper three-quarters of this lake is owned by the state—the Nahmakanta Unit Preserve—and the other quarter is owned by the paper company. I lease this land from the State of Maine. I have to get permission to build anything, and I can't cut any wood here because I'm in a no-cut zone. So we have to lug all our wood in.

"The camp has quite a history. Our oldest cabin is from around 1900 and was built by a trapper who lived here with a Native American woman. And she was amazing. She decorated the entire inside walls and ceiling with birch bark, all cut out and tacked up in patterns. We call it Indian Camp. She hung up pictures and one is of the Roosevelt family. It seems Roosevelt stayed in Indian Camp while he was president."

During the late afternoon and through the early evening we could hear what sounded almost like loons. I was told, emphatically, that it was bears howling. It was certainly the first time I had ever heard such a thing and it was an eerie, exhilarating, wild sound echoing out from the forests and over the lake.

Jean: "I have three daughters and six grandchildren, and five have been here so far. They love it. Dan comes in regularly and has a cabin he uses. When he's gone, I'm the only resident west of the east-line section of T1R11 [that is, in the entire township], but I don't mind. In fact, I cherish my time alone. I'm not a recluse by any means, but I've never regretted my decision to move out here. For some reason, I'm supposed to be here. It shows in so many little ways."

45. WAPITI CAMPS

AP/HK

OWNERS: Frank and Anita Ramelli

ADDRESS: Patten, ME 04765; 207-528-2485 (camp); 508-481-0398 (winter)

SEASON: May through November

ACCOMMODATIONS: Seven log cabins (two to three bedrooms) with indoor plumbing and shower, wood heat, electric lights and refrigerator (not on generator), porch

RATES: $55 per day per person (AP); $295 per week per family (HK)

ACCESS: I-95 to exit 58. Take ME 11 north to Patten and turn left onto ME 159. Go 10 miles west to Shin Pond. Cross the bridge and take the next left. Go 2 miles on a dirt road into camp, at the end of the road.

$F_{rank:}$ "We are the only cabins on Wapiti Lake, or Davis Pond, as it used to be called. It is a spring-fed lake 1 mile long by half a mile wide and 72 feet at its deepest, and is stocked with brook trout. You can see Katahdin, right there at the end of the lake, from the porch of every cabin. We like to say, 'This is where the road ends and the trails begin.'

"These camps have been around since 1912. The history is that there were two women, a librarian and a schoolteacher from Bangor, who came up and stayed at what used to be a big hotel called the Shin Pond House. During their stay they would hike in here with friends for a picnic. It was a field with cows—they just liked the gorgeous view. Well, they went to the owners, the Webber family, who were the largest exporters of hardwood in Maine in the early 1900s, and got permission from them to lease the land. They built the lodge first, then tent platforms, and then it was so popular they built cabins on top of the platforms. And it has been serving sportsmen ever since. In fact, we're the oldest bear-hunting camp in the Patten area.

"We bought the camps in 1985. We're from Massachusetts, although we spent 23 years in Austria traveling around behind the Iron Curtain. I used to go hunting with my father at Maynard's and loved sporting camps. I retired when I was 50 and bought these. And I hope to pass them on to my son. My wife's from Germany and likes cooking, and so was fine with the idea of doing this. We used to come to Maine together and she said she always wanted a little nest, and this was the closest thing to it."

46. WHITE HOUSE LANDING

AP/HK, SCA

OWNERS: Candy and Bill Ware

MANAGERS: Linda Higgins and Bill Ware

ADDRESS: PO Box 749, Millinocket, ME 04462; 207-745- 5116; Web site: www.mainerec.com/ware.html

SEASON: Year-round

ACCOMMODATIONS: Three cabins (one to three bedrooms), with space heater, gas lights and stove; two cabins have running water and toilet; one has an outhouse; all share a central shower

RATES: $19–39 per person per day; tent sites, $15 per day

ACCESS: I-95 to exit 56 (Medway). Take ME 157 north through Millinocket. Follow signs to Baxter State Park. Before reaching the park, look for the North Woods Trading Post on the right side of the road and park across the street near the boat landing. The Trading Post has a phone booth (but it's best to call ahead for pickup time at the boat landing).

Inaccessible by car, the camps are a 10-mile boat trip up Ambajejus Lake (4 miles long) with a spectacular view of Katahdin (one of Thoreau's favorites), into "the Gut," where Ambajejus, North Twin, South Twin, Elbow, and Pemadumcook Lakes join up, and then 6 miles up Pemadumcook (a Native name meaning "a lake with a rocky bottom") to camp. The cabins are basic, and the main lodge is made of logs with a spacious dining area and large picture windows.

Bill: "Our cabins are named after local lakes, Debsconeag, Nahmakanta, and Minister, and two have the only flush toilets in T1R10 [Township 1, Range 10 of the "unorganized territories" in Maine], which is where we live. When my sister Candy and I first

White House Landing

came in here, we brought an 850-pound Vulcan restaurant stove up behind a snowmobile." *Candy:* "Not only that, but when we got it here it was April 1 and all the snow had melted off the hill to the lodge. So we parked the sled down on a stream and spent two hours shoveling snow onto the front lawn so we could bring it up. All the log siding for a cabin came up by boat, and all the roofing material. We generally go through sixty 100-pound propane cylinders a year. The gas we sell snowmobilers we have to haul up here. If I sat down and made a list, it would be tons and tons of stuff. Literally.

"In the fall they do a 10- to 14-foot drawdown of the lake, because the dam generates electricity for the paper mill and they're sort of building themselves an electricity credit. And also, that way when the snowmelt starts, there aren't any flooding problems. Now salmon and brook trout spawn in the spring, but togue [lake trout] spawn in the fall. They lay their eggs in shallows, so you don't want to draw the water down to the point where the eggs are on dry land and dry up. So biologists net the togue, put a transmitter in their tummies, and then follow them with a little beacon. And when the togue stop moving, they know that they've built their nests. Then they bring the state divers in, who find the nests and set the amount of drawdown.

"When we were investigating having a business on leased land—

which sounds scary, but most businesses in any city lease—one of the things we learned was that the paper companies can't use this land anyway because it's so close to the water, a good percentage of it is field, and we're within a mile of the Appalachian Trail. They definitely stay away from a corridor of the AT. Actually, if most of northern and western Maine wasn't owned by the few paper companies, it would be a patchwork, developed and fenced, and you wouldn't have a wilderness. It's gotta be at least a third of the state that is still wilderness because it's a farm for trees."

Bill: "ITS 86 comes right through our backyard. On a good day we'll see two or three hundred snowmobiles come through here. People leave Greenville usually, go to Kokadjo 25 miles west of here, come across to our place, have a meal, fill up with gas, and maybe continue on 30 miles to Millinocket. Some start at Canada on the west, go all the way across Maine for a week, and end up in Canada on the east side. We had two couples through here that were doing that for their honeymoon.

"Last winter, January 24, I was bringing a $50,000 snowmobile-trail groomer from here to Kokadjo, and it went into 24 feet of water. This was in 20 inches of ice, and it had been 10 degrees below in the night. It turns out there was a crack that ran down my route for 3 miles. And there was water in the crack. I went 150 feet trying to get on good ice. As I started to break through, I tried to jump out, but the door had me by the waist and took me under the water. When I got away from the sucking of the water, I saw the hole and pulled myself up. I had four layers on top, three on the bottom, with big heavy polar boots. I don't know how I swam up. A guy named Benjamin Moore came by in a snowmobile and brought me back. It was 1 mile to go and my hair froze instantly. No one was expecting me till dark. That hole was frozen hard enough for a man to walk over in 3 hours. It took eight days to get the machine out and $10,000 worth of fixing. Three times we had skidders down to get it out. They weigh 25,000 to 50,000 pounds, and my groomer weighs 10,000 pounds, just to show you. I was back grooming trails two weeks to the day after it happened. Had a moment of silence out there where I went through, because I very nearly lost my life.

"The state is now rerouting the snowmobile trail around Nahmakanta Stream and onto a bridge. I hire a nighttime operator to groom from here to Kokadjo four times a week—takes 10 to 12 hours roundtrip. I do the Mary-Jo Trail during the day on Tuesdays, which takes 9 hours."

Linda: "We're so busy here feeding snowmobilers, we can barely keep up. It's exhausting. Once a week he goes out and fills up a pickup truck with groceries and supplies. Wednesday and Thursday are my baking days. I don't want to see another whoopie pie by the end of the season, I tell you. Snowmobilers are great people, though." *Bill:* "They're a very appreciative bunch, particularly if you've got a well-groomed trail. We had a snowmobile group from southern Maine who had a ceremony for me here in the lodge 'cause they said this was one of the best-groomed trails they had ever been on."

Whoopie Pies

> 6 tsp. shortening, 1 cup sugar, 1 egg, 1 cup milk, 1 tsp. vanilla, 5 T cocoa, 2 cups flour, 1¼ tsp. baking soda, 1 tsp. salt

Cream together shortening and sugar, then egg, milk, and vanilla. Add the rest of the ingredients. Drop by tablespoonfuls on an ungreased cookie sheet and bake at 425 degrees for about 15 minutes. Cut in half and fill with 1½ cups confectioner's sugar, 12 T shortening, and 12 T marshmallow fluff creamed together.

The North Maine Woods

For the purposes of this book, this region includes "everything else" north of Baxter State Park, bordered to the east by ME 11 and by the Canadian boundary to the north and west. (Maine is surrounded on three sides by Canada.)

Many of the sporting camps in this book are located in remote or pristine spots. I suspect, to visitors from major urban areas, that the State of Maine itself seems remote. It is, to some degree. That is its charm—it is one of the last outposts of the American wilderness—and that is why so many people are drawn to sporting camps in the first place. But it is here, in the North Maine Woods, that even the Maine resident comes head to head with the concept of "vast wilderness." You can drive around for days and for hundreds of miles without seeing streetlights, telephone poles, or paved roads. Mileage is posted on small metal or wooden rectangles in trees, wildlife meanders on or beside the right-of-way, pulp trucks and pickups outnumber cars. Piles of logs, lumber camps, and busy loggers attest to the fact that this region is a huge network of tree farms, Maine's largest cash crop. When you venture into this region, it is best to remember the old Boy Scout motto—and be prepared. Please refer to the sections "How do I get there?" and "What should I bring?" in the introduction of this book.

Getting there: Many of the sporting-camp owners in this region suggest flying in to their camps. A number of owners are pilots themselves and can pick you up at a set rendezvous and fly you directly to their dock. The closest airport is in Presque Isle (rental cars available). Floatplanes are available through Northstar Outfitters, Portage, 207-435-3002, and Scotty's Flying Service, Shin Pond, 207-528-2626, as well the services from Millinocket and Greenville. Driving times vary wildly depending on the location of camp. Generally, driving time from Portland is 4–6 hours; from Boston, 7–9 hours; from New York City, 10–13 hours.

Guidance: For further information, contact North Maine Woods, PO Box 421, Ashland, ME 04732; 207-435-6213.

47. BRADFORD CAMPS

AP, SCA

OWNERS: Igor and Karen Sikorsky

CAMP ADDRESS: Box 729, Ashland, ME 04732; 207-746-7777

WINTER ADDRESS: PO Box 778, Kittery, ME 03904; 207-439-6364

SEASON: May through November

ACCOMMODATIONS: Eight log cabins (each sleeps two to six people) with woodstove, gas lights, indoor plumbing, shower, porch; two outpost cabins; no pets

RATES: $80–100 per person per day

ACCESS: I-95 to exit 60. Turn left onto ME 212 west and go 10 miles to Knowles Corner. Go right onto ME 11 north, 31 miles to Ashland (last gas). Go left at the four-corners (staying on ME 11 north), go 1 mile, cross the Aroostook River, and turn left at the T intersection. Drive 0.75 mile to the Gateway Store. (You can call the camp from here.) Take the right-hand fork onto a dirt road. Go 5 miles to the North Maine Woods gate (fee: $18 per person). From the gate, take the left fork. Go 10 miles, cross the Machias River, and take the left fork. Go 15 miles and take a right at the sign for the camps. Follow signs about 19 more miles into camp.

One of the cabins at Bradford's Camps

After driving a maze of logging roads along vast tracks of forest, you reach Bradford Camps by emerging onto a spacious lawn with a quarter-acre of gardens lush with flowers and vegetables, surrounded by picturesque log cabins. Smoke rising from the chimney at the main lodge in the distance and the no-cars-in-camp policy all contribute to the traditional sporting-camp feel and the sense of having come to a place set apart.

Igor: "Bradford's was started in 1890 by Will Atkins, who came up here from the Rangeley and Moosehead Lake areas. The camps are named after Governor Bradford of Massachusetts, an ancestor of Milt Hill, the third owner. We're located at the headwaters of the Aroostook River watershed on Munsungan Lake. It's a mile by 4 miles long and 123 feet deep, with lake and brook trout, landlocked salmon, and smelt, and is bounded by 1400-foot Munsungan Ridge on the south and 2,300-foot Norway Bluff on the north. You should see these hardwood ridges in the fall-foliage season with the sunset hitting them. It's magnificent! They're the dividing line between the Aroostook and Allagash watersheds. The Aroostook empties into the St. John River, which heads north and east into New Brunswick. Most rivers everywhere else flow south, but the waters in northern Maine all flow north.

"At one end of Munsungan is a thoroughfare with a path to Chase

Lake, where we keep a canoe for our guests. We also have two fly-in-only outpost camps: Big Reed Pond and Bluffer Pond. The Big Reed Pond camp is special to us for a couple of reasons. First, it's in the middle of a 5,000-acre preserve owned by The Nature Conservancy, with the largest old-growth forest in New England. Second, the pond has blue-back trout, *Salvelinus alpinus oquassa,* and this fish is found in only 10 other lakes in the world, all of them in Maine!

"For our first-time guests, especially, we really want them to be guided. Not only will they learn how and where to fish here, and have a little history and lore of the area, but they'll also be able to get to some of the outlying fly-fishing ponds. Munsungan is a smelt-driven fishery, which means the fishing is primarily trolling. And we have 50 waters within a 20-mile radius of us. With a guide, our guests can have a total fishing experience, plus guides are a sporting-camp tradition we believe in upholding.

"The way I got into this is really a lifelong thing. I started when I was 10 going to Gary and Betty Cobb's boys' camp. I went there for 12 successive summers and eventually helped run it. When that closed, I helped at the Cobbs' Pierce Pond sporting camps next door. I took architecture in college and spent 12 years in the building industry, but those early experiences were pretty well ingrained. I built Karen her first fly rod, and our honeymoon was a fishing trip to Alaska. Our honeymoon suite was a 16-foot Winnebago; our first vacation was a canoe trip down the Allagash. We kid each other that we have yet to take a vacation where we haven't had to buy fly dope and long johns.

"We decided not to have kids and so devoted our energies to this major project. After spending four years staying at different sporting camps, we knew what we wanted: classic, historical camps in good condition and in a remote, pristine location. We were invited to some Maine Sporting Camp Association meetings and almost everyone tried to talk us out of buying a camp, said it was no place to make any money. But in February of 1996 we called the Youlands, the former owners, and it all happened in one breath. Less than six weeks later we closed on the place and we were in here opening up camp on April 26, having left our jobs the week prior. I had been with a roof-truss manufacturer and Karen had worked eight years in the clothing industry—product management, traveling to the Orient several times a year. And here we were owners of a sporting camp and in less than two weeks we had full ice-out, 20 guests, cabins cleaned, water running, food on the tables! Gary Corson, our head guide, and his wife, Diane, our cook, are now in here with us, but we sure had a firsthand initiation.

"I'm in the midst of creating some hiking trails around here now. I've put in about 10 miles so far, and we're offering some family trips in the area. We have some canoe trips, like on Munsungan Stream or the Allagash 15 miles away. We can also arrange a white-water rafting trip on the Penobscot River. And at camp we have a 10-station sporting clays course. So there's a lot to do in addition to the fishing or hunting. For hunting we have thousands of acres of excellent cover for grouse, deer, and bear.

"We have a 20-year lease with Seven Islands Paper Company. They're known as a 'green company,' with good cutting practices and policies. They don't have a mill they have to feed and they don't spray herbicides. They believe in sustainable stewardship, and the view from camp will never change. To give you an idea, they've recently leased out 10,000 trees, and eventually it will be 60,000, to a maple-sugaring operation—Munsungan Maple Products. They make maple syrup right over there at Norway Bluff and deliver it to camp by boat."

Dark Star Cupcakes

> 8 ounces cream cheese (room temperature), 1 egg, ⅓ cup sugar,
> ⅛ tsp. salt, 1 cup semisweet chocolate chips, 1½ cups flour, 1 cup sugar,
> ¼ cup unsweetened cocoa, 1 tsp. baking soda, ½ tsp. salt, 1 cup water,
> ⅓ cup vegetable oil, 1 T white vinegar, 1 tsp. vanilla

Preheat the oven to 375 degrees. Line muffin tins with cupcake papers.

To make the filling: Blend the first four ingredients with a wooden spoon. Fold in the chocolate chips and set aside. *To make the batter:* In another bowl, combine the dry ingredients and mix well. Add remaining ingredients. Blend thoroughly. Fill cupcake papers ¾ full with batter. Drop 1 heaping tablespoon of filling into the center of each cupcake. Bake 35–40 minutes.

48. CROOKED TREE LODGE AND CAMPS

AP
OWNERS: Gloria and Nick Curtis
ADDRESS: PO Box 110, Portage Lake, ME 04768; 207-435-6413
SEASON: Year-round
ACCOMMODATIONS: Four cabins (each sleeps two to six people, dorm-style) with indoor plumbing and shower, electric lights, automatic heat

RATES: $25–60 per person per day
ACCESS: I-95 to exit 60. Take ME 212 west 10 miles to ME 11, then follow ME 11 north to Portage. Turn left at Coffin's Store onto West Cottage Road. Go 2.5 miles to the camp sign on the left.

Gloria: "We're right across the road from Portage Lake, which is shaped kind of like a U. It's about a mile wide, 24 feet at its deepest, and is 10 miles from the inlet to the outlet. It's part of the Fish River chain and has brook trout and landlocked salmon. The log lodge here used to be a private home—we converted it and built the cabins. They're made out of cedar, planed at the mill down the road. We're planning on building a couple more. We'd been working at other camps, Moose Point and Red River Camps, and we just wanted to have a place ourselves. We have 33 acres of land and have made a trail to ITS 85.

"We're both from here. My mother's family is from Portage and Nick's family is from Portage. The town has a golf course and a little beach and there's a tennis court by the town hall. The Portage Lake Snowmobile Club has poker runs and suppers and there's ice fishing on the lake. The Aroostook Center Mall, movie theater, and restaurants with Saturday-night bands are nearby. It's not an industrial town; there's a lot of hunting and fishing in the area.

"I used to live near the fire station and every time the alarm went off, no matter what time of day it was, I'd just show up. And I was almost always the first one to the fire. Initially, I'd just follow them around and grab furniture or do whatever I could do. Just 'cause I know I'd want someone to do that for me. Eventually I was voted in—I believe it was 1985—so now I'm the only woman in our 15-member volunteer fire department. We have Scott air-pack training and have to study things like the 'Firefight 1' booklet for structure fires. The alarm goes off and guests all figure my husband's going to jump, but it's me. I love it! The Maine State Forestry Department is in Portage, so some of our group fight forest fires.

"We have people in now from Virginia and West Virginia who are hunting bear with hounds. There are three men to a guide. Nick is one and we hire the others. They have different breeds of hounds, like blueticks, black-and-tans, and walkers—which are a good-sized hound and got their name, we were told, because of their large feet and long toenails. They can run up a tree! The dogs travel up here in carrier boxes in the back of pickups. It takes a couple of days to get them here.

Out back we have 55-gallon drums for them, filled with hay. They all wear radio-tracking collars and the hunters have the receivers. This group of nine guys has 26 dogs. We have one woman who's here with three children. They're out of school and have been hunting with their parents since they were little. They follow the hounds by car, kind of like orienteering but not by foot, until the bear gets treed and they hear the hounds baying. They hunt bobcats the same way in winter, and coyote."

Looking around, I notice a canoe paddle in the dining room with lettering that says, "Coming to Crooked Tree Lodge is not a matter of life and death, it's much more important than that." In the living room area are several chairs made with snowshoe caning. *Gloria:* "I learned how to weave those snowshoe chairs from Jim Holmes, an old trapper who lives in town. We have to get cowhide, take the hair off it, and cut it in strips. You weave it up wet and then it dries up hard. You can also use moose hide. Once it's dry you varnish it—otherwise your dog might chew on it and eat up your chair!"

Spanish Rice

"This serves 12," says Gloria, "and, as you'll see, it's not fast food. But it's our real specialty."

Boil a whole chicken in a large roasting pan with 10 quarts of water. Debone the chicken and save the chicken juice. Debone 4 pork chops and cut them into chunks. Fry the chunks in 2 T oil with all the cloves in a small head of garlic.

Cut the chicken into pieces and put it in the bottom of the roasting pan. Put the pork-chops pieces on top of that. Next pour in 7 cups of Uncle Ben's long-grain rice. Add 2 cans of drained, French-style green beans and 1 can of drained peas.

Crush the tomatoes from a regular-size can of whole tomatoes and add that. Add 1 T of saffron filaments to 4 cups of the chicken juice, bring to a boil, turn off the heat, and let it steep 10 minutes (it gets yellowish). Pour this over the mixture in the roasting pan. Then take the rest of the chicken liquid and cover the ingredients, leaving 2 inches of headroom. Cover with foil and bake at 300 degrees for 1 hour. Take it out, add more liquid to cover the ingredients, and cook another hour until done.

49. FISH RIVER LODGE

HK/AP, SCA

OWNERS: Jim and Kathy Lynch

ADDRESS: Box 202, Eagle Lake, ME 04739; 207-444-5207; e-mail: fr-lodge@ainop.com; Web site: http://www.mainerec.com/frlodge.html

SEASON: Year-round

ACCOMMODATIONS: Eight cabins (one to three bedrooms) with indoor plumbing and shower, gas or wood heat, electric light and refrigerator, gas cookstove

RATES: $60 per couple per day, $350 per cabin per week (HK); $60 per person per day, $350 per person per week (AP)

ACCESS: I-95 to exit 58 (Sherman Mills–Patten). Go north on ME 11 to the town of Eagle Lake. In the middle of the village, at the general store, turn right for 1.5 miles on a paved road to the camps. By the time you've reached Eagle Lake, you are only 18 miles from the Canadian border and 6 hours north of Portland. The camps are at the end of a paved road, just 1.5 miles from ME 11 and the conveniences of Eagle Lake village.

K*athy:* "Don't confuse us with the Eagle Lake in Acadia National Park or Big Eagle next to Chamberlain Lake. We had a woman call us once, 'I'm here in Bar Harbor and I can't seem to find you!' Our Eagle Lake is part of the Fish River chain of lakes in the St. John Valley. It's 18 miles long. Being on a lake is great for family vacations, and we're very family oriented. That's our biggest growing sector. Sporting camps aren't just for hunting and fishing. The photographic opportunities are great, for example, and we just had a couple who got engaged while they were here."

Jim: "For beginning canoeists, a good trip would be the Fish River from the head of it and down. It's a two- or three-day trip meandering down through the North Woods with no white water."

Kathy: "We're fortunate here because over 9 miles of lake beyond the camps are all Maine Public Lands, which can never be built on. Our guests have access to about 26,000 acres of public lands. Eagle Lake was settled in 1840 by Sefroi Nadeau, a Canadian Frenchman, and Richard Woods, an Irishman. The town was incorporated in 1911 and was given its name because of the eagles in the area."

Jim: "This whole area used to be called Lincoln School Site instead of Aroostook County. The camps themselves were started in 1928 by Charlie Wiles, a lumberman. They were built for his wife because she wanted to start a business. She did very well, and they kept adding on to the lodge and building cabins. They called them Charles Wiles' Lake View Camps. When we bought them, in 1993, they were called Camps of Acadia and we changed it to Fish River Lodge because, like we mentioned, it was getting confused with Acadia National Park.

"I taught for 13 years at a vocational school. Then I started my own outdoor-equipment business in Cumberland. We decided when the kids were out of high school we'd do something in this business. We looked around until we found camps that were reasonable, plus we wanted to be easily accessible and have a good lake. We're at the very end of what they call Old Main Street here, so we have a paved road into the camps. We're on public utility, public electricity. Eagle Lake here is 18 miles long, 2½ miles wide. It is the last lake on the Fish River chain of lakes from Fish River Lake, Portage Lake, St. Froid Lake. In an easterly direction, we can go to Long Lake, across Square Lake, and back into Eagle Lake.

"If anyone came to me saying they wanted to purchase a set of sporting camps, what I'd tell them is manage a place for a year, see what it's all about, the ups and downs of the business. Then make your decision. And instead of going to a bank, have the owner finance it if possible. That way you're going to get a better interest rate, plus you won't have the headaches. A survey is worth it, but that should be the owner's expense. The majority of camps are on leased land. But we couldn't do that. We wouldn't be able to sleep at night."

Kathy: "When we first got here I was fishing off the dock one day and people coming by said, 'You can't catch any fish off the dock.' Well, a couple weeks later we had a 10-year-old boy who caught a 17-inch salmon off that dock. He was beside himself!"

Jim: "Basically Eagle Lake has landlocked salmon, brook trout, and togue. In the wintertime they catch cusk up here. We also have white suckers, chub, and jack smelts [the large smelts]. For ice fishing, they plow a two-lane highway right down the lake from the center of town. And there'll be anywhere from 30 to 40 ice shacks right in front of the camps here. The lake is 80 feet deep in front of the camp, and the deepest part is between 140 and 180 feet, depending on the time of year. It's fly-fishing-only, artificial lures, the month of September on the Fish River and the Thoroughfare between Eagle and Square Lakes. At any other time of the year it's whatever you want to do: trolling, plug fishing, worms, whatever.

"Hunting is great in the fall, good bear hunting, very good moose hunting. If a guy can't get a moose up here, he shouldn't be moose hunting. Deer hunting—there are some big deer. It's not uncommon to get a 250-pound buck, but you have to be a hunter because the territory's so big. There are thousands and thousands of acres with nothing. Plenty of logging roads for partridge [ruffed grouse] and woodcock, or 'timberdoodles' is what we've always called them. You're almost guaranteed a bear. We have three guides available, plus I'm a registered Maine guide.

"We're very fortunate that rabies hasn't come this far north, or heartworm problems, or Lyme disease. There is a strain of rabies coming in being carried by raccoons that there is no cure for yet. So if you see a raccoon walking around in your yard that's lethargic, chances are it's got rabies. Fox and coyote also carry rabies. With all the anti-trappers and fur people, pelts aren't worth anything. So the trappers aren't trapping them, and the hunters aren't shooting them. Pine martins, fisher, and skunk don't usually have rabies."

Kathy: "Hunting does have its uses. For every deer that's shot by a hunter, the biologists say 10 starve during the wintertime because of the cutting and the building, especially in southern Maine. I mean, when you build a house or mall in the middle of their field where they spend the winter, where do you expect them to go?"

Jim: "Do you know there are probably more moose killed on the highway than they take during the hunting season? And it happens in the deep woods by the logging trucks. They can't stop, no way, and the moose dies." *Kathy:* "If a deer comes out of the woods, it'll stop by the road, look, and then jump out. So if you're paying attention, you'll see a deer first. A moose comes out of the woods, takes four or five steps out of the trees, gets in the middle of the road, and stops. There's no warning. I came back from Cumberland one night and I had three of them come out in front of me. One of them was a fairly close call—for the others I was able to slow down. The lights make them blind and totally unpredictable." *Jim:* "Not only that, but a moose, being dark, is very hard to pick up. You've got to watch for the eyes to glow, to reflect the light. But moose eyes don't glow as much as deer eyes for some reason. One thing about a moose, he could be jogging alongside the road right beside you and all of a sudden, he'll just turn in front of you. And they trot right along at 35 miles an hour." *Kathy:* "We had friends come up here. The wife was in the passenger seat and there was a moose running right beside them. Her husband kept going faster and faster because he was afraid the moose would get ahead and dart in front and he wouldn't be able to stop the car in time. And the moose kept right up with him! Finally, they just stopped and let the moose go. She said she couldn't believe it—she's looking out her window and there's a moose right there!"

Turkey Stuffing

Kathy: *"This is enough for a 20- to 25-pound turkey. I usually fill the turkey (both openings) with water and drain several times. When you stuff the turkey, always cook immediately or store the stuffing in the refrigerator until you're ready to cook the turkey."*

> 2 loaves bread (with homemade bread, use 1–2 loaves, depending on the size of the loaf); 1 roll pork sausage; oregano, Bell's seasoning, parsley, rosemary, sage (all 1–2 tsp.); salt and pepper to taste, 1 green pepper, 2 onions, heart, liver, and neck

Break bread into a large bowl that can take hot liquid. Stir the bread so it gets exposed to air and starts to dry out. Cook the sausage until brown. While sausage is cooking, put heart, liver, and neck into a saucepan with 2 cups of water. Boil 10 minutes. Drain and keep the water/broth. Chop peppers and onions and add to the sausage. Sauté the mixture and then add to the broth. Cut the liver and heart fine and add to sausage. Add seasonings to taste. Cook on low for ½ hour. Add sausage mixture to the bread. If it's too moist, add more bread.

50. JALBERT (WILLARD) CAMPS

AP/HK, SCA

OWNER: Phyllis Jalbert

ADDRESS: c/o Dana Shaw, 6 Winchester Street, Presque Isle, ME 04769; 207-764-0494

SEASON: Year-round

ACCOMMODATIONS: Three log cabins with central outhouse and sauna, gas lights, woodstove, running water, screened-in porch; one cabin has a full kitchen; also outpost cabins along the Allagash

RATES: $100–125 per person per day, includes boats and all meals (five-person minimum group rate); $50 per day per person (HK)

ACCESS: I-95 to exit 58. Take ME 11 north to Portage. At Dean's Motel in Portage, turn left. Turn left (follow the signs) and pay at the gatehouse. Follow the main logging road south of Portage Lake. Turn left at Dead Horse Gulch and continue to the bridge at the base of Round Pond, where you need a boat pickup to get to the camps.

I visited Jalbert Camps in the middle of winter and participated in one of their winter-camping expeditions. Jalbert's (pronounced "Jalbear") is on a 2-acre peninsula in Round Pond along the Allagash, and most people come upon the cabins while canoeing the wilderness waterway. In winter you get to walk on water while trailing a toboggan-load of gear, sleep in a cotton tent with a portable woodstove, use a bucket or outdoor privy, reach the luxury of log cabins, and generally have an incredible adventure.

Phyllis: "In the late 1930s my grandfather, Willard Jalbert, used to come up here for hunting, guiding parties, and fishing. He was a lumberman." Maine guide Dana Shaw continues: "He was born about 15 miles downriver and spent most of his life on the Allagash. 'Moose-towner' is the name that's given to people who live in the Allagash area." *Phyllis:* "They're mostly of Scotch and Irish ancestry, perhaps mixed with French, too. My grandfather was considered to be a real Moosetowner." *Dana:* "After the war, Willard and Willard Jr., Phyllis's father, and her uncle Bob decided they needed to build a camp here, and that's how the camps started in 1946."

Phyllis: "This was true wilderness in those days. Let's see, it's 35 miles to Allagash Village from here. We used to put in below Allagash Falls and sometimes we could make it here in a day, if nothing went wrong. Otherwise, my father would leave us along the river somewhere and go back to town and get what he needed. We have another camp downriver. It was one little cabin at first and they kept adding rooms on and now it's the Hilton of the Allagash. There were a lot of other log cabins along the river, which have since burned down because of the Allagash Waterway protection."

Dana: "The reason we're able to offer camps in a state preserve is as a result of Supreme Court Justice William O. Douglas. He took a trip through here and Phyllis's grandfather and father and I were on that trip. This was back in 1960. He said to us, 'This will be destroyed unless it's preserved.' So he went back to Washington and sent Stewart Udall, secretary of the interior at the time, up here to investigate. They really wanted this to become a national preserve." *Phyllis:* "But the state didn't want to lose control of the area." *Dana:* "So the state bought these buildings and burned down all the structures along the river except Nugent's up in Chamberlain Lake. This was in 1966. And they allowed the Jalberts to lease them back for a percentage of the gross income. And that's how we were able to hang on."

Phyllis: "My father and brother died in 1976, in a car accident to-gether, and then my uncle died in a plane crash coming up here in 1980. My cousin ran the camps for five years, but he just wasn't of the nature to do this, so he gave it up. We've given our hearts to this place and to see it, poof, handed over to someone else—it was close. I was the only person in the family who came forward and tried to keep it. I was terrified—terrified. The grunt work that went into this place is un-believable. That huge stove over there came up in a canoe! I mean they dumped it in the river several times, they portaged it across the falls. It was a major operation. I was 9 when this cabin we're in was built. I remember them putting in the 'picogee,' the top log. And then, all of a sudden, it wasn't going to be part of us anymore? I spent a whole year putting together papers—lawyers want papers, a proposal. There were people who wanted this place, and some who felt it should be burned down and returned to wilderness. And our position is that this has always been a working river, a log-driving river with log cabins along it. Anyway, we presented the proposal, the governor had to sign it off, and I got it. We started in '86 with a 10-year lease and a 10-year option. The state is happy because the cabins are in much better shape now. We're not open like many of these other camps; people don't just drop in here. They only come in by special appointment. We runs trips mostly, at this point."

Dana: "We start our fishing groups around May 1, ice-out. We feed people, and some bring their own food. The fishing is all wild brook trout, and it's actually pretty good still. We have fishing until mid-June, when the water starts warming up, and then we start our family-type groups."

Phyllis: "We organize Allagash canoe trips. The classic trip starts at Telos Lake and ends up at Allagash Village and takes about 7 to 10 days. Or you could do shorter sections. For the most part, the Allagash has flatwater and Class I and II rapids, making it ideal for a wide range of canoeists. And then in the fall we have hunting both at base camp here and at Whittaker Brook, a camp 8 miles upriver. We have coy-otes in the area, and you can hunt for them after dark.

"We started our winter camping in 1988, and 1992 was our pilot year for taking off from here on foot, with no snow machine backup and no dogs. From here to our tent site is about 4 miles. Then we go 4 miles above that and stay in a cabin, then 2 more miles, and then we swing back and stay in the tents again. We'll pull our made-to-order cotton tents and gear behind us on special easy-run toboggans Dana made.

The author winter camping at Willard Jalbert Camps.

"It's so beautiful here in winter. Here's how you can sleep outside, even if you don't have a tent: You make a snow cave. First, you want to have some snow! Then you use a snowshoe or shovel and heap up an elongated mound of snow about 10 by 7 feet long and about 4 or 5 feet high. As you heap the snow on, really pack it down. The weight of the snow will keep pushing down and it will settle. When it's set, in about 2 hours or so, you can just dig it out. Be careful not to dig too close to the outside or it will collapse. Keep about a foot of snow all the way around. You can measure some twigs or boughs to a foot and place them around the top of the cave, so when you dig it out and come to a stick inside it means you've gone to the foot mark. The secret is to make the opening very small—just enough to crawl down into, and with the inside having just enough room to turn over and move around some, but not so large that your body heat can escape. And it actually warms up to a little below freezing when you're in there, even if the temperature outside is 10 or 20 degrees below zero."

Dana: "In the old days, this river was run in 20-foot Old Town guide-model or E.M. White double-ended canoes that were good for poling and paddling. Then they brought in a 2.5-horsepower motor. But you put that on and the stern would tend to drag down. So over the years the canoes kept getting broader in the stern, with a flare in the bow and midsection so the water would roll out, not in. My first canoe was a Gallup canoe built in Fort Fairfield, Maine, and it just worked so much better than the old canoes. But I broke it in two trailing the thing, and I was heartsick. So I built myself a mold. I wanted my canoe to be bigger, longer, deeper, wider, with the same general features of that Gallup canoe. And my canoe came out much better than I expected. The material on the mold is cedar covered with sheet metal. The reason for the sheet metal is when you drive the little tacks in and the tacks hit the metal, they clinch. Now I had a hauling canoe which could work well with a 10-horsepower motor and float over bars at maximum speed without hitting rocks."

Dana: "Back when I was beginning to guide, a young fella in my 20s, the 'Ole Guide' was talking about giving these people a bear scare." *Phyllis:* "My grandfather was called the Ole Guide because he didn't want to be called the O-L-D guide!" *Dana:* "Well, these guests were egging to see a bear. So he got me to one side and says, 'Hey, go get that bearskin hanging alongside the cabin and drape that over you and you go rutting around out there by the woodshed. And then we'll grub around with a flashlight and when you see the flashlight,' he says, 'you duck.' So, of course, I was out there grubbing around and he says to these people, 'Did you see him?' And everybody says, 'Oh yeah, I saw him.' Well, the Ole Guide, unbeknownst to me, had a shotgun. And he loaded that thing and he fired a shot. Can you imagine! I didn't know who fired that shot, and here I am with a bearskin draped over me! Now that's a Moosetown story, and trick!"

PJ's Oatmeal Sundaes

Phyllis: *"Cereals provide powerhouse nutrients—paddle power. But you first have to convince people to eat it! This does the trick."*

> 2 cups water, ⅓ cup raisins, 1 cup rolled oats or five-grain cereal, 2 T oat bran, 2 T wheat germ, 2 apples (precooked with ⅛ cup water, 1 tsp. vanilla, ½ tsp. cinnamon, and 1 T maple syrup)

Combine water and raisins in a saucepan. Bring to a boil. Reduce heat and add oats, wheat germ, and oat bran gradually while stirring. Add the apples, vanilla and cinnamon. Reduce heat and cook for about 5 minutes. Spoon into bowls and top with any combination of nuts, seeds, fruit (fresh or dried), and milk or yogurt, along with real maple syrup, if you have some.

51. LIBBY CAMPS

AP, SCA

OWNERS: Matt and Ellen Libby

ADDRESS: Drawer V, Ashland, ME 04732; 207-435-8274 (radio phone) or 207-435-6233; e-mail: matt@libbycam.sdi.agate.net

SEASON: May through November

ACCOMMODATIONS: Eight log cabins at the home camp (sleep two to six) with indoor plumbing and shower (two have a shower-tub combination), skylight in roof, gas lights, woodstove; 10 HK outpost cabins; well-behaved pets welcome

RATES: $100–325 per person per day, includes boats

ACCESS: I-95 to exit 58. Take ME 11 north approximately 40 miles and turn left at the sign for the camps, onto a road that will take you through the town of Oxbow. Continue to the North Maine Woods Gate ($21 fee). Continue on a dirt road about 20 miles, following signs. For quicker access, camp seaplane pickup is available at Presque Isle airport or at Matagamon Lake near Patten. Van pickup at the airport is also available.

Libby's is tucked in the forest with some old and some very new cabins built of massive spruce and balsam fir logs. Matt Libby has been handcrafting log buildings as long as he can remember. Inside, home-made quilts add warmth and skylights add light.

Matt: "The Libby family came to Maine from England in the 1660s. Two of my great-grandfathers were original settlers of Oxbow, the closest village to camp down the river [Aroostook River] about 35 miles. In the 1850s C.C. 'Ike' Libby moved to Oxbow, which only had a number for a name. Here, miraculously, he met a woman, Melissa Trafton, daughter of another original settler, Eben Trafton. They had farms and supplied the loggers coming in here around the 1880s. Then, around 1885, they started Libby Hotel. At the time, there was a man named Will Atkins who was running sporting camps on an island here on Millinocket Lake. Will's customers would come and stay at my grandfather's hotel on the way through. Then in the 1890s my grand-father and his brother Will decided to get into the sporting-camp busi-ness, and they bought the island camps from Will Atkins, who went off and built Bradford Camps—which wasn't called that then. They also got another set of camps, Spider Lake Camps. The saying was, '50 camps [cabins] in three counties, half a million fish waiting for your line,' or something like that. The dining room on the island was twice the size of this one here—70 feet long. And back then they thought it

Matt and Ellen Libby

was too rustic to have your lodge look like logs, so they sawed them in half to make them look like boards. They'd have a cow they would swim over in the spring. The chore boy, my uncle Charlie, used to walk the cow up the trail from Oxbow 25 miles, cross the river, and then swim across the lake, leading the cow, so the guests would have fresh milk.

"Then the two brothers decided that my grandfather Ike would run the town end and Will would run the camp end. Will died in 1938 and left what he had to his sisters. Well, they came up, and to make a long story short, we lost all the camps. So in 1938, my dad, Allie, and three customers from the island bought a new set of camps here on the mainland, which were built by Will Atkins' son, 'Sleepy.' After two or three years the camps on the island were sold to Maine Public Service Company. They wanted to flood every lake on the Aroostook so their dam in New Brunswick could save the spring high water to use in the summer and the fall high water to use in winter. They flooded the lake with about 7 extra feet of water and let us have some of the cabins on our island. I was on the raft in the late '50s when we moved them across the lake, just a 4-year-old kid.

"Dad started with three cabins here and built River Camp, a two-day paddle upriver, and then built Chandler Pond Camps. In 1950 he bought his first seaplane, because he wanted to get to the little ponds. He got a lease to build a camp on Big Caribou Pond just before he died. This was in 1959. He was 46 and Mom would have been 42. Here she is, a lady back in the wilderness, no communications, four sons, with me as the youngest. All her supplies had to be flown in by Ray Porter, a pilot out of Shin Pond. Before Dad died she'd bought a new washing machine, a boat, and a tractor, which they brought in by cutting the footpath wider. So here she is, the first winter after he dies, and all she's got is bills. And no husband. So she sold the plane—for $700!—and the farm equipment. Then after another year, she got her spirit back up, kept running the camp, and built the one Dad had planned to build at Caribou Pond. In '68 she built the dining room. My brothers and I did the work. She took out a small-business loan for $10,000 to do it. That was a lot of money back then and everybody, especially guys, said a woman would never be able to do that, no way, leased land and all. But she did it. She paid it all off." *Ellen:* "Early. She's an amazing woman, really."

Matt: "Mom did it all and sent four boys to college. She remarried in '69 to John Gibson, who managed half a million acres for Seven Islands Land Company, which included land for one of our outcamps. In '68 we got our first 'road.' I can remember the last 3 miles took an hour—just crawling. You could walk ahead faster. Everybody'd get out and walk while the guy drove the stuff in. We had that right up until '89. I went to the University of Maine [Orono], like all my brothers. And my sophomore year I met Ellen. Best thing that could ever happen to me." *Ellen:* "You've got that on tape!" *Matt:* "And I guess probably our first date I told her about the camps." *Ellen:* "The first 5 minutes after I met him." *Matt:* "Yeah, well. I didn't appreciate camp until I got away from it. Growing up you think this is just an old camp in the woods. And then when you find out that everything else is just an old town with a lot of people, you start to see what you have. So our junior year Mom was talking about selling and we decided to buy her out. We got married in college." *Ellen:* "Because we had guests coming in here the day after graduation!"

Matt: "I started flying in 1977, the first year after we took over and in '87 I got a floatplane. That's one of the special things about our camps. We have a vast area we cover, but the plane can get us to one of our remote outpost lakes in 10 minutes. The big lake here [6 miles long by a mile wide, 60 feet deep] is fished in the winter [brook trout and landlocked salmon], so the smaller lakes and streams are better for fly-fishing. So we can fly you out to our Chandler Pond or Lower Hudson Pond camps. They're housekeeping and we limit those to a three-day stay." *Ellen:* "Everyone wants to go to there."

Ellen: "We spent the winters of '81 and '82 in here. The kids didn't get sick until we went to town to do a few sportsmen shows. Matthew was 1 and Alison 2½. A few years ago we had a family reunion. It was the first time in 15 years that the four boys had been together." *Ali:* "Gramma was here." *Ellen:* "So it was special. We built an addition to a cabin in honor of it."

Ali: "I love it here." *Matt Jr.:* "Living in here you think it's going to be so boring. There's no TV or anything, but there's tons of stuff to do—go for a walk, ride your bike, go fishing, hunting, whatever you want to do."

Ellen: "The first hunting season I was here a fellow brought in this deer liver that filled the bottom of the sink. I looked at this thing and thought, How do you cook it! Well, the old fellow who worked for Elsie, Matt's mother, said, 'You know, liver and onions.' Well, I'm sure if it didn't taste just like the bottom of your shoe, it wasn't even that good by the time I got through with it!"

Matt: "Deer season takes a lot of preparation. For one thing, you're heating uninsulated camps that time of year, which takes a lot of wood. I get up at 3:30 and we'll have breakfast at 5 AM. We'll head out the door probably 5:30, so they'll be in the woods 15 minutes to a half an hour before daylight. Hunting has been getting better over the years. The only problem now is they've cut down too many of the deeryards, so the limiting factor is the wintering areas. The hunters go on a deer run [trail], or on a deer 'scrape line,' which looks like a patch of open dirt. The buck will usually break a limb above the scrape and put a scent there from around his eye or by his ear and that will key some deer to what is there, and then a doe will come by and urinate there. So that's an active spot. There may be several of these scrapes within half a mile. You build the hunters a little ground blind, for cover, and then they'll wait. Usually 2 or 3 hours is all they can stand in the cold. During this time the guide is looking for new areas, maybe trying to get deer out of their beds and running down their natural runs. We'll come back, pick hunters up, maybe show them the new areas, try to stalk some deer if they're quiet enough, which they seldom are, and have lunch. The first hour and a half is prime. The deer may be moving out of their bedding area into their feeding area, or vice versa. But if there's a full moon, a lot of times the deer will feed at night and bed all day.

"A trophy buck here would be over 190 pounds. In Maine, if a hunter gets one over 200 pounds, he gets into the Big Bucks Club. There are probably 800 to 900 a year taken that are over 200 pounds. A lot of guys could care less about weight. Their first trip up they want horns. And they aren't interested in just the deer meat. Most of them come from great hunting states like New Jersey and Pennsylvania. Their deer may not be much bigger than a German shepherd, but it's good eating. Down there the bigger deer are culled out by the hunters. Up here, 10 or 15 percent of the big deer are killed by hunters. We have about as many deer in our area as we can hold. Any larger and one harsh winter could wipe out 50 percent of them, because there's no place for them to winter. They don't winter in a clearcut or on a ridge no matter how many trees are on it. They have to have 'black growth.' A deeryard is mostly black spruce. We call it black growth because you have such a heavy overstory of conifers that it's dark in there. It keeps out the snow. If you go on a hardwood ridge, you'll be up to your waist, say. Down in the black growth, you're up to your knees, or less. There's a lot of food down there for them— lichens off the trees, mosses, and as the season gets harsher they'll start on the tips of cedar trees. If they can't reach the cedar, they're probably going to die. They'll eat hardwood buds. And in a logging area, the deer will come in and feed on fallen birch tips. When a tree falls, all the tops are available to eat and it's also great cover. Summertime, deer feed on just about anything that's green—moss being the least preferred, to ferns, raspberry leaves, and water plants being the most favorite. In the fall they like old-man's beard, which hangs on spruce and fir trees and looks like Spanish moss.

"I think northern and southern Maine is like black and white as far as hunting, trapping, and outdoor issues in general. You find a lot of people moving into Maine from cities where there are no deer or moose who think, 'You can't kill them.' But come on up to northern Maine and stay here for a whole season and see if you have the same feeling. I think that if there's to be no hunting in an area, it ought to come from the people who live in the area. Let us use our own judgment and our biologists—we hire biologists to look at the herd—and let's listen to them. Every single human has in him the need to provide for his family. People must realize that. Here you need to harvest against fire and disease, and it's a renewable resource."

In 1990 the Libbys expanded with Riverkeep Fishing Lodge in Labrador, Canada, and in 1993 Libby's became an Orvis-endorsed lodge, the first one in New England.

Tunnel of Fudge Cake

Matt: *"Ellen's fresh-baked breads and pastries have saved the day many times when the fish decided not to bite or the deer decided not to appear. Without the long line of talented Libby women, the repeat customer list would undoubtedly be short."*

> 1¾ cups softened butter, 1¾ cups sugar, 6 eggs, 2 cups confectioner's sugar, 2¼ cups flour, ¾ cup baking cocoa, 2 cups chopped nuts
>
> *Glaze:* 1 cup confectioner,s sugar, ¼ cup cocoa, enough milk to mix to the right consistency

Beat together the butter and granulated sugar. Add eggs, one at a time. Gradually add confectioner's sugar and blend well. Stir in flour, cocoa, and nuts by hand. Pour into greased and floured Bundt pan. Bake at 350 degrees for 55–60 minutes. Cool upright in the pan on a rack for 1 hour. Invert on a plate and drizzle with glaze.

52. LOON LODGE

AP/MAP/HK
OWNERS: Mike and Linda Yencha
ADDRESS: PO Box 480, Millinocket, ME 04462; 207-695- 2821 (radio phone)
WINTER ADDRESS: PO Box 2469, Wilkes-Barre, PA 18703; 717-287-6915
SEASON: May 1 through November 30

ACCOMMODATIONS: Five cabins (one log outpost cabin) with wood or propane heat, gas stove, gas refrigerator, gas lights, no running water; central shower house has toilets, sinks, electricity, and hot and cold running water; bring blankets or sleeping bags and towels; pets welcome

RATES: $20–55 per person per day; $120–325 per person per week

ACCESS: I-95 to exit 56 (Medway). Take ME 11/157 through Millinocket. Follow signs to Baxter State Park and go 10 miles to the North Woods Trading Post (right side; last phone and gas). Turn **right** onto Golden Road and go 2 or 3 miles to the Great Northern checkpoint (register, no fee). Go 18 miles to Telos Road (sign), turn right and go 13 miles to the next checkpoint (fee). Continue 8 miles and turn left (sign). Go 26 miles, following signs. Pass a lumber camp, then take a right and go 2.5 more miles to camp.

Mike and Linda mail out three pages of written directions with three accompanying maps for people driving into camp. Loon Lodge is 96 miles from Greenville, 78 from Millinocket, and 91 from Ashland—or, as they explain it, 3 hours from any town. The cabins, basic with a cozy, attractive log lodge, are set on a knoll overlooking 1½-mile-long by ½-mile-wide Round Pond.

Linda: "Round Pond has perch, lake and brook trout, and land-locked salmon. One advantage to our remoteness is that we're the closest sporting camp to Lake Allagash, which is hard to get to and totally pristine. Round Pond is the central hub near the headwaters of three of the most famous watersheds in New England: the Allagash, the Penobscot, and the St. John Rivers. We have a wide variety of terrain around here and lots of wildlife. The alder swamps and beech ridges attract upland birds such as ruffed grouse and wood-cock. The shallow ponds and swampy lowlands attract ducks like black ducks, teal, mallards, wood ducks, mergansers, and Canada geese. There are over 5,000 acres of water you could fish without getting out of your boat.

"Since the nearest paved road is over 50 miles away, and then you have to go almost another 30 miles to get to a town, this place is for people who really want to get away from it all. That's what happened to us. Mike was doing Boy Scout trips when we found this area, and we fell in love with it. We had a hard time getting the lease from Seven Islands because they thought we were too young. But we got it in '84, stayed in a tent that first year, and have been here ever since.

"One of the things we did was to put in a thousand-foot driveway to make it easier for guests to get in here. The other thing that's made a big difference is our new shower house, so people can have bathroom and shower facilities."

Mike: "We get a lot of people here from Pennsylvania, I suppose because we're from that area. A lot come in for hunting season in groups. We only take 10 hunters a week and 40 for the whole season, and we generally do all meals for these guests, although they can stay at our housekeeping cabin 5 miles north of here. We pay extra to the paper company to reserve over 100,000 acres of forest for our sole use during bear hunting. I personally guide every hunter and bait every stand myself.

"Deer hunts in northern Maine mean big bucks. Granted, we don't have the numbers you can find in southern New England, but we make up for that in size. Bucks that dress out over 200 pounds are taken out of camp every season, and there are a few roaming around out there that are over 300 pounds. We have millions of acres of unposted land available to our hunters. And that's something you seldom see in this day and age."

53. MACANNAMAC CAMPS

HK/AP, SCA
OWNERS: Jack and Sharon McPhee
ADDRESS: PO Box B-A, Patten, ME 04765; 207-528-2855 (radio phone)
SEASON: Year-round
ACCOMMODATIONS: Seven HK log cabins; newer cabins have full utilities, older or more remote cabins have outhouse, no running water, gas lights, woodstove, porch. Main lodge: AP, three rooms, all utilities.
RATES: $25–35 per person per day (HK); $100 per person per day (AP)
ACCESS: I-95 to exit 56 (Medway). Take ME 11 through Millinocket to the right-hand fork for Ripogenus Dam. Cross the dam onto Telos Road and go 38 miles. The Telos gate fee is currently $15 per person per trip for Maine residents, $21 per person per trip for nonresidents. A sign for the camps is on the left.

Macannamac Base Camp has a spacious main lodge surrounded by luxurious gardens. Inside is a fieldstone fireplace, and sliding doors lead to a deck that looks out on Haymock Lake. There are guest accommodations on the second floor, and the place has a bed & breakfast feel to it. Nearby are new and airy log cabins. Pilot Jack McPhee provided one of the highlights of my research by flying me, in his Piper Cub,

Macannamac Camps

to outpost camps on Cliff and Spider Lakes, where guests have a lake to themselves.

Sharon: "Haymock Lake here is 3 miles by 1 mile and 65 feet at its deepest. Spider is smaller, 2¼ miles by 1 mile, and Cliff Lake is 1¾ miles by ½ mile. They all have lake and brook trout and whitefish and they're all general-law fishing.

"At first we came up here to Spider Lake and built a family cabin in 1973. We decided to start in the sporting-camp business in 1983 and built two cabins that year on Haymock Lake. In '85 we built another cabin on Haymock and in '87 we constructed the main lodge and put up another cabin on Spider Lake. In '96 we built another cabin on Haymock. And the cabin on Cliff Lake makes seven, all of them new. We built these places with the hope that people would come in and have the feel of being in their very own camp. So we spaced the cabins for privacy and each has its own dock, driveway, and woodshed."

Jack: "We did this all because we wanted to live here and had to figure out a way to make a living. We lease from Seven Islands. Our cabins are on property controlled by an organization of landowners called North Maine Woods, and visitors coming here register and pay fees to pass through their gates. There are a number of these gates around the North Maine Woods. Our gate system is operated from May through November."

Sharon: "We both retired in '85. I was a dental hygienist and Jack was a game-warden pilot. This was his area, the northern third of the state. My father was a game warden in Patten in the 'good old days,' so I knew this way of life. When he was a full-time game warden it was a 7-days-a-week way of life. Now it's hourly. My mother taught fifth grade and music for 35 years. Jack's mother was a schoolteacher, and Jack himself was a nice, sensible math and English schoolteacher from Patten until my father got ahold of him and eventually got him the pilot job out of Eagle Lake in '67. We have two daughters and one grandson, and we encourage families to come here. Pets are also allowed. Our English setter here, Bandit, is 11 years old and we always put a picture of him in our brochure to show people that pets are welcome."

Jack: "That's our whole philosophy—that people can treat our camps like their own. Our landlord [Seven Islands] is bombarded with people who want to own a private camp on perhaps an otherwise pristine lake. Our camps alleviate some of that wilderness sprawl. It makes no sense spending thousands of dollars a year owning and maintaining a camp that spoils a wilderness setting, when you can come to Macannamac and have your own remote cabin and only spend $300 or $400 a week. No other camps in this area fit the criteria of full utility housekeeping."

Sharon: "The name for our camps is a traditional one. *Macannamac* means Spider Lake—where we started out—in Abenaki. The Abenaki Nation was here and the Penobscot tribe came up through here. Haymock Lake is *Pongokwahemook* in Abenaki."

Jack: "Now that I'm retired as a warden pilot, I seem to still get in a lot of flying time. Most of what I do is airborne radio tracking, called felonics, which tracks critters that have radio devices on them. I cover bears, moose, martin, fisher. And we've been able to tell, with this tracking, that on average most years 2 or 3 percent of the female black bears and martins of reproductive age are killed. With black bears, we've been mapping out their dens. We have a ground crew that goes around from January through March and checks out the dens. We've been doing this for 15 years. Actually, I've been at it so long I kind of get attached to some of the animals I track. I followed one bear for 15 years who was live-trapped and given the ID number 159400 and a radio collar. Those who fly, though, call the bears by names. I tracked another bear that covered 75 miles in 48 hours, and that's for me, in a straight line, in the air. Imagine what the bear did! It's hard to stalk a black bear—so even if I were to tell a hunter where I saw one, it would still be hard to get. So our tracking is for research, not for game hunters."

Sharon: "After our fall hunting season, we get a lot of vacationers in for winter. There's ice fishing and snowmobiling from January through March, and we create our own cross-country ski trails with track setters. For many winters we had a group of ministers who came in here for three weeks of rest, discussion, and study. In spring, around the middle of May, Jack and his second wife, Joanne, lead wildflower tours. We have a lot of fairy calypso orchids, just the size of your thumb, which are very beautiful. They're quite rare—some horticulturalists spend a lifetime looking for them. We also have pink, white, and yellow lady's slippers, and hepatica, a white flower that blooms here very early, before the grass. Actually, the first flower out is coltsfoot, or dandelion flower. Nothing else is out. It's the same yellow as a dandelion and the flower blooms in the snow before there are any leaves. The leaves come out in late summer, strangely enough. We also have bog orchids, along with red trillium—gorgeous wildflowers. The tour is half a day long and we have people from the New England Wildflower Society who come up especially to do the tour, as well as other people. Even our driveway is flanked by purple fireweed and goldenrod."

Lemon Bars

Sharon says, "In the lodge we're traditional American Plan and serve meals. I'll give you one of the favorite desserts."

> 1 cup flour, ½ cup chopped walnuts, ½ cup canned shortening, 1 cup confectioner's sugar, 1 cup Cool Whip, 8 ounces cream cheese, 2 cans lemon pie filling

Mix flour, nuts, and shortening. Press into a 9x13-inch pan. Bake at 350 degrees for 10 minutes. Mix sugar, Cool Whip, and cream cheese and spread on cooked bottom layer. Pour and spread pie filling on top of previous layer.

Spread an additional cup of Cool Whip over that and sprinkle ½ cup chopped walnuts on top as garnish.

54. MCNALLY'S CAMPS

AP, SCA

OWNERS: John Richardson and Regina Webster
ADDRESS: HC 76, Box 632, Greenville, ME 04441; 207-944-5991
SEASON: Year-round
ACCOMMODATIONS: Six log cabins (sleep two to eight people) with indoor plumbing and shower, gas lights, wood heat
RATES: $70 per person per day
ACCESS: I-95 to exit 56 (Medway). Take ME 11/157 northwest to Millinocket. Go through Millinocket, bear right onto Baxter State Park Road, and go 10 miles to a left-hand turn for the West Branch Region, where there is a gate. Tell the attendant you're going to McNally's and you won't have to pay a fee. Continue up Golden Road 18 miles, then take a right-hand turn onto Telos Road. Go 15 miles to the North Main Woods gate (the fee is $7 per person for Maine residents and $14 per person for nonresidents; no fee for children under 12 and adults over 70). Go 8 miles to the Chamberlain Bridge parking area. From Chamberlain Bridge, drive northwest 50 miles over John's Bridge and through Clayton Lake. After the ranger station, turn sharp right and continue 6.5 miles to a right-hand turn (watch for the sign) into camp.

John: "Will McNally, who many consider to be the father of North Maine Woods sporting camps, had a son, Dana, who built this place in 1951. Both men had a flair for designing and building. We just bought these camps [in 1997] from Mycki, Dana's wife. We're on Ross Stream, originally called Chemquassabamticook, or 'place of many fish.' And there are a lot of trout. It's a classic fly-fishing stream: general law with a one-fish limit in the fall. And there's whitefish and togue in the lake [the stream is on the north end of Long Lake, 500 yards outside the Allagash Wilderness Waterway]. We offer a 30-mile motorized canoe trip from Nugent's, our other camp, to here. It's a great way to see remote Maine and still sleep in a bed with a roof over your head. And did I mention ice fishing, cross-country skiing, snowmobiling, snowshoeing, and great hunting? We've got it all covered!"

Mycki McNally, lithe and sharp as a tack at 83, offers another definition for Chemquassabamticook: "Friends once sent us a sign with the Indian name and I asked Dana, 'What does that mean?' Without skipping a beat he turned to me and said, 'Squaw, you no-good cook—go home!'"

Dana's manuscript, *Bush Happy,* is typed on the back of letterhead that lists Will McNally's holdings: Big Fish Lake, Round, Ferguson, Island, Moccasin, North, and Beavertail Ponds, and First, Second, and Third Chase Lakes. Mycki notes that was 100 years of continuous operation of McNally camps—quite a North Woods empire. Three of McNally's camps are in Dana's book: Wilderness Island, Red River, and McNally's.

As Dana writes:

> Mose McNally, Dad's father, was one of the finest lumbermen in this section. He came from Fredericton, New Brunswick, and made his way up the St. John and then Aroostook Rivers to settle in Ashland. He got driven out of Scotland for stealing chickens, according to Dad, William (Will) Parker McNally, next to the youngest of five boys, who became the camp hunter. Dad remembered that at that time, in the early 1900s, there was no such thing as game laws, and there were no deer, but plenty of caribou.
>
> During the years while I was away from Maine, I had learned to hunt ducks, and after coming home and going into business with Dad, the thing I missed above all else was good duck hunting. I got Wilfred Atkins, the local game warden, known as "Sleepy" around here, interested in duck hunting around Portage and Fish River Lakes. In the fall of 1950 we had a hard freeze early in October and most of the ducks left our hunting grounds. One of our guides, Herber Umphrey of Fort Kent, had also become somewhat duck conscious. So one afternoon he and I and Sleepy loaded the Pacer with a tent, sleeping bags, and a bit of grub and flew into the Allagash country to try and locate a few. When we flew over the marsh where Chemquassabamticook Stream enters Long Lake, hundreds of ducks flew up out of the many small pot holes. So we landed, carried our duffel ashore, tied the plane down for the night, and set out for what turned out to be the fastest duck shooting any of us have ever experienced before or since.
>
> It was a beautiful, clear afternoon, just cool enough to be comfortable walking. We set out abreast and about twenty to thirty feet apart, walking toward the pot holes. A small bird flushed ahead of us and from the view I got of it in flight, it looked to me like a woodcock. I had never hunted any woodcock, but the markings on the back of its head and rump pretty well matched pictures I had seen. Sleepy said, "What kind of bird was that?"
>
> "A woodcock," I answered. "Is the season open on woodcock?"

"Yes, but are you sure it was a woodcock?"

"Sure," I said. "Didn't you see the markings on its back?"

About that time another one took off and within the next five minutes we must have seen at least half a dozen. The more we saw, the more convinced I became that they were woodcock until I finally shot one. We picked it up and decided it was indeed a woodcock. During the next few hours we ended up with an even bag limit each. Also, the marsh was literally alive with Black Ducks that day. They would flush out of the tall grass only fifteen to twenty feet ahead of us, circle around unperturbed by our shooting, and fly straight back over us as though they had never seen us. It was like shooting Pheasant in a corn field! By the time we had hunted back to where we had left our duffel, we each had our limit.

The sun set on three very happy hunters that evening. And what a beautiful evening it was, too. The surface of the lake was as calm as a mill pond, the air was warm and it felt more like an evening in June than mid-October. As we boiled coffee over a driftwood fire, we decided that there was no sense in bothering to pitch the tent. We would just put it over us to keep out the dampness and lay under the stars. We laid there for hours after supper, watching the fire, telling stories, and listening to the ducks talking out in the marsh in front of us—one of those evenings that come but once in a lifetime!

There's more to the story. Dana and pals were awakened by a deluge and eventually had to take off into the teeth of a gale out of the north, "colder than a banker's heart." They landed in Portage, where

Sleepy piled out, taking only his woodcock as a gift for his supervisor. When Herber and I walked into the cook camp at Fish River, Mycki took one look at our "woodcock" and wanted to know what we were doing bringing home a bunch of jacksnipe when the season had been closed on them for years! A few days later, I landed at Portage and Sleepy was waiting for me on the dock with a copy of Roger Tory Peterson's *A Field Guide to the Birds* in his hands and a most unkind expression on his face. It seems that our warden's gift to his supervisor had definitely been a mutual surprise!

During the following winter they made plans to build at the stream. Dana says, "I could hardly wait to fly back there, so shortly after opening up camp on Fish River in early May, Allie Frieman and his son, Dick, both of Sayville, Long Island, hopped into the Pacer and we took off for the Allagash country." When they reached Long Lake they saw a large bay rather than the marsh, since the spring water was up about 10 feet.

> We chose a site on a high bluff overlooking the lake and what had been the marsh. There was a good spring nearby and plenty of the right sized spruce logs not too far away. Above the campsite, about three quarters of a mile up the stream and on the same side, Cunliffe Brook leads back half a mile into Cunliffe Lake, a wild, remote little body of water that provides some of the best trout fishing in this part of the country. At the junction of Cunliffe Brook and the stream there was a burned over area of roughly one hundred acres very sparsely grown up into white birch and patches of wild raspberry. An old tote road passes just behind the campsite and runs up the stream and through the burn to Cunliffe Lake. This looked like a good bet for bear, deer, and grouse and so it has proved to be. About July we had been granted a lease on the chosen campsite by the International Paper Company and were ready to start building.
>
> There seemed no easy way to get a horse in there so our plans were to make only a simple cabin with logs small enough to be carried on our backs out of the woods. What we call a "post camp" or cabin made from short logs standing on end. Except for the sills and plates, all the side logs are about six feet six inches long and not more than eight to ten inches in diameter. Three or four of the guides, with me and Dad, who was doing the cooking, flew in and landed in front of the campsite. We pitched a tent up on the bank, cut a supply of wood, made ourselves some bough bunks on the ground, and staked out the base of the camp. By that time it was getting late, so we launched the eighteen foot aluminum canoe I had flown in previously and caught ourselves a mess of brook trout for supper. When we climbed the bank after cleaning the trout, we could smell the coffee boiling over the open fire and Dad had a batch of biscuits browning in the outdoor baker. Trout never taste the same as they do when freshly caught and cooked in the open. After we cleaned our few dishes, we sat around the fire and Dad got to reminiscing about his early days in the woods.

The next day they started building the cabin. They cut long-lasting cedar logs for sills and rigged a parbuckle to get them up the high bank from the stream. A parbuckle in this case was a long rope with each end fastened to a stake about opposite the ends of the logs, but up on the bank. The center of the rope is then dropped down the bank and under the log and the rope is long enough so that this middle can be dragged back up the bank before it brings up around the log. Three or four men then pull on the middle of the rope and the log rolls up the bank on the rope. This is also the method used to get the ribs and other long logs to the top of the cabin from the ground.

The next job was to hew off the floor sills, place them over the mud sills, and notch and lay the floor timbers over them. Now we cut four plates, hewed off one side flat and notched in the ends so all four surfaces would be at the same level. We then put a good big post upright on the floor sills at each corner and hoisted the plates on to them and spike the posts, plates, and sills in place. Then you need to cut, carry in, and spike the upright logs, which will be the walls, between the plates and sills, leaving the openings for the door and windows. After we had filled in the walls, we determined the pitch of the roof and layed and spiked the two gable ends and put the ridge pole in place on them. We then notched rafters into the ridge pole and the plates and were ready to board in the roof. We had now been away from Fish River for five days and had to leave for home camp. But during the summer, two or three of us would fly over and work on the cabin and by the middle of September it was about ready for the hunting season.

Thus started McNally's Camps. Eventually five more cabins, a main lodge, and an enclosed garden and outbuildings were constructed. In the main lodge, a well-appointed kitchen looks out on a dining area where guests eat family-style at long tables. A living room with a fireplace is off to one side. Overlooking the stream outside, the Indian-name sign—Dana's "Squaw no-good cook"—remains. Of course this description of Mycki as a cook runs counter to all reports. She asks, "Do you know the only sandwich that won't freeze? Peanut butter and bacon."

Reggie's Raspberry Jell-O Pie

Combine 1 cup water, 1 cup sugar, and 3 T cornstarch in a saucepan and bring to a boil, stirring constantly. Remove from heat and add: 3–4 T strawberry or raspberry Jell-O. Stir well to blend and dissolve Jell-O. Add to precooked pie shell filled with fresh raspberries. I use a graham-cracker crust. Cool and enjoy.

55. MOOSE POINT CAMPS

AP, SCA

OWNERS: John Martin, Patricia Eltman, Michael Michaud
ADDRESS: PO Box 170, Portage, ME 04768; 207-435-6156
SEASON: Mid-May to mid-December
ACCOMMODATIONS: 10 log cabins with indoor plumbing and shower, gas lights, wood heat, porch; pets allowed
RATES: $65 per person per day; $330 per person per week
ACCESS: I-95 to exit 58. Take ME 11 north to Portage. Turn left at Dean's Motel and left onto Toll Road (camp sign). Pay a fee at the gatehouse and continue 17 miles to the camps following signs (black lettering).

Moose Point Camps is a set of classic, honey-colored log cabins ranged around a peninsula jutting into Fish River Lake. The cabins form an irregular T shape with the low main lodge at the top-left portion of the T. There is a comfortable sitting area with sliding glass doors, and a main hallway leading through the kitchen into a sunny dining area with long tables. Native American drawings and artifacts grace the walls and shelves, gifts from participants of a tribal gathering.

John: "The original camps were built in 1908 and were purchased in the 1930s by Dana West, who had them for 25 years or so. Then in the late '60s they were bought by Rose and Bill Mitchell, who occupied them for 23 years. I ended up with them in the fall of '91 and then Pat and Mike joined up. I worked in a sporting camp as a kid, Camps of Acadia [now Fish River Lodge], at Eagle Lake. My uncle and aunt owned those camps for some 20 years. And I worked there from seventh grade through high school. I mowed lawns, brought in wood. I always wanted to own a set of sporting camps after I retired as state representative from Eagle Lake [including 19 years as Speaker of the House].

"One of us is always at camp on weekends. Our manager, Clayton Dube, has been with us since '91, and Karen McGough is our cook. The place was called Moose Point Camps when I got it. It was the Mitchells who put up the wooden moose out on the point. It's actually just two pieces of wood: The body of the moose, the front leg, one back leg, and the head are all one piece. One leg in the front and one in the back are add-ons. And then they put on the antlers.

"We're open until 'black powder' season, for muzzle-loading guns. Remember Davy Crockett? His gun was a muzzle-loader. We've had black-powder season in Maine since the mid-'80s. For the fishery,

Moose Point Camps

we're located on the shore of the west wing of the Fish River chain of lakes. We've got trout, landlocked salmon, togue, and whitefish. It's called Fish Lake by some and Fish River Lake by others, and it's 5 miles long. Fish runs into Portage, which runs into St. Froid, and then into Eagle. And if you start at the other end, on the east side of the chain, there's Long Lake, then Mud, then Cross, then Square and Eagle. There's only one portage, at a falls, and that's after you leave Fish. Otherwise you can canoe the whole thing. You could put in at Carr Pond, which is the headwater of Fish Lake, and go down to Eagle Lake in about two days."

Pat: "I do marketing and advertising, and I oversee the kitchen and food operation. I go in to the camp as much as I can, but I live 312 miles away and it's easier for John."

John: "I live only 36 miles away, in Eagle Lake. I can literally go 1 mile from my house and be on woods roads the rest of the way."

Pat: "Mike's from Auburn, so that's halfway up. People forget it's a big state. I go practically from one end to the other when I go back and forth from Portland. I have been doing sportsmen's shows and mailings; I do a lot of that some years."

John: "The camps were in pretty good shape, but there's always work to be done. We put in underground gas lines for propane, so now we don't have individual tanks at each camp. We put in the internal water system, dug a well, leveled the road in. We built an icehouse in the fall of '92 because that summer we used about $1,200 worth of ice. Every time people would come in, I'd say, 'Bring ice.'

Pat: "It's interesting, the generations that come back to camp. You know, their grandfathers came and they're coming with their grandchildren. People like the seclusion and no interruptions by phone or fax."

John: "We actually have quite a few in that situation."

Pat: "Mike is the bookkeeper right now, and John gets to oversee everything. He's the CEO."

John: "I've never understood that title at all. I mow lawns—"

Pat: "We all chip in. Whatever needs to be done, we do it."

Boiled Dinner

> One 8- to 10-pound ham with bone, 1–2 large onions (quartered), carrots, turnips, potatoes (all in large chunks)

Place ham with onions in a large pot, cover with water, and bring to a boil for 1 or 2 hours at steady low boil. An hour or two before serving, add carrots, turnips, more onions (if desired), and potatoes, enough to feed the number of people being served. Potatoes go in last. Cook until the potatoes are done. Place the ham in the center of a platter and arrange the vegetables around it.

56. NUGENT'S CAMPS

AP/MAP/HK, SCA

OWNERS: John Richardson and Regina Webster

ADDRESS: HC 76, Box 632, Greenville, ME 04441; 207-944-5991

SEASON: Year-round

ACCOMMODATIONS: 12 log cabins (one or two bedrooms), each with outhouse, gas lights, woodstove, porch; share central shower house; pets welcome

RATES: $60 per person per day (AP); $35 per person per day (MAP); $25 per person per day (HK).

ACCESS: I-95 to exit 56 (Medway). Take ME 11/157 northwest to Millinocket. Go through Millinocket, bear right on Baxter State Park Road, and go 10 miles to a left-hand turn for the West Branch Region, where there is a gate. Tell the attendant you're going to Nugent's and you won't have to pay a fee. Continue up Golden Road 18 miles, then take a right-hand turn onto Telos Road. Go 15 miles to the North Maine Woods gate (the fee is

$7 per person for Maine residents and $14 per person for nonresidents; no fee for children under 12 and adults over 70). Go 8 miles to the Chamberlain Bridge parking area for boat launching to camp. (In winter, continue across the bridge and drive another 8 miles to Nugent's 2.5-mile snowmobile trail.)

Nugent's Camps are located along the Allagash Wilderness Waterway, a world-renowned destination for canoe enthusiasts in summer and snowmobilers in winter. The cabins, nestled on a knoll on the north shore of 2½ by 18-mile-long Chamberlain Lake, offer respite for weary travelers, no matter what their mode of transportation. The camps are rustic, and state rules require that they be kept that way. They have dock facilities for boats up to 26 feet. (*Note:* Before camp, there's a bridge with a 7-foot clearance.) Guest come to troll for lake and brook trout and whitefish or to hunt in the remote woods.

John: "In 1936, Al and Patty Nugent came here on a homemade raft and built these camps together out of the wilderness. They built them specifically for hunting and fishing. This was, at the time, a public lot they got—50 miles north of Millinocket, between Allagash Mountain and Baxter State Park. A pretty spot.

"We're both from central Vermont. Our house there was in the woods, but it just wasn't a big enough patch of woods, so we began looking for bigger patches."

Regina: "I had worked for the state of Vermont as an office manager for 10 years, so it was kind of a career switch for me, going into the sporting-camp business. But I grew up in a rural area, at the end of a dead-end road, so it was not a big switch in that sense."

John: "We happened to see an ad from Webber Oil in the *Maine Sportsman* for someone to run their private camps. We looked it up on the map and it was right around Mount Katahdin, which is where we'd decided we wanted to be. So we started at Rainbow Lake Camps and, oddly enough, that's where Patty Nugent started, too. She must've been there in the late '20s, early '30s. We stayed there close to five years. Then we went to Lake Clark in Alaska to work, but everything fell through on that. Meanwhile, a friend saw a notice in the Bangor paper that said the State of Maine was putting Nugent's up for bid. You see, the state owns these camps. They bought the Nugents out, basically forced them to sell. Al and Patty took the money and leased the camps back from the state for $20 a month, I think it was. All the years it was assumed that Parks and Recreation would burn these

John Richardson and Regina Webster at their camp along the Allagash.

buildings when Patty was gone, because they wanted just wilderness. But Nugent's Camps were so well established, as were Jalbert's, that people pushed to save them. So the state passed a law and the camps were protected.

"The state awarded the lease of the camps to us in 1987 with one 10-year lease and two 5-year extensions. The Bureau of Parks and Recreation determines what we can and cannot do. Any improvements we make on these old log cabins have the same codes that apply for a new building in Augusta! And I have to follow strict rules about where I can cut. There's a lot of red tape and rules now, for all the sporting-camp owners. There are people who say Alaska's different, or northern Québec, but it's the same everywhere probably." According to the Bureau of Parks and Recreation, the State of Maine has 30 parks, 20 historic sites, and around four commercial sporting camps leasing land.

John: "When we came in here, Patty was getting too old to run the place by herself. And it was sad she had to go. I mean, she loved this place, but she just couldn't physically stay here anymore. When she left, she was an unhappy soul till the day she died, because this was her home."

John and Regina became the owners of McNally's Camps in 1997 and have thus become, as Regina puts it, "stewards" of two camps that were run by women who were legends in their own time, Patty Nugent and Mycki McNally. Indeed, sporting camps owe their longevity to the fortitude of women like these—other names include Alys Parsons (Lakewood Camps), Violette Holden (Attean Lake Lodge), Elsie Libby (Libby Camps), and women such as Phyllis Jalbert and Maggie McBurnie carrying the torch now—wilderness women all, who kept the camps running long after their husbands had died.

John: "I suppose wilderness is relative. I mean, you can drive up here from a major city in a day's time and think, gee, this is nice, nobody's around. There are still some nice remote areas in Maine, and I think this happens to be one of them. The whole Waterway's a good concept and I'm glad it's run on a state rather than a national level. I believe it's the only one run that way. It was established in 1971, the first federally designated wilderness and scenic river. It has a 15-member advisory board, which I'm on. When it started out, it had a lot of use. Big groups of 30 or 40 kids from summer camps, for example. Now we get campers, but in smaller groups. The Allagash flows north, which is somewhat unique as far as rivers go. The Waterway is 92 miles long, and it begins at Allagash Lake and ends upstream from Allagash Village.

"We have a canoe trip we offer. You leave Chamberlain in the early morning, go to Lock Dam, and from there to Allagash Stream, Eagle Lake, Churchill Lake, and Chase Rapids, where your gear is portaged by the park rangers. Ice-out up here doesn't happen until the middle of May, so in June it's fairly exciting water. And it's so beautiful. You start with big lakes and wide green areas, views of Katahdin. At Churchill it starts to close in to ridges and hills. Boats are allowed on Telos and Chamberlain Lakes. On Eagle Lake you can have canoes with up to 10-horsepower motors, but no boats, and Allagash Lake is canoes only, with no motors. Most people start their trip at Chamberlain Bridge or Churchill Dam. There are several outfitters in Allagash Village that rent canoes and shuttle people around." One is Allagash Outfitters, Box 149, Allagash, ME 04774; 207-398-3277.

Regina: "We also host naturalist groups in the summer, like for the Audubon Society. But by the same token, John and I are not anti-hunting. We get a lot of hunters and fishermen. We like to see the people who at least give some thought to where they are and what they've got around them. And we really do get a lot of people who appreciate it."

John: "We're open year-round: January and February, May and June, and November are our busiest months. We don't close down and we generally don't take a vacation somewhere else because we find that there are very few places we'd rather be than here."

Reggie's Togue "McNugent's"

> 1 large togue (or whitefish), 1 cup stale beer (or water), 1½ cups Bisquick, 1 egg, sprinkle of pepper, 1 tsp. garlic salt

Fillet togue or whitefish (this should be done when the fish is freshly caught). Chunk the fillets up into 1-inch cubes. Combine ¾ cup Bisquick with pepper and garlic salt. Mix the other ¾ cup Bisquick with egg and beer (or water). Dip fish chunks into the dry ingredients first, then dip into beer batter. Deep-fry in 2 inches, or more, of oil, four or five pieces at a time. Cook 2 minutes or until golden brown.

57. RED RIVER CAMPS

AP/HK, SCA

OWNERS: Mike and Rhonda Brophy

ADDRESS: PO Box 320, Portage, ME 04768; 207-435-6000 (summer); 207-528-2259 (winter)

SEASON: May through November

ACCOMMODATIONS: Nine log cabins (one to four bedrooms; three cabins are HK equipped) with wood heat, gas lights, indoor plumbing; HK includes linens (bring towels)

RATES: $40–80 per person per day (AP); $35–40 per person per day (HK)

ACCESS: I-95 to exit 58. Take ME 11 north to Portage. Turn left at Dean's Motel and then fork left at the Great Northern Paper Company road (dirt). After the North Maine Woods tollgate, take a right-hand turn (sign) and go 12.5 miles. Turn left after the logging camp. Bear left all the way in, going another 8.2 miles. The camp driveway, on the left, is steep and rocky.

Most of the cabins at this classic sporting camp form a gently rising horseshoe around the mowed hill to the left of the main lodge. Tucked down by the water's edge at the end of the slope, the lodge has a cozy feel. The logs for the buildings have a reddish brown stain. There are a couple of cabins right at the water's edge, and another cabin awaits guests on the island for which Island Pond was named, an easy paddle away.

Mike: "Around 1886, a man named Chapman married a woman with a lot of money, took all her money up here into the woods, and built a set of camps, a private retreat." *Rhonda:* "And it was the island that was built on first, in 1887." *Mike:* "The main lodge, the cabin on the hill in back of the lodge, and the guide's cabin were built prior to

1900. Actually, the guide's cabin was originally a schoolhouse."

Rhonda: "Families would come in here, and while the adults went out fishing, the kids would stay. They would hire a tutor to teach the kids. When we redid the walls in there, we found slates with math problems and things like that."

Mike: "The bell on the dining room was originally the schoolhouse bell. And there was a two-chair barbershop up on the hill. The camp on the island was just one big room, nothing there but a fireplace and a piano; that was the dance hall." *Rhonda:* "We would like to know where that piano is!" *Mike:* "Yes. No sign of the piano around today. Throughout the years, all the previous owners have taken a little bit with them each time they left."

Rhonda: "But we've had guests come—I think our oldest one remembers what it was like from 1928—and the traditions and history have just been passed down by word of mouth. Up until about the '40s, it was a private complex."

Mike: "Herschel Currie bought it right after World War II. He had worked here as a caretaker for the former owners: the Christies and McNallys. After Chapman built it, the story goes, his wife got tired of him spending her money and the place got sold to the Whitman family. They owned several textile mills in Massachusetts. And they bought it as a family compound.

"The people coming in here came to Portage on the B&A [Bangor and Aroostook Railroad]. They got off the train, got in a canoe at Portage Lake, canoed up the lake and up Fish River as far as Fish River Falls [20 miles]. There was an outpost camp at Fish River Falls, which is still there today. It's no longer part of this. When Dr. Christie's daughter got married, he gave her the camp on the island as a wedding present, but because of the lease arrangement with the paper company, they considered this all one lease and wouldn't split the island off from it. So instead he gave her the camp at Fish River Falls. Anyway, people would spend the first night at the falls, and the following morning they would either walk or come in by horse and wagon the 10½ miles to here.

"We're in the southeast corner of Township 15, Range 9 [T15R9], which is Public Reserve Land. The camps sit on the north shore of Island Pond, which is roughly half a mile long by a quarter mile wide, and 44 feet at the deepest. It's fly-fishing-only for brook trout. Most of the ponds around here are fly-fishing-only. We have 25 lakes and ponds to fish within a 5-mile radius of camp. We're one of the very few places in Aroostook County that have areas restricted to fly-fishing-

Red River Camps

only. We've got canoes spread all around for people who come in here and want to go to these other lakes and ponds. Several are within walking distance, others you go to by boat. The state has done a good thing blocking off some of the roads in the area to make the ponds a little harder to get to, which cuts down on the fishing pressure and on the poaching. Plus it's a good walk. The state does have a cabin in the area, but other than that, we're the only taxpayers in town!

"This Reserve Land has four ponds that support a population of arctic char [blue-backed trout] that came down in the Ice Age. Only ten bodies of water in the whole state support a population of arctic char, and we've got four of them here: Gardner, Deboullie, Pushineer, and Black. It's a rare fish, but not endangered. They don't get very large, but just the fact that they survived that long, and are still surviving on their own, is amazing. They were trapped here when the glaciers receded." *Rhonda:* "They look a little like brook trout, but they're a separate species.

"When we first started driving in here, we used what Pete and Chris Norris, the previous owners, had used, which was the North Pond Road. But the bridges kept washing out and you'd have to drive down the riverbank and up the other side. In the fall, if it was the least bit icy, I remember getting stuck in those rivers. The more you tried to get up on the other side, the more the water would splash and freeze, and you were basically just building an ice valley. So we stopped using that and went up through the village of St. Francis at the Canadian border [the camps are only 20 miles from the border]. It wasn't a great road, but passable."

Mike: "We used that maybe a year. It was about 22 miles long and probably a 2-hour drive. The earlier road was 29 miles in and took an hour and a half anyway. Next we used Chase Pond Road."

Rhonda: "At that point, we actually owned a car. All we ever had before was a Jeep. But I could drive in only to a gravel pit and then I'd have to unload everything into the old Blazer and continue on. It was loud and rattly, but at least it got us over Chase Mountain. That was actually the worst part of the road, and it would wash out terribly sometimes. Then there were beaver dams we'd have to get through."

Mike: "About 40 miles in over Chase Mountain."

Rhonda: "And that was an adventure when it was icy—you'd look down and wonder if you were going to make the corner! Big Brook Road we didn't use too much. These are all just tote or logging roads. And then the state bought this township from the paper company, so instead of leasing from the paper company we were involved with the state. And the state started talking about an access road. They wanted the general public to be able to get into this state-owned land. This was 1986. On a lot of lakes, there are public camping spots, which is fine. They surveyed campers and published the results, and 75 percent of the population surveyed said, 'Leave it the way it is. The rough access adds to the adventure and keeps it remote.' So the state put the road in from St. Francis anyway! But we did have an easier way of getting in and out. Now access is the easiest it's ever been, due to the logging operations, as they have been harvesting near this area."

Mike: "I started working here as a guide in 1975 when the Norrises owned it."

Rhonda: "He would just work during deer season. He was here at camp when I had my first child. My father radioed in, but Mike was out guiding at the time. Dad told Chris and she met him at the door when he got in and said, 'You're a father!' And then, in 1979, when he came home he said, 'Pete and Chris are looking for someone to run Red River Camps until they can find a buyer.' Well, we were very poor—we still are, but that's OK—and Mike said, 'Do you think we could run it for six weeks in the springtime?' And I said, 'Sure. I could do that.' Jennie was 9 months old and Matthew was about 1½. Well, Mike grew up in this type of life and loved it. I didn't know anything about it; had no clue. I had only been in here once, in 1978. It was in October, the trees were bare, it was cold. I was here maybe an hour. So that's all I knew about Red River Camps! Anyway, we came in the following spring. And the longer we were here, the more Mike kept saying, 'Maybe we can do this.' And I'm saying, 'I really want to go home!' I had left my home, the kids were in a strange place, it was busy, and it was a lot of work. It was like a dream to him; he really wanted to do it. And so we did. That was in 1980. It was really hard for five years, and then things began turning around.

"In 1982 we started something we still do. For a week each summer we take a group of approximately 20 to 25 special-needs people. We just turn the camps over to the residential staff. I cook and clean and everything and they handle the clients. In the fall we have a few bird hunters and two weeks of deer hunters. Then Mike stays and does some trapping." *Mike:* "In the past I trapped for martin and fisher. Trappers today are catching less martin than in previous years. My feeling is that 95 percent of these so-called trappers are riding up and down the roads, jumping out, and setting a trap here, a trap there. None of the traps are more than 100 feet away from the roads. But you get back up on a ridge, and you can get all the martin you want. You know what a sable coat is? That's pine martin. They eat mice, rats, some carrion, bugs."

Rhonda: "This township supports a plant, the arctic sandwort [*Minuartia rubella*], a plant of national significance, which grows on the talus slopes of Deboullie Mountain. This particular flower was found in 1980 and is found in only one other place in New England, and nowhere else in Maine. Over on Deboullie, there is a natural ice cave where even in the middle of summer you can reach in and grab a chunk of ice. It's because of the rock formations. There's a channel of arctic air that keeps it frozen all year."

Mike: "The old Pushineer Dam is the beginning of the Red River. They used to float logs down here and then down the river to St. Froid Lake. And then they'd put them on railroad cars at Eagle Lake." *Rhonda:* "It's called Red River because there is rust formation in certain rocks which causes the river to look red in places. At Crater Pond, over the knoll, you can see the Cliffs of Galilee. They go 500 feet straight into the lake. It's probably the most beautiful of all the beautiful ponds in the area because of those cliffs. There's really just so much that's unique here." *Mike:* "We're talking about 23,000 acres our guests can use!"

Cheesecake

For crust: To 2 cups ground graham crackers, mix in ⅓ cup sugar and ⅓ cup melted margarine. Press this up against the sides and bottom of a 9-inch spring-form pan.

For filling: Blend three 8-ounce packages of cream cheese, 1 cup sugar, 3 eggs (added one at a time), and 2 tsp. vanilla. Beat until creamy smooth. Blend in 1 cup sour cream.

Bake 50–60 minutes at 325 degrees until set. Leave in the oven with the door ajar for 1 hour. Top with favorite topping or serve plain.

58. ROSS LAKE CAMPS

AP/HK

OWNERS: Mary and Curt Shilling
ADDRESS: PO Box 606, Clayton Lake, ME 04737; 207-695-2821 (radio phone, Folsom's Air Service)
SEASON: Year-round
ACCOMMODATIONS: Four cabins (sleep 4 to 10 people) with wood heat, gas stove, gas lights, gas refrigerator; bring your own bedding (AP and HK); cabins share two outhouses and a shower house
RATES: $15–18 per person per day (HK); $300–750 per person per week (AP)
ACCESS: I-95 to exit 56 (Medway). Take ME 11/157 northwest to Millinocket. Go through Millinocket, bear right onto Baxter State Park Road, and go 10 miles to a left-hand turn for the West Branch Region, where there is a gate. Continue up Golden Road 18 miles, then take a right-hand turn onto Telos Road. Go 14 miles to the North Maine Woods gate (fee). From here it is 61 miles to camp on the connecting logging road.

Follow the orange arrows instead of the yellow brick road to Chemquassabamticook Lodge on Ross Lake and, like Dorothy, you'll find lots of adventures on the way—not the least of which is navigating the 3.2-mile camp driveway. The camps, stick built and stained dark brown, are set in a cozy clearing within a stone's throw of Ross Lake.

Mary: "Curt and I bought the camps in May of '94. We married in April that year and moved up here two weeks later. And it gets better! I had never even seen this place! We brought in two U-Hauls and a car and sank all three vehicles up to their axles in mud. So we had to walk in, 5½ miles in the pouring-down rain. Married a whole two weeks. Thank goodness it was dark when we got in here and I didn't see it,

Hunting buddies at Ross Lake Camps

'cause I was exhausted and the place needed work. I knew nothing about sporting camps. My first husband had died and I was burned out from the medical field. When Curt started talking about camps back in Pennsylvania, he'd already been to Maine hunting for seven years. I said, 'This is something you've always wanted to do, so let's go for it.'

"Our business lease is from Seven Islands company, and we live in here. In the winter we have snowmobilers in from Greenville—usually Pittston Farms—and we sell gas if people let us know in advance. We also have ice fishing. This year [1997] an 8-year-old boy from Mapleton [between Ashland and Presque Isle] caught a 6½-pound togue and won the fishing derby out of Ashland for a $250 prize. He was just so happy! He caught it right out front here, last day they were here. The father and his friends were getting ready to leave—they'd spent all their time down the lake but they set up a hole here—and while they were packing up, the kid caught the fish!

"The camps were built in the early 1960s and originally were owned by Bill and Alma Mower. We're the third owners. When Curt and I do our shopping we go into Presque Isle, 3½ hours away [Millinocket is also 3½ hours away], and we go in every week. I serve fruit and veggies as much as possible. We have peas and tomatoes in our garden.

"Ross Lake has a natural reproducing population of togue and brook trout, whitefish, and cusk. We also have over 160,000 acres available for hunting with beechnut ridges, clear-cuts, and cedar swamps. We had hunters in here last week from Pennsylvania, and we asked them why they picked us over another sporting camp. They said it was because they spoke to us at one of the three sportsmen's shows we do a year, and we didn't promise a catch of fish or animal but simply laid out what was available. Like with deer hunting, I don't know when it's going to snow. I don't have any control over Mother Nature or a person's skill. What I will guarantee is we're not fancy here, but if our guests have their meals in the lodge, they are going to be full when they get up from the table."

Curt: "I used to make bear bologna. In Pennsylvania people eat a lot of bologna, and with bear you don't get a lot of good cuts of meat. Back in 1963 I worked for the parks department in Montana, and in Pennsylvania I worked 22 years as a deputy in the conservation office as a game warden, so I love the outdoors. I was active in the Boy Scouts and helped at Loon Lodge sporting camps. When I first came to Maine, back in the early '80s, I went to Hardscrabble Lodge near Jackman. Maine is the last wilderness left in the eastern United States and I wanted to come live and work up here. My father ran three nursing homes and I met so many people that said they wished they'd done something or other in their lives. I realized I was in my 40s and it was time to go out and do what I'd always dreamed about if I was ever going to do it. Mary's the one who encouraged me. She's one of a kind. It takes the right woman to live this kind of life. People told us it would take five years before we made any money. This is our fourth year, and it looks for the first time that we're going to break even. But that's not as terrible as it would have been to us. Things people on the 'outside' feel are important don't seem so important when you get in here."

Mary: "The one thing we miss is our families. So in December we go back down to Pennsylvania to be with everyone over the holidays. Then we're ready to come back up here for the winter season."

Snickerdoodles

> 1½ cups sugar, ½ cup softened margarine or butter, ½ cup vegetable oil, 2 eggs, 2¼ cups all-purpose flour, 2 tsp. cream of tartar, 1 tsp. baking soda, pinch of salt

Heat the oven to 400 degrees. Mix the first four ingredients. Stir in the next four ingredients. Shape into 1½-inch balls and roll in a mixture of ¼ cup sugar and 2 tsp. ground cinnamon. Place 2 inches apart on a cookie sheet. Bake 8–10 minutes, or until set. Cool. Makes 4 dozen cookies.

59. UMCOLCUS SPORTING CAMPS

HK/AP, SCA

OWNERS: Al and Audrey Currier

ADDRESS: General Delivery, Oxbow, ME 04764; 207-435-8227

SEASON: Year-round (closed April)

ACCOMMODATIONS: Six log cabins (one or two bedrooms) with wood heat, gas lights, gas stove, gas refrigerator, porch; central shower house; no pets

RATES: $30 per person per day; $180 per person per week (HK)

ACCESS: I-95 to exit 58. Take ME 11 north approximately 40 miles and take the left-hand turn to the town of Oxbow. The Curriers' house, on the right, serves as the town post office and the camp headquarters. Check in at the office in back.

Umcolcus's cabins are arranged in a horseshoe around the new (1997) main lodge. With this handcrafted addition, the Curriers can now offer American Plan and "rustic retreats" for groups and organizations. The site is relatively open, looking out on the Umcolcus Deadwaters, with a stream running along a wooded portion of the property and into the clearing.

Al's roots in the area go back a long way: "The site itself is a hundred years old, but the cabins there now are not the original ones. My grandfather was a guide and caretaker for the original camps which belonged to the Hines family out of Portland [Maine]. And as they all got older and the group all broke up, 'for 1 dollar and other valuable considerations' the camps, were turned over to my grandfather.

"The name itself is from the Umcolcus Lake. That gets a little confusing because there's an east and west branch to Umcolcus Stream. We are actually on the west branch, which has its headwaters in Cut Lake. The camps are about 5 miles below the lake. There's a big deadwater right in front of camp called Cranberry Pond. Cut Lake is a small lake, shallow, with some trout, so people mainly come in to relax, canoe, hike, hunt, cross-country ski, and snowmobile. We're within 10 minutes of ITS 85."

Audrey: "I got involved in Umcolcus Sporting Camps by being married to Al, of course. We spent the second night of our honeymoon at camp. I had seen the camps once before we were married. His father was running them for hunting season at the time. Then we just started going in on weekends, and as we had children, we'd go in with them. We kept working on the biggest cabin, trying to maintain that as a family cabin. And then, somehow, some hunter and his crew started renting it. We've had the camps since 1972.

"We live full time in Oxbow and our daughters, Tori and Debi, traveled 20 miles to Ashland for school. I'm originally from Ashland, but we've been living here since 1975. I'm also postmaster of the area. The post office has been in this same family and same house since 1917. The mail for the townspeople goes into an antique wooden general-delivery mailbox unit. I put the mail into the small units and hand people all their mail. The population of Oxbow is probably around 80, but I also service 26 general-delivery customer boxes and then there are 14 highway contract boxes in there."

Al shows me an album: "That's my grandfather and that's Jack Dempsey, the boxer. He used to come up with his trainer and go into camp. The old main lodge had two bedrooms, and that's the one we made into a family camp. The old cook's cabin was torn down. One of the other camps was big, with two fireplaces. Dad said it had a hearth so wide you could get right up and lay down on the top section. That camp was struck by lightning.

"So we had a lot of building to do. Fortunately, we've had a lot of help from friends. We felled the logs and took them to a mill where they were two-sided and brought back to the site. Then we built the camps, weekends mostly. You can use white pine, spruce, cedar. I personally like spruce—the original camps were spruce logs. Then we protect the wood with a clear preservative. We've gone away from oakum for caulking and use regular fiberglass insulation. We cut it in strips, lay it on top of the log, staple it, and just keep layering up. You could construct a camp in a month if you set right up to do it. It's quite a process. And then once you go inside and make it into a housekeeping unit, it's like a home. The old camps were on what they called the mud sill. They started right out on the ground, and you don't get any ventilation. Eventually the camp would settle and the dead log would be right in the ground. Our new ones are set in a cement slab and then on hemlock puncheons. They're the foundation that the floor stringers for the camp are built on, so we can get under the building and have an air flow. We have some cabins with cathedral ceilings. Inside we framed the bottoms in, put heavy plastic, and then boarded up and down with pine boards. We did the same thing, on a bigger scale, with the main lodge, which in addition has a large fieldstone fireplace.

"Besides building the camps, we also built the road coming in here. It used to be an old tote road for horses, and then we started coming in with old four-by-four army trucks, chains on all four wheels. Over the years I've re-corduroyed sections of the road and bulldozed and graveled to get it to the point where you can get in here with a car or pickup. A corduroy road is a base of wood you lay in a swampy area, where it's just mush. You lay the logs crosswise and cover them with gravel. In the wintertime, I plow for the town of Oxbow and some county roads. I also do land excavation, put in sewer systems, landscape work, so luckily I have equipment to use for the camps. I've been well over 20 years on the camp road. A few years ago we had a logging operation come in and chew up all the work of 20 years. So we're at the road again. It's just the way it goes, I guess."

Audrey: "We work hard to make a nice place for people to relax. And more and more people are coming in to do simply that. They say this peace and quiet just can't be bought."

60. WILDERNESS ISLAND

AP, SCA

OWNERS: Mike and Carol LaRosa
CAMP ADDRESS: PO Box 220, Portage, ME 04768; 207-435-6825
WINTER ADDRESS: PO Box 847, Groton, MA 01450; 508-448-5450
SEASON: Mid-May through October
ACCOMMODATIONS: Eight log cabins (one or two bedrooms) with indoor plumbing and shower, wood heat, gas lights, limited handicapped-accessible; one cabin has a fireplace
RATES: $95 per person per day, includes use of nonmotorized boats
ACCESS: I-95 to exit 58. Take ME 11 north to Portage (last supplies or place to call camp). Go left at Dean's Motel and then fork left at the Great Northern Paper Company road (dirt), where there's a sign for the camps. Pay the toll at the North Woods gatehouse. Follow camp signs 17 miles to the boat landing.

Mike LaRosa tries to greet every guest at the dock. Such warmth and enthusiasm permeates 10-acre Wilderness Island, formerly known as Zella Island or Fish River Camps. As Mycki McNally, daughter-in-law of the original owners, relates, a woman named Zella Mileau was the first female guest at camp, so they named the island after her. The McNally clan saw this spot as their home camp. Eventually the original lodge just became too small and Mycki's husband, Dana, had a dream one night of a six-sided lodge: "But he realized the corners would be too sharp, so he made it eight-sided, octagonal—that way

Wilderness Island vegetable garden

he could have a wide building but it didn't have to be terribly long. It's 50 feet across by 30 wide. He built a three-sided chimney with rocks from the island. The logs rest on the chimney for support. After a heart attack, he directed construction from a hospital bed until he could get back to work."

Mike: "There are a lot of stories about Wilderness Island. The camps were founded in 1895 and may be the oldest operating sporting camp in Aroostook County. It used to be a stopover. People would come in from the town of Portage, spend the night, and continue on to the Allagash. One of the cabins has the date of 1909 on the wall with all the guides' initials on there. And it's my understanding that where our cabin number 3 is used to be the main lodge. Dana McNally was an architect and he also made all the furniture in the lodge. It's 30 feet from the floor to the top of the fireplace, which is a conversation piece itself. I've looked at the lodge over the years and a lot of those cuts are very difficult to make, the logs in the ceiling fan out from the chimney—it's gorgeous. It had to take a lot of planning before they even started building. I mean, it's really complex. The windows are actually storm windows put in the wrong way, so you can slide them back and forth. And the windows in our big cabin are 10 feet long by 5 feet high. They brought those up in a canoe, crated, from Portage all the way up the Fish River chain, coming in the east side of the lake. That's

23 miles in a car, but it's a lot farther by boat because the river snakes around so. Trouble is, it takes 4½ hours to get here by canoe *without* a heavy, tippy load of windows. I love that story, and I hope it's true!

"I'm very prejudiced about Wilderness Island, but there's not a camp in the North Maine Woods I've visited that I wouldn't be glad to stay the night or a week. We used to vacation on Moosehead Lake and were thinking of retiring there. I thought that because I do a lot of woodworking, I would open up a little Papa Geppetto–type shop. Then we went to a real estate office on the last day of our vacation and this place popped up. When I saw it was an island I just couldn't believe it! So we bought the island in January 1985.

"Carol is a consultant. She does work for computer companies and takes time off to work here during our season. We have three boys, Mike, Eric, and John, so this is a family business. The island is 9.6 acres. When the water's low, it might be even larger! It's shaped like a spade in cards. We can see the landing from the main lodge, and if you drive, we'll look for you for an hour before your estimated arrival and keep looking for you till dusk. If you don't show up, we'll contact the main gate and try to find you. We have direct radio contact to a woman named Wilza Robertson, who answers our calls.

"We've come up with several package deals for our customers, which have proved to be very popular. We have a five-day retreat, a long-weekend special, a two-for-one package. These all include a flight in, use of boats, all the meals, everything. Or people do their own trans-portation. Also, we do a lot of dinner business—people coming in from Fort Kent, Caribou, Presque Isle, Mapleton, Washburn. Every Sunday we have an international buffet, like Mexican, Spanish, Hawaiian—which someone told me was crazy. 'How can you have a Hawaiian buffet in the middle of the North Maine Woods?' But we do it! And it works! The first year we had 107 people come in. And we were dressed in Hawaiian shirts and pants, wearing straw hats. We deco-rated the main lodge with Hawaiian paraphernalia, and I'm having a ball with it! We cook Chinese, genuine Italian, Arabic—whatever you want. If we don't know how to cook it now, we'll know by the time you get here! Carol and I cook, or I do it alone when she's not here. Our first year I didn't know how to cook well and I was scared every day. Terrified! I mean, people are paying for what you're cooking, and I wanted it to be really good. I don't think anyone could make me go through that first year again. I'm not proud of doing things I don't like to do, but I am proud of trying to do them well, and I now feel great about the cooking because I know our guests enjoy it. Carol doesn't even need a recipe most of the time.

"For me, the most important thing when you're getting ready to serve a meal is the last 7 minutes, because you've got to do several things at the same time. I cook with a lot of timers and each timer has a different sound. I know all the sounds of those timers, so I know when the muffins are done, when the beans are just about right, when the coffee is done—6½ minutes perked. I've got that all down in my head, and that's the '7-minute challenge' to cooking.

"I've got to show you some pictures of my garden! We've been trying to grow a garden here, well, every single season. We have good wax and string beans, peas and broccoli, but they're cool-weather crops, so you expect them to do well. Plus these things would grow in cement, I think! But the soil was mostly clay. So every year we've worked on it. We separate all our garbage, and anything we can put in the garden we put it into what we call the garden bucket. And when that's full we go out and trench it into the soil. We've been doing that since 1985. And then we have horse manure in there, so we have a great-looking garden. I don't even want to harvest it, it's so beautiful! We have guests that come here, Alice, and they get their bucket and little knife and go out and harvest their own beans, and we'll cook them for their supper. They love doing that.

"The way we get our drinking water is interesting. It comes from a spring across the lake, halfway up a mountain. It's all PVC pipe down the mountain, underneath the lake, and back up onto the island, and then up a 40-foot tower—over a mile and a half of PVC pipe. The best part of this system is it's free and it doesn't have to be run by generators, so the camp can be quiet and peaceful. It's probably the purest water you're ever going to drink because by the time it gets to the lake it's run the gamut of rocks and pebbles and really filtered out.

"I'll tell you a cute story about hummingbirds, Alice. One day, in the springtime, when we'd just bought the island, I was walking to the main lodge and something buzzed right by me. I thought it was a bee making a huge noise. When I talked to Carol, she said it had to be a hummingbird. Well, I'd never seen a hummingbird before. The first thing Carol did was go out and buy feeders, and it was just an incredible thing. Here I'd never seen one and now there were 15 to 18 hummingbirds buzzing around a feeder! They are intelligent and aggressive. When they're upset, they fan their tails out for stability. We haven't built the machine yet that can outperform them in the air.

"Before we came here I was planning to retire, but I'm working harder than I did my entire life! I was in the hotel-motel business in Massachusetts. When I first bought this place, people said, 'What's he doing that for? He's not a hunter.' I don't hunt. I don't fish. I don't do any of those things, and here I am in the sporting-camp business. But it's not really the old idea of hunting and fishing, it's really vacationers. Alice, there are two types of businesses when you run a sporting camp, and a lot of people don't understand that. When you come in the main lodge, you're in the restaurant business. When you leave the main lodge, you're in the recreation business. In the main lodge, you're on my turf, and I know how to take care of you. I don't have to be a big sportsman to run a sporting camp. I can get a guide. This is a business of hospitality. Any time you're dealing with people, you're in the business of hospitality. That's a big product. When someone says, 'You're a good host,' my answer to that is, 'I'm a good host because you're a good guest.' And that is absolutely true. When people come into the North Maine Woods, I don't care whose camp they're coming to, they're at your mercy. They really are, because if they don't like your food, where can they go? There's no place around here but Dean's Motor Lodge, which serves good food, but it's 23 slow, logging-road miles away. If you get hungry at 2 in the morning, and some people do, you're at our mercy again. So I make sure they get plenty of food and that they know where the refrigerator is. Every cabin has a flashlight and they know they can come into the main lodge at 2 AM. They know where the bread and meat is, where all the fixings are, so they can make a sandwich. We say everyone needs a time to retreat, and we want people to relax, unwind, and enjoy. Stress doesn't even make it to our island; it's out there back at the boat landing somewhere!"

Ham Kebabs

Mike: *"Two pounds of ham serves five people, so figure accordingly. The secret to this is the glaze."*

> For each person: 4 one-inch cubes of baked ham, 3 pieces tomato, 3 pieces green pepper, 3 pieces onion, 3 mushrooms
>
> Glaze: 1 cup packed brown sugar, ⅓ cup peach (or other fruit) juice

Skewer kebabs, starting and ending with a piece of ham. Put tin foil on a barbecue grill (or on a cookie sheet in the oven). Combine glaze ingredients until liquidy. Brush kebabs with glaze. Cook, turn, and brush. Cook until vegetables are the way you like them. We like them still crunchy.

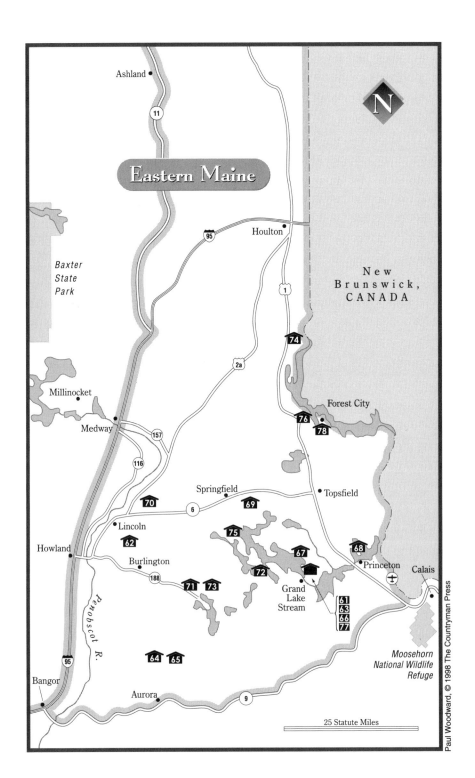

Eastern Maine

PART THREE
EASTERN MAINE

The camps in this section are grouped into one region, which includes the area east of I-95, bounded on the south by ME 9 ("the Airline") and everywhere else by the Canadian border. In terms of landmarks, the area is bracketed on the west by the Penobscot River system and on the east by the St. Croix flowage. A large and interconnecting series of lakes, ponds, and streams make up what is known as the Grand Lake Stream–St. Croix watershed area, which serves as the focus for a majority of the camps in this region. The unique feature of sporting camps in Grand Lake Stream Village (there are four or five others not included in this book because they are currently for sale or not operating, or they do not meet the criteria, either in age or appearance) is that they form a close community while maintaining their individuality. Guests can experience a village as well as a camp community. It is the personality of the owners that sets the tone of each camp and attracts kindred clientele.

The waters in this forested land support bass and salmon as well as togue, perch, and other fish. Many of the camps are close to New Brunswick, Canada, and an annual International Festival in August celebrates the good relations between neighbors. The main cities and towns in this region are Bangor (Maine's second largest city) in the "south," Lincoln as the gateway to ME 6, and Houlton to the north. Calais ("CAL-lus"), at the end of the Airline, is Maine's busiest border crossing. Just west of Calais is the Moosehorn National Wildlife Refuge, established for the study and protection of regional species, particularly migratory birds, waterfowl, and deer. This sparsely populated section is also an agricultural center for Maine's blueberry and potato crops. In the autumn, the blueberry barrens form an alternative fall-foliage experience. The blueberry stalks turn a bright magenta, while the needles of the softwood "hackmatacks"—that is, tamaracks, or larches—glow golden against the green of evergreens and the brilliant blue skies.

Getting there: Commercial airlines fly to Bangor International Airport, which has rental car services. KT Aviation (207-945-5087), Lucky Landing (207-945-5087), and Telford Aviation (207-990-5555) fly out of Bangor, and Central Maine Aviation (207-827-5911) flies out of nearby Old Town if you want to take a floatplane or hire a regular plane to fly you into Princeton airport. If you arrive in a private plane, Princeton has two 4,000-foot runways and is 5–15 minutes from Grand Lake Stream area camps. Driving time (taking I-95) to the Lincoln area from Portland is 3 hours; from Boston, 5 hours; from New York City, 10 hours; to the Grand Lake Stream area the drive from Portland is 5 hours; from Boston, 7 hours; from New York City, 11–12 hours.

Guidance: For further information contact the Greater Lincoln Chamber of Commerce (207-794-8065) or the Grand Lake Stream Chamber of Commerce, PO Box 124, Grand Lake Stream, ME 04637.

61. COLONIAL SPORTSMEN'S LODGE

AP/HK

OWNERS: Steve and Pat Takach
ADDRESS: Grand Lake Stream, ME 04637; 207-796-2655
SEASON: May 1 through October 15
ACCOMMODATIONS: Five cabins with indoor plumbing and shower, electric lights, automatic heat, porch, and satellite TV
RATES: $50–95 per person per day (AP); $30–60 per cabin per day (HK)
ACCESS: I-95 to Lincoln. Take ME 6 east to US 1 at Topsfield (40 miles). Turn right onto US 1 and drive south 14 miles. Turn right onto Grand Lake Road at a sign for the camps. Go 10 miles to the village store in Grand Lake Stream, turn right, then take the left fork over the bridge. A sign for the camp is at the base of a knoll. Take the left fork up a hill and turn left at the sign.

Colonial Sportmen's main lodge, a white farmhouse, sits way back and up on a knoll of carefully mowed grass. Cabins, off to one side and near the trees, head down the hill toward Grand Lake Stream itself, visible and audible from the lodge's long porch.

Pat: "These camps were the first commercial sporting camps in Grand Lake Stream. The earliest brochure I have is from 1908, but before that they took care of the high mucky-mucks when the world-famous tannery was in business. You can see where the chimney was from here. There's nothing left of the building, but it was on the site where our fish hatchery is now. It was originally called Ovananiche Lodge. *Ovananiche* is the Indian name for landlocked salmon. And they had an outcamp called Sunset Camps on West Grand Lake. It was started by a Mr. Rose and a Mr. Boyton, who belonged to the New York and Boston yacht clubs. They then sold to Weatherby's, and at that point some of the oldest camps or cabins were moved to Weatherby's. The place was then bought by a man named Peabody, who was going to have it as a private estate, and he sold off some more of the camps. The result is we have only three of the original cabins.

"When the camps were first operating, the settlers cut all the trees to build the town. There was basically nothing here except one family—it was the tannery that brought people. Before the town became a 'plantation,' we were what the state calls an unorganized township, which means the state oversees the territory. In the early days a guide used to get $3 for one person, $4 for two, and the rates for camp were $2.50 a day and $15 a week.

"This area is famous for its fishing. Fly-fishing for landlocked salmon in the stream opens on April 1. About the middle of May, the first fly hatches produce top-water fishing with dry flies. In the fall, when the water cools, spawners return. Grand Lake Stream is 2 miles of fast water, boulder falls, and deep pools. Grand Lake, beyond the dam, has been noted for its landlocks since the late 1800s. It is 19 miles long with over 100 miles of shoreline, and most people prefer trolling around it. We also have brook and lake trout, white perch, and pickerel. Plus, you can't find any better fishing for smallmouth bass, especially the first three weeks in June. For those who want saltwater fishing, we are only an hour's drive from the Machias River—which has 60 miles of public water for Atlantic salmon fishing—and from Passamaquoddy Bay and New Brunswick."

An old brochure gives some trolling information:

> With his craft moving about two miles an hour, the fisherman, comfortably seated, pays his line out slowly, till about one hundred feet is in the water. He may get a strike during this process, or he may be in dreamland when the visitor arrives . . . the rod dips suddenly. The reel screams. The old hand snubs his fish for a second to insure the hold, and the game is on.
>
> The togue tugs hard, shakes his head savagely, rarely breaks water, but fights every moment, making his last spurt when he sees the landing net. His worst trick is to roll over and over at this moment and sag heavily, often breaking tip or line; and, if netted safely, this move is sure to mean a snarl.

The brook trout is a racer under all conditions. With a free lake, his rush is less dangerous than the spurt for the sunken bush (in a stream); but the pleasure is balanced by the fact that the brook trout run large in the lake.

The ouananiche is the finished acrobat and strong man, resourceful, almost tireless, and a relentless fighter. When he calls, there is rarely any doubt in the mind of the fisherman as to the nature of his guest. He has evidently spent the winter with a storage battery. An ouananiche may break water a dozen times while on the hook and appreciates the value of a good finish. Woe to the novice who does not watch for that last dip! Once in the net, he is a glory, marked like his lordly cousin, with fine indigo spots on a coat of burnished silver. And, further evidence of fine breeding, he improves on acquaintance. Broiled over the coals, he wins the heart and stays with you like a man. A few hardtack, a pound of salmon, and a pint of coffee make one fit.

An even older brochure, 1908, asserts:

It is unquestionably true that nearness to nature has an elevating influence upon heart and character. Nature is a school of all the hardier virtues. What, for instance, can impart a more effective lesson in patience than a day's fishing? These quiet places, fortunately, are not beyond the reach of people of moderate means, to whom the "call of the country" means peace and freedom, not the mere shifting of the scene of social dissipation and rivalries.

Broccoli Salad

1 bunch broccoli, ½ cup raisins, ½ cup pecans, 1 small onion, ½–1 pound bacon (fried crisp)

Dressing: 1 cup mayonnaise, ½ cup sugar, 2 T cider vinegar

Chop up everything but the raisins. Mix together. Make the dressing and mix it into the salad. Let sit for an hour before serving.

62. EAGLE LODGE AND CAMPS

AP/HK, SCA

OWNERS: John and Tami Rogers
ADDRESS: PO Box 686, Lincoln, ME 04457; 207-794-2181
SEASON: Year-round
ACCOMMODATIONS: Five log cabins (one or two bedrooms), with indoor plumbing and shower, wood heat, gas lights, gas stove, gas refrigerator, screened-in porch
RATES: $60 per person per day (AP); $55 per cabin per day (HK)
ACCESS: I-95 to exit 55. At the US 2 intersection, go straight. At the ME 155 intersection, go left. At the Penobscot Valley Hospital, go right 2.8 miles to a four-corners. Turn left and follow the signs to camp, 3 miles.

Even though the town and all its modern conveniences are only about 20 minutes away, by the time you get to Eagle Lodge and see the familiar log cabins and main lodge you are in "camp mode." As the driveway dips down and into the woods, the experience starts to feel "right." Only 50 miles northeast of Bangor, Lincoln has 78 square miles of land, making it the largest township east of the Mississippi. There are more than a dozen lakes and ponds with public access, including the Penobscot River and its bass fishery, within the town's borders.

Tami: "We bought the camps in 1994—looked at them in June, and by July they were ours. We weren't really in search of a sporting camp per se, but it was a meant-to-be situation. In the beginning we worked so hard it was unbelievable. By the time we'd been here eight months, we had a group of hunters that left a $100 tip and we decided it was time to splurge and take the kids, Greg and Courtney, out. So we went to Bangor for dinner and a movie. We were at the restaurant and went into the bathroom to wash up. I met up with John on the way out and we both looked at each other, shocked. Did you see yourself in the mirror? We hadn't looked in a mirror for eight months! But, you know, it was the best winter. We had no radio or TV. We went through one or two books a week, all of us. It was a real connecting time."

John: "When you don't have a TV or radio, you can hear what's going on around you. We'd listen to the ice—there are air bubbles underneath frozen water that build up and you get this sound we called the heartbeat of the earth.

"The camps are on Folsom Pond, which connects to Crooked Pond, and both are a mile long and wide and have smallmouth bass, pickerel, and white perch. Upper Pond is the headwaters and that has

Eagle Lodge and Camps

brook trout. The Penobscot River is 15 minutes from here and we fish that—50 to 100 smallmouth bass a day is common.

"We have a lot of hiking trails and do guided rock-climbing trips, even for people who've just learned how to spell 'rock'! We have an excellent hunting season. For winter we're on the ITS 81 snowmobile trail and provide food and lodging for snowmobilers." *Tami:* "Yes, we can provide all these things, and more, but what we really offer is nothing. If you want to sit on the front lawn, in the peace and quiet, and watch eagles, that's what you can do."

John: "The camps were built in the early 1920s by a Dr. George Averell from Lee, Maine, who built Lee Academy. The original lodge was elaborate, with flush toilets—this is in the '20s—but it burned and they built another one right off. Teddy Roosevelt was here when he was in Bangor. This was when he was governor of New York.

"The driveway's only been here since the late '60s. Prior to that, they had a set of rollers to crank boats down and every Thursday they'd get to town by boat. The Sharkeys, father and mother and three daughters, bought it in the late '30s. Mr. Sharkey was a schoolteacher who worked two jobs all year so he could take the summer off to come here. If you wanted to stay with the Sharkeys, you'd wait at the railroad station— there was no telephone communication—and they'd swing by to pick you up. One crazy aunt would come in on a floatplane with bags of groceries. The three sisters would come in here, without husbands, by canoe at night and lie on their backs and look at the stars and roll down the hill. One sister painted an oil painting of the camps. They come each year; they're hooked forever." *Tami:* "These women have really touched our lives. They've told us wonderful stories about growing up here that have really brought the history to life for us. Their parents finally relented and said they could stay up one hour later, but then went around and set the clocks ahead 1 hour all summer!"

John: "When the sisters were teenagers and had their cousin around, there were four buddies in town who spent one winter building four canoes, all alike. They called themselves the Four Aces. They put motors on these canoes and would race around the lake trying to get the girls' attention. Well, Pa had to go to town and there's the guys hanging out in their boats. So he calls to the guys and says, 'I'm headed to town to get reflectors for your canoes.' 'We don't need reflectors,' they say. 'It's for me,' he says, 'so I can get a bead on it to shoot you guys out of the water!'"

Tami: "Some of these guys have been back, one on a motorcycle. He's always loved one of the sisters. The sisters' grandmother died here, and their mother died many years later on the same day. Their father tried to die on the same day but passed away a few days ahead. I believe the passion and love of the former generations for this place is still here in these walls and around us. Magical and special things happen at Eagle Lodge. We have logbooks in the cabins and people write such beautiful things it makes you cry."

John: "On May 3, 1997, we started something that is turning out to be a wonderful and popular addition. That was our first Maine Guide School session. We get the people who come ready to take the Maine guide test. It's rigorous, but they end up prepared and seem to have a worthwhile time. We're planning on doing this at various times year-round."

Deep-Dish Moose Stew Pie

Tami: *"You can use beef instead of moose."* John: *"This is so good it makes you want to go out and shoot a moose, even if you don't hunt!"*

> 2 pounds cubed moose meat, ½ cup flour, 1 tsp. salt, 1 tsp. basil, 1 tsp. thyme, pinch of five-spice powder, 4-plus cups water, 3 peeled and sliced carrots, 2 chopped onions, 5 medium potatoes, 3 T cornstarch, pastry for single piecrust

Combine flour, salt, and herbs and dredge the cubed meat. Brown the meat in an oiled heavy saucepan. Add 4 cups of water and simmer for 2 hours. Add vegetables and more water if needed. Thicken with cornstarch after the veggies are cooked. Pour into a baking dish and cover with the pastry. Bake at 350 degrees for 20–25 minutes.

63. GRAND LAKE STREAM CAMPS

HK

OWNERS: Nancy and Gary Betz

ADDRESS: PO Box 17, Grand Lake Stream, ME 04637; 207-796-5562

WINTER ADDRESS: PO Box 276, Milbridge, ME 04658; 207-546-2930

SEASON: May through October

ACCOMMODATIONS: Five cabins (one to two bedrooms) with indoor plumbing, wood heat, gas or electric lights, porch; central shower house; pets welcome

RATES: $21 per person per day

ACCESS: I-95 to exit 54 (Howland) or exit 55 (Lincoln). Take ME 6 east to Topsfield (40 miles), then take US 1 south 14 miles to Grand Lake Road. Take the right onto Grand Lake Road and go 10 miles to the general store in Grand Lake Stream. Turn left along the stream. A camp sign will be on the right.

Grand Lake Stream Camps is a cozy compound right along the shore of Grand Lake Stream with a lived-in, homey look. A guest oversees Nancy's refinishing project, Gary putters among the outsized plants in his lush vegetable garden, a guest's dog meanders slowly by while his family prepares for a bike outing. The cabins are a dozen yards from a homemade swinging bridge that spans the gurgling stream.

Nancy: "We've been running these camps since 1973, but we actually started coming here in 1966." *Gary:* "We had a nice little hometown in New Jersey, but two developers showed up and doubled the size of the town. It was too late to save what we'd had, so I had to leave. I was a surveyor at the time and Nancy worked for a pharmaceutical company until we had our family, a boy and a girl. So we bought these camps. I was 29, and now my son has bought Nicatous Camps when he was 29!

"The history of the place is that a man named Hill Gould came here when he was 70 and built the original two cabins, Mallard and Teal. He was a guide and lived in the farmhouse right down the road. Then

Gary and Nancy Betz, Grand Lake Stream Camps

he sold to Jack Page, who sold to a Captain Elliott, who was in the merchant marines. Captain Elliott had looked all over Maine for a place he liked, and when he saw this spot he decided this was it. He purchased the camps in 1948 and had it 25 years until we bought it. He put in the three other cabins. From the stream, we have boat access to Big Lake, so we have the best of both worlds."

Nancy: "The people of Maine almost lost this beautiful area. It all started in October 1992 when the Land Use Regulatory Commission [LURC] wrote us a letter asking if we wanted a public hearing. Georgia-Pacific Company [GP] was planning a 30-lot subdivision right along the stream, if you can imagine! We got other signatures on the petition and had the hearing in the schoolhouse. It was a packed audience and about 30 people spoke. The Passamaquoddy Indians said there used to be a campground for them on our site. And we have found Indian heads and pottery here. The falls area used to be their burial grounds, and they wanted it protected."

Gary: "We were getting ready to put the place on the market because we'd already been through this twice, once in New Jersey and once at North Conway, New Hampshire, where we used to live in the winter. And we knew we wouldn't want to live here [with a housing development]. We found out a lot of other people in town felt the same way. Most of the people who live in Grand Lake are here for a good way of life. You sell your way of life, what you really care about, and you may get rich quick, but you slowly feel real poor."

Nancy: "Anyway, it took us almost three years to get approval from Georgia-Pacific to buy the land and be successful in raising the money. There are only 180 full-time residents here, but we said we'd give $5,000 and then we increased that to $10,000. The Maine Coast Heritage Trust really helped, L.L. Bean gave us $50,000, the Land for Maine's Future gave us $70,000, and about 400 individuals raised more than $90,000. The purchase included a 500-foot easement on the other side of the stream. It was incredible. I mean, we'd had no background with this kind of thing. We honestly didn't know what we were doing at first. But you learn, and it was something that people felt strongly about. We had our celebration in October 1995 and it turned into a real media event. We put up a tent at Little Falls and Governor King came, and Leon Gorman, the head of L.L. Bean, and Bucky Owen, commissioner of inland fisheries. Leon Gorman had presented Governor King with a fishing rod and the governor caught his first salmon at Little Falls. He is so charismatic—what a speaker. He gave his speech in waders!"

Gary: "It would be great if we could do what happened here on a larger scale. I think the idea of a Maine Woods national park would be a good idea. I think we should take all the major watersheds in Maine and protect the land around them and the islands in them."

Nancy: "There's so much history in these places. I've somehow ended up as president of the historical society and there's a book written by Minnie Atkinson around 1918 called *Hinckley Township* which tells a lot about the village."

According to the book, the Passamaquoddy tribe, who live in this region, formerly used the east bank of Grand Lake, *Witteguergaugum,* or "landing place," as a portage from Grand to Big Lake so frequently that even the rocks are worn. The tribe was able to maintain its obscurity from outside intervention (both Native American and European) by living in a "vast waterway which afforded hiding places." Jesuit missionaries established a spiritual foothold with the tribe, and that religious allegiance was not swayed when the English took over the region in the early 17th century.

However, the tribe took an active part in the Revolutionary War on the American side. After the War of 1812, the region reverted to the English, who planned on making it a Canadian province called New Ireland, but the Peace of Ghent returned it to the United States. The area was called the Hinckley Township after Samuel Hinckley, a probate judge from Northampton, Massachusetts, who paid $9,711.18 for the 30,770 acres in 1811. The first white natives of Hinckley were the children of David "the General" and Ellen "Aunt Nellie" Cass, who came to Big Lake in 1820. In 1810 a dam was built across Grand Lake Stream and "pioneering languished" but logging flourished. Logs were floated down the lakes or down the West Branch of the St. Croix River to Milltown, near Calais and St. Stephen, 30 miles away. In 1869, "the turnpike" was built right to the stream to service what was to become the largest tannery in the world. Sportsmen started arriving the very next year, "hiring Indian guides and fishing only the stream." The instant village unofficially took the name of its famous stream and officially became Grand Lake Stream Plantation in 1897, when the village formed its own government. The tannery closed in 1898 and by 1900 the population had plummeted from over 500 to 221. But sportsmen had found their mecca, and the rest, as they say, is history.

Nancy: "People come up here to experience the beauty, be someplace that hasn't been developed, hasn't changed. And these undeveloped places get fewer and fewer. We know. We have kids here right now who were given the choice of Disneyland or Grand Lake Stream and they said they wanted to come back to Grand Lake. It's partly this spot, and partly because of my kidlike husband taking them out in the middle of the night in the Jeep to watch the bears! The time just flies here. We love our people, some of them come three times a year. As we say, you either love it or you don't. But if you come here to Grand Lake Stream and love it, you get hooked for life."

64. GREAT POND LODGE

AP, SCA

OWNER: Ed Musson
ADDRESS: HC 31, Box 530, Aurora, ME 04408; 207-584-3541
SEASON: May through November
ACCOMMODATIONS: Six cabins with outhouse, electric lights, wood heat; shower in the main lodge
RATES: $225 per person per week, includes boat transportation to camp and use of boat while at camp
ACCESS: I-95 to exit 48 (Bangor). Cross the bridge to ME 15 north and follow signs to ME 9 (Eddington). Continue on ME 9 east through the village of Aurora to the camp sign and the 6½-mile access road to the boat landing and the camp boat.

Great Pond Lodge is situated on an island in Great Pond and is accessible by a 5-minute boat trip. The cabins are of frame construction, stained a dark brown.

Ed: "Locally it's known as mountainy pine siding with 'live-edge' boards. It's just like clapboards, only the bottom edge is wavy [the 'live' edge is unmilled, as it comes off the tree]. The clapboards run 10–12 inches wide. They cut the trees at the end of the lake, floated them down, and hauled them to the mill. I worked at Leon Williams Lumber Company for more than 25 years, until 1985. The beauty of working there was I could have November off to guide for hunting. I did anything and everything. When you raise five kids, and you're broke, it takes quite a lot of work to keep things going.

"I've been plumbing inspector since 1976. I still do that. I've got 16 of the unorganized townships and 12 regular towns. I'm licensed by the state but hired by the towns. In the unorganized territories, I'm appointed by the state. There's somewhere over 200 inspectors in the state. I got involved in the first place because the federal government was polluting the lake and I didn't appreciate it, living on the lake. So I just got the book, read it, took the examination, and the town appointed me. Then the next town over hired me, and it sort of snowballed. It's very lucrative for the time you apply to it. You go in, issue the permits, and then see that the work is done according to the permit. The unorganized townships are the worst because it's all back roads and sometimes it's hard to find the place. Like when I go from here to, say, Nicatous Lodge and back it's 150 miles.

"Anyway, my grandfather came from Bridgton [Maine] and I always wanted to be in this area. We had our first daughter the December we came up here. And my wife, Doris, went back to New Jersey with her parents and came back in the spring. She passed away a few years ago, but she helped all those years with the camp. The year she died was the first summer the camps weren't open. I just couldn't do it.

"The original Great Pond sporting camp was built in the early 1900s by Guy Patterson. It wasn't here on the island, but right across from where we are now. The area itself was settled mostly for logging purposes. I agreed to buy the camp in 1946, right after the war, and it came with this island. One of my hunters from Philadelphia lent me some money. He came up every year—died must be 10 or 12 years ago now. I've had two people die here, both of them heart trouble. One was a hunter, the other a fisherman. So, anyhow, with the help of quite a few friends, we managed to get this place ready for the 1952 hunting season. Then I think it was the following year that Canada was closed to hunting because of the hoof-and-mouth disease and I had more hunters and we killed more deer than in any other year. Forty-six deer went out from this island.

"Great Pond is kind of L-shaped, running mostly northwest–southeast with a branch going sort of southwest to the outlet. There's three inlets—Main or 'Buffalo' Stream, Dead Stream, and Collar Brook. And Union River flows out of here to the ocean. The deepest water is 45 feet, so it's a warm-water fishery: bass and pickerel. There's some brown and brook trout, but actually I rely mostly on the hunting here. For a bear hunt, the first thing that happens is Wayne, our game warden, goes down to the bakery and gets some day-old jelly doughnuts. That's for the bear! I've had three women hunters in here as I can recall, but my son-in-law Rob Grant works at a gun shop in Ellsworth and he says there are more women hunters now than there used to be."

Rob: "I figure it may be because more men are incorporating their wives into the picture so they'll know what it's all about. This here [touring the room] is a Maine Antler and Skull Trophy Club mount. Ed has four of the trophies, with the certificates. It's very rare for somebody to get as many as four trophies. The first year, a deer would have no antlers. And generally, the second year he'd have spikes, 'devil's horns.' But you can't tell. The one I showed you was a year and a half old and had eight points. A deer that starts getting old, his antlers will decrease in size because he's not physically fit. You can tell his age by his teeth. Same way with a moose. Ed has mounted all this stuff [two rooms in the lodge are full of trophy mounts] himself."

Ed: "A fellow from down in the village was a taxidermist and he showed me how. Because of the different anatomies, every one of them is different. But it's easy to learn. I don't tan the hides, I just salt-cure them. After awhile they get as hard as a piece of wood. Depends on how fresh the hide is, maybe takes a month. To mount it, you get the mannequin made and soak the hide in a solution of water and borax to get it soft and pliable. Moose needs to cure longer than deer because the hide is thicker. And with bear I salt it, same as I would a deer hide, and when it's dry, a couple months later, I scrape the salt off, soak it in water to get off the salt, and then soak it in gasoline to cut the grease. The difference between tanned and raw hide is the rawhide is cured with salt and tanned is cured with other chemicals. A tanned skin will stay the same size. A piece of rawhide will shrink.

"You came in here on what's called the Airline, Route 9 from Bangor to Calais. Originally it was dirt and narrow. Pretty rough. It's the main freight line now since they discontinued the railroad. I think they call it the Airline because it goes 90 miles in a straight line. And I believe that when they were ferrying planes out of Bangor during the war, heading to England, the Airline was one of the landmarks they used. Actually, it wasn't even plowed through to Calais until the 1960s.

"I gave a speech at the Hancock County Planning Commission one time and somebody asked me what makes sporting camps so special. To me, what it always reminded me of was coming home for Christmas. Because someone like old 'Pop Shelly' from Philadelphia, he wouldn't see his buddy from Florida from one hunting season to the next. Once a year these people get together to see each other again. And those friendships carry through over the years. I think it's important."

In-the-Bottle Salad Dressing
A recipe from Marianne Wiles, the Great Pond Lodge cook:

Using a regular size (Heinz) vinegar bottle, pour in ¾ cup tarragon vinegar. Add extra-light olive oil up to the place on the bottle where it starts to bulge out. Add 2 tsp. dried basil, a couple of garlic cloves that are partially cut through, and a rounded tsp. of sugar. Shake well. Put in a little water to thin out a bit (it will be the consistency of olive oil). Pour in ⅓ cup ketchup and shake well again.

65. GREAT POND WILDERNESS LODGE AND CAMPS
HK, SCA
OWNER: Otis Godley
ADDRESS: RR 2, Box 482, Eddington, ME 04428; 207-745-6728
SEASON: Year-round
ACCOMMODATIONS: Five log cabins (sleep two to eight people) with wood heat, gas stove, gas lights, gas refrigerator, gas grill; central shower house and bathroom; bring sleeping bag, blanket, pillow; pets welcome
RATES: $40–240 per cabin per day
ACCESS: I-95 to exit 48 (Bangor); follow signs to ME 9 east. Take ME 9 east through Aurora and turn left onto Great Pond Road. Go 6 miles to the first right, then go 1.3 miles and turn left. Continue 3 miles to Stud Mill Road. Turn left and go 3 miles. At mile marker 19, turn left and go 2 miles to camp.

O*tis:* "This place was started in 1904 by a man from Maine called Guy Patterson. He originally had a place on Long Pond and then came over here. It was always run as a sporting camp even though there were logging operations nearby. I've found old logging equipment in the woods around here. I'm the fourth owner in all these years. Ed Musson, on the island across there, owned them before me.

"The camps sit up on a knoll overlooking the lake and all the cabins are on the water. Great Pond is 2 miles long and about half a mile wide, shaped like a boot, with brown trout, pickerel, bass, and some brook trout. There's a big field with a volleyball net and picnic tables as you drive in. We have 300 feet of beach, which is where we have our cookouts at night, and you need sunglasses for our sunsets!

"Hunting is as good as you'll find around here. We have about a dozen deer hanging around camp most of the time. I guide, but if I'm out by myself, I won't shoot a good, big deer anymore—save it to seed the next generation. The property behind my camp hasn't been cut for about 50 years and is the only good place within 10 miles that is natural for the deer. There may be a couple thousand acres in that public lot, owned by the state. We're also surrounded by thousands of acres owned by different paper companies. I own this land, 17 acres, so I have a lot of protection. Moose are a common sight. Many mornings guests look out their front porch to see a moose feeding in the shallow water near the inlet. We're in the southeast zone for moose hunting here.

"I grew up hunting and fishing with my father, and owning and operating a sporting camp is something I've wanted to do for 20 years. But I was in no position to do anything about it because something like this takes a lot of money. I just stumbled into this place when I was out snowmobiling with a friend. It was in a state of disrepair, which is why, in June 1990, I was able to buy it. So I've been playing Mr. Fix-Up. Right now I work for UPS, but this is what I plan to retire to, hopefully within the next 10 years. I'm a Master Guide and have another Master Guide who helps me, Walter 'Butch' Myers. I couldn't possibly do this all on my own. Butch and I and the others in this business for the long haul are here because we like it. It's in our blood. I mean, today practically everyone we know is getting ready to sit down and watch the Super Bowl, but we're out at camp getting things ready for our '98 winter season, when we'll be feeding and fueling snowmobilers. I put in a central shower and bathroom facility, and now we're concentrating on making this a full-service winter snowmobile destination, open 24 hours from Thursdays through Sundays. We're a mile from ITS 84, with a side trail leading right to the lake. Also in '98 we'll be doing bear hunting. It's slow, but exciting, getting closer to the goal of being in here full time.

"This is a great year-round spot. We want to show our guests the beauty of the area, show them a good vacation. Sometimes funny things happen, though, no matter what we do. I remember one time we had a father and son at camp and we'd shown them where to fish. I had to go into town in the afternoon, and when I got back they hollered for me to come over and see the mess of trout they'd caught for supper. Well, I came over, and here they were eating away on chub! I had to laugh—pretty high-bred chub. We also have guided canoe trips on the Machias, Union, Narraguagus, and St. Croix Rivers. In the fall, this is a great place for what we call leaf-peepers. Eagle Mountain is near us, and each year at the height of the fall foliage, we take our guests who want to go up to the top of the mountain for a view of the autumn colors. On the way we go through a place that in the 1800s was a town of over a thousand people, but now is nothing more than a couple of brick ovens by a big spring, some rock foundations, and some old apple trees. It used to be a tannery, but when the hemlock-bark source dried up, so did the town. Marjorie and George Baker wrote a book about the town called *Munsungan to the Sea*. That's the Indian name for the Passadumkeag watershed we're in. A nice connection is that Marjorie is the daughter of Guy Patterson, who built this place. The book describes how they'd go into their cabins—these were really basic with no windows, and dirt floors—and they'd start a fire to smoke the mosquitoes out. And then they'd go in to go to sleep. Marjorie and her husband used to snowshoe 70 miles a week trapping beaver. That's when women were women, Alice!"

66. INDIAN ROCK CAMPS

AP/HK

OWNERS: Ken and JoAnne Cannell

ADDRESS: PO Box 117, Grand Lake Stream, ME 04637; 1-800-498-2821 or 207-796-2822; e-mail: indianrockcamp@nemaine.com

SEASON: Year-round

ACCOMMODATIONS: Five log cabins (each with two bedrooms), with indoor plumbing and shower, electric lights, wood and automatic heat, porch; pets welcome

RATES: $62–82 per person per day (AP); $27–45 per person per day (HK)
ACCESS: I-95 to exit 54 (Howland) or exit 55 (Lincoln), then ME 6 to
Topsfield (40 miles). In Topsfield, take US 1 south about 15 miles to Grand
Lake Road (right turn, sign). Go 10 miles to the village of Grand Lake
Stream. As you enter the village, look for the CANOE sign on the left by
tennis court. The camps' driveway is above a church on the right.

Indian Rock Camps are within walking distance of Grand Lake Stream
village as well as Weatherby's Camps. But as is typical with sporting
camps, the place has its own character in a little world set apart.

JoAnne: "We've had these camps since 1987. Ken and I always fished
and hunted with our dads when we were young. I was brought up in
Bath and Ken in North Windham, on Sebago Lake, so we're both
Mainers. Basically, we found this place by accident. We were on a trip
and got lost driving back roads. We came to Grand Lake Stream and
fell in love with the area. At the time Ken was a mason and I was a
hairdresser. We'd raised a son and he was off and married and we decided before our daughter was off we were going to do what we wanted
to do. We live here year-round and are the only ones who feed people
in the winter. After October 15 we do reservations for all meals, but
during our regular season we're very flexible. If guests call ahead, I
will cook anything they want off the menu. And whenever they want
to eat they tell us and that's when I'll serve them. There are about
85 people who live full time in Grand Lake Stream, and it grows to
around 200 with the summer residents. The sporting camps are really
the only major industry in Grand Lake.

"The camps were started in the late 1800s. They're the third oldest
camp here. It was originally one cabin that belonged to a Mr. Yates and
because of the tannery it grew. It was and is one of the few places with
a barn. The sportsmen who came here originally were rich gentlemen
from the Boston area who had stock in the tannery business.

"Ken is the only registered Maine guide in Grand Lake Stream who
owns and operates a sporting camp. Grand Lake has a very active
group of guides. In fact, we have the largest single guides association in
the state. We run a fly-fishing school and maintain mountain-biking
and snowmobiling trails. We just had a bird-watching group in from
Texas, and we encourage hunting with a camera. For gun hunting,
the bear, in particular, is good. Many people come up for historical
reasons, to see the Passamaquoddy lands and artifacts.

"Ken is a Micmac and we celebrate the Native American culture during the same time as the July Folk Arts Festival by having a tribal gathering, with drumming and workshops, here at Indian Rock Camps. Native tribes come in traditional dress and do beadwork, carving, make moccasins—someone painted on deer and moose hide.

"The Passamaquoddy reservation surrounds us, and they have concerns about the cutting of ash trees and sweet grass by the sides of the road because they use these for their beautiful baskets. They showed me arrowheads from Mount Kineo, way over at Moosehead Lake, that are here because they were used for trading. There have been an ongoing number of intermarriages between the Passamaquoddy, Micmacs, and Penobscots, but there is still a real sense of their history as individual tribes and as a people. It is a very spiritual culture.

"We are very interested in tradition and history and nature. We have a collection on the porch of natural objects like big wasp and hornets' nests, and family heirlooms, and I collect old fishing creels, reels, and rods. We have a gift shop that features antiques, Indian artifacts, and items by local craftspeople. For us, this area is like the old Maine. We want to develop it focusing on the natural resources here rather than on property development—just another way of looking at property development. And because of this we have people coming from all over the world to see the town that raised its own taxes—we voted down $5,000 and raised it to $10,000—to save our stream from the traditional property development. By developing the property in its natural state we are allowing its long-term use by many people.

"Each year we have one very special time called Celebration of Life Week, which we open up, free of charge, only to families who have children with cancer. The town is invited to a cookout before the families leave and everyone gets involved. The guides volunteer their time, the townspeople help with cooking and cleaning up, our next-door neighbor does magic tricks, another neighbor sings. We started this in 1996 because of our daughter, who is doing beautifully and even fly-fishing again. It will always start on August 10, which is when her tumor was found, and is also our anniversary, and go until August 17."

Fall Soup

This is good for any vegetable you may have in the refrigerator, and it tastes even better in a day or two.

> 2 pounds hamburger, 2 medium onions (diced), 6 potatoes (peeled and cut in chunks), 6 to 8 carrots (cut in chunks), cooked cabbage (cut in chunks), one stalk celery, other veggies you have

Stock: 5 beef bouillon cubes, 2–3 T "kitchen bouquet" herbs, dash Worcestershire sauce, ½ tsp. garlic powder, ½ gallon water

Sauté hamburger and onion in a little bit of butter until hamburger is brown and onion transparent. Place stock ingredients, hamburger/onion combination, and all vegetables in a large, heavy pot. Bring to a boil, lower heat, and simmer for several hours if possible (or until carrots/potatoes are cooked). Serves 12 to 15.

67. LEEN'S LODGE

MAP/HK, SCA
OWNERS: Dick and E.J. Beaulieu
ADDRESS: Box 40, Grand Lake Stream, ME 04637; 1-800-99-LEENS
WINTER ADDRESS: PO Box 92, Newport, ME 04953; e-mail: leensldg@mint.net; Web site: http://www.mint.net/leensldg
SEASON: May 1 through October 31
ACCOMMODATIONS: 10 log cabins (one to four bedrooms), with indoor plumbing and shower, woodstove or fireplace, gas backup heat, electric lights; pets welcome
RATES: $65–125 per person per day (MAP); $75–80 per person per day (HK)
ACCESS: I-95 to exit 54 (Howland) or exit 55 (Lincoln). Take ME 6 east to Topsfield (40 miles), then US 1 south about 15 miles to a right turn (sign) for Grand Lake Stream. Go about 9 miles. The right turn (sign) to the camp is prior to the village. The dirt camp road is 2 miles long.

Leen's is located on 23 acres, on spring-fed West Grand Lake. The cabins dot a peninsula and circle a cove. Two stick-built housekeeping cabins are hidden away on a wooded knoll a short stroll from base camp. The main lodge has a large dining room, and the adjacent Tannery Room is a sitting room and gaming area with a whimsical fish mobile and other classic camp artifacts. Both rooms have large, west-facing picture windows for sunset viewing.

E.J.: "Leen's began in the 1940s and we're only the third set of owners, so there's been a lot of continuity in spite of the fact that it was closed briefly before we bought it. Cassey and Jack Williams were the original owners and then the Stan Leen family ran it.

"I'm a Mainer—born in Presque Isle, grew up in Augusta, and later lived and worked in Cape Elizabeth. I kept moving south until we came up here and I reversed the trend! When I was growing up, my mother ran a tourist home in Augusta, the Kennebec Pillars, so I grew up in the hospitality business. I can't remember a night when we didn't

Leen's

have 10 or 12 people, like the chief of police, the attorney general, senators, living with us. We used to have interesting discussions around the dinner table. Summers we'd go to Shin Pond. My uncles owned private camps there and were friends with all of Jake's Rangers, the informal group [including Jake Day, the artist] from the Shin Pond–Chesuncook area that Edmund Ware Smith made famous in his book *One-Eyed Poacher in the Maine Woods*. As a teen I'd split the summers between Shin Pond and the County—Aroostook, Presque Isle— and that's when I learned to fish. I went to college at the University of Maine and majored in journalism and English. From there I went to Portland, where I worked as a reporter for Portland papers, was a technical writer and editor, and worked in human resources. But I wanted to be my own boss. Running Leen's has given me the opportunity to pull everything together. Plus you pick up accounting, business management, and a few other things along the road.

"Dick was brought up in Van Buren, the St. John Valley, and went to Hussen College for a degree in business. He works full time selling commercial and industrial lighting. His territory is the entire State of Maine, so he knows the state very well. Because of where he grew up, he speaks French fluently and loves having guests who speak French. We have a blended family of five grown children and decided to ease up a bit and move to an area that was more secluded. This is a dream for Dick. We wanted a business we could develop so when we retired we could do it full time. It just came sooner than we'd expected, but it's perfect for us, as it turns out. We saw Leen's on a Saturday and made an offer on Monday—this is in 1994—and here we are.

"We have guests from all over—Russia, Africa, Australia, the UK, Europe. And we have huge family reunions here. We've got cabins off by themselves that can accommodate a lot of people. The Leen-To has eight bedrooms, the Landlocked cabin has two bedrooms and a loft, and our Cove Cabin has four bedrooms. They all have bathrooms, full kitchens, living rooms, so it's like a family compound. They usually eat at least some of their meals in our dining room. I used to do all the planning for meetings of 400 to 600 people when I worked at the bank, so I've coordinated a lot of public events. I know everything a big group needs ahead of time: transportation, menus, special dietary restrictions, it all goes like clockwork.

"Until I moved here, I never realized how much there is to do in Washington County. I love the festivals. There's the Blueberry Festival in the beginning of August in Machias, the Salmon Festival the weekend after Labor Day in Eastport, the International Festival in Calais, and of course we have the Grand Lake Stream Folk Festival the last weekend in July. You can go whale-watching out of Eastport every Tuesday, drive over to Campobello, New Brunswick, for a tour of President Roosevelt's summer retreat, or cruise along coastal villages on the *Bay of Fundy* sloop. We have golf courses, hikes, canoe trips, a wildlife refuge, and the village has a couple of tennis courts. There's just so much to do. We're trying to take advantage of this by offering all sorts of specials like guided kayak and canoe trips and wildlife and birdwatchers' tours, a women's fly-fishing school, a photography workshop. We have all the freshwater attractions, plus the ocean is only an hour away.

"The owners of sporting camps in the area got together and formed an association, and we got a grant to develop a plan for a series of pedestrian and biking trails. Mountain biking is becoming really popular. We rent out bikes, and we're hoping to map out trails, provide signs to mark scenic points, and have educational information on plant and wildlife species. We all try to work together. Each camp has a different feel and the owners all have different personalities. So if someone doesn't particularly like one place, they have information about other spots. We want guests to build a rapport. It's all about finding the right fit with owners and guests. I've been serving as the secretary for the Maine Sporting Camp Association, so I can see how this working together extends throughout the industry. It's good for owners and guests alike. I mean, the bottom line is we all want to enjoy our time together. People find it a real catharsis here, a respite, a haven. They want a place to go where time stands still, where they can take their watches off and have no responsibilities or commitments. When you're at a sporting camp, you revert back to body time. People who come here metamorphose. They come out of their shell from their high-stress, competitive world. They blossom and surprise even themselves. We love having families here. We have games for the kids in the lodge, we have campfires at night. You look up at the stars, at the clear sky, with your family around you, and you realize how good this is for the soul."

68. LONG LAKE CAMPS

AP/HK, SCA

OWNERS: Sandra Smith and Doug Clements

ADDRESS: PO Box 817, Princeton, ME 04668; 207-796-2051; e-mail: longlake@nemaine.com

SEASON: Mid-May through October 31

ACCOMMODATIONS: 13 log cabins with wood heat, electric lights, porch, indoor plumbing and shower; pets $5

RATES: $55–65 per person or couple per day (HK); $75 per person per day (AP)

ACCESS: I-95 to exit 54 (Howland) or exit 55 (Lincoln). Go through Lincoln on ME 6 east to US 1 at Topsfield (about 40 miles). Go south on US 1 to Princeton. In Princeton, take a right-hand turn onto West Street (at a sign for the camps). Go a couple of miles to the camp sign on the right (beyond the airport) and drive 2 miles in to the camps.

Long Lake's cabins sit at the water's edge, their dark-stained logs blending with the tree trunks of the surrounding tall pines. A main lodge rests, like the hub of a wheel, in the midst of the compound. It may be the large number of cabins, or the location of the main lodge, but one expects kids and counselors to come tumbling out the screen doors. A swimming area, a dock, and a boathouse full of games and books add to the summer-camp feel.

Long Lake Camps at sunset

Sandra: "The history of these camps begins in the early 1940s with Maine guide Eddy Jones. He described the atmosphere as a 'quiet woods camp with the easy informality that goes with log cabins and wood fires.' We have the same philosophy and are very laid-back and flexible. Not formal at all. I think we may be the only sporting camp that doesn't have set times for meals. We don't wait on our guests hand and foot. They can come in the kitchen if they like. In fact, we just had a guest who cooked us dinner, which was great!

"We bought these camps in May of '97 after spending the past ten years involved with other sporting camps. We liked these camps because we thought they had a wonderful location, and we thought they were good camps for family vacations because people can do things here or do a variety of things within an hour or so drive. Also, there's an airstrip right up the road from camp, which makes us easy to get to.

"We're located on the south side of Long Lake, which is part of a huge water system—West Grand Lake, Grand Lake Stream, Big and Lewey Lakes, the Grand Falls Flowage, and the St. Croix River. All of the waters from West Grand and Big Lakes drain down through Long Lake through the 'neck' right in front of the camps. Landlocked salmon pass through this neck every fall and spring. There are also over

20 miles of interconnected waters that offer some of the best small-mouth-bass fishing in New England. In the fall we have grouse and woodcock hunters who can either bring their own dogs or use a guide's. We don't have kennel facilities, so people bring whatever works for them. One mile up the lake on the opposite side is a Passamaquoddy Indian reservation and on one side of us the state owns a site for the University of Maine at Machias, so we have some protection."

Bottomless Cookie Jar Cookies

This is Sandra's signature tradition. Guests can get cookies whenever they want.

> 1 cup each butter, brown sugar, and white sugar; 2 tsp. vanilla; 2 T milk;
> 2 eggs; 2 cups flour; 1 tsp. each salt, baking soda, and baking powder;
> 2½ cups old-fashioned oats; 12 ounces chocolate chips; 1½ cups
> chopped walnuts

Melt butter. Add sugars. Add vanilla, milk, and eggs. Mix. Sift dry ingredients together and add. Stir in walnuts and oats, then chocolate chips. Drop by spoonful 1½ inches apart on greased cookie sheets. Bake at 350 degrees for about 5 minutes or until golden. Makes about 5 dozen.

69. MAINE WILDERNESS CAMPS

HK

OWNERS: Terry and Paula McGrath
ADDRESS: HC 82, Box 1085, Topsfield, ME 04490; 207-738-5052
SEASON: Year-round
ACCOMMODATIONS: Seven cabins with indoor plumbing and shower, wood or gas heat (some with fireplace), electric lights, full kitchen facilities, porch; campsites are available, some with water and electrical hookups
RATES: Cabins $35–60 per day, $210–375 per week; campsites $10–30 per day, $60–180 per week
ACCESS: I-95 to exit 55 (Lincoln). Take ME 6 east for 34 miles. Turn right at a large sign for the camps and go 3.5 miles to Pleasant Lake. Pickup at Bangor International Airport is available.

You emerge from the camp's access road onto an expanse of lawn with unobstructed views of Pleasant Lake. The cleared area is surrounded by 40 acres of forest with footpaths in the woods and along the shore. The camps are a mixture of cabins and campsites, which, although not the traditional "look," give guests options and seem to coexist in harmony. The camps are a ¼-mile portage from the Grand Lake wilderness waterway. The centrally located log main lodge is full of outdoor curios, and has a shop for guests.

Terry: "This was originally the Duck Lake Club founded in the late 1870s. They had three places: the original one on Duck Lake out of Springfield, this one here on Pleasant Lake, and one down at Pocumcus Lake which they called the Birches. Guests would be boated down into Junior Lake, Junior Stream into Scraggly Lake, into here and then back. This is all in one day. The head guide got $2.50 for paddling all day and he had to give $1.25 back to the Duck Lake Club. The other guides got $1.25. The club is gone, the Birches is now private, and there's us open to the public.

"The first mention of a building here is in 1917. This main lodge they called the clubhouse and the name of the original cabin is the Gold Brick. This was all potato fields, and you can see they had a barn, cattle, and a huge bathing beach. Unfortunately, most of the sand is gone now. The club owned this place until 1949. Then Roy Spencer, who was the head guide at all three places, bought it. In '72 it was sold to a retired commander from the Coast Guard who changed it into the Maine Wilderness Canoe Basin and used it for canoeing, biking, and hiking trips. They brought kids from all over the world. He owned it until '85. Then a couple of retired policemen from Massachusetts bought it and they ran it for one year as the same thing, for the kids. There is a club of people who worked here as kids and they have a group within that of ones who met and married here. And there were five. We had a reunion of 51 of them the second year we were here. They rented the whole facility and they came from all over—98 or 99 percent of them are very successful people.

"I bought the camp in '89 from the retired policemen. I own 43 acres, almost ¾ of a mile lake frontage. Practically all the rest is owned by Georgia-Pacific lumber company, so there's basically nothing else on the lake. I've been an outdoors person all my life and have wanted to do this since I was a little kid. I was an antiques auctioneer and lived in Poland [Maine] before we came here. My wife, Paula, was all for it. When I met her, she was a teacher in Rhode Island and, like most teachers, had always taught in standard schools—20 or 25 students. She now teaches kindergarten, first, second, and third grade all at one time and has nine kids in a two-room school in Brookton, 20 miles away. She's never missed a day. The whole month of April she goes out on a four-wheeler.

"We're here at the very beginning of the Grand Falls Flowage. This lake is 1,500 square acres, 120 feet deep, a cold-water fishery man-

Maine Wilderness: Terry McGrath

aged for lake and brook trout and landlocked salmon. General law. And we do have white perch and bass. Outward Bound has a nine-day canoe trip out of here. The kids have been on the ocean for two weeks in open sailing ships before they come here. It's a month-long deal. They won't even let the kids come to the store here in the lodge. One kid tried to bribe a counselor 11 bucks for a candy bar!

"This area has always been known for hunting. We have moose, bear, and bird hunting. There is a little bit of goose hunting and a little duck hunting, for black ducks. And then on canoeing—we have a complete outfitting business here. We do river and lake trips, mostly three to five days. We rent canoes and provide transportation, take you out and pick you up. St. Croix is across the Canadian border 30 miles away. That's where they put in, and most of the lake trips are circle trips back to camp.

"These baskets around the room here my wife made. Some are my personal collection. There are Indian wall baskets, for pinecones, and this one's called a buttock or melon basket, because of the shape. You can bounce them off the floor, they were done so well. This big basket here is a feather basket for pillows and quilts. This is an Indian creel for fishing. It was made by a local fellow from Enfield, a well-known Indian carver, Albert J. Nicola. He made snowshoes, pack baskets, Indian baskets. The Passamaquoddy Indians are just down below us on Big Lake, which is off the Grand Lake Stream road. And this here's a spruce-gum box. When the loggers worked out in the woods, they were only home three or four weeks a year. They would carve these boxes at night. The lid would slide out and they'd put spruce gum inside the box and bring these home for Christmas presents. This is the old green paint, probably from 1830, 1835. They had a chisel they'd drive into a tree and spruce gum would run out. It'd get hard like candy—tastes terrible. And here's some pottery called flow blue. The blue was painted on the inside. It was then baked to a certain temperature and the blue would actually flow through the piece. It was popular from the 1870s to the 1920s. The inside would be very little blue. They had maybe 75 patterns they did this in. The best one is Scinde. Basically, the more blue, the better.

"The big wood item hanging on the wall is called a log caliper. There's a scale on the top—see those little numbers? And a wheel on the bottom. If you find one with a wheel, we're talking $500 to $700. The wheel went up the tree, then you read off the scale and that would tell you how many board feet the tree would yield. Fellows called cruisers went through woods and told buyers how much wood they could get out of an area. Speaking of wood, we have big Norway pines here. We have loggers in here all the time wanting to cut them for telephone poles. They send them into Canada to be made into poles and then they get shipped back. All the loggers see is the money in those trees, but we plan to watch them fall and die."

70. NESTING LOON CABINS

HK

OWNER: Bill Fay

MANAGER: Sheila Harnden

ADDRESS: HC 65, Box 3974, Lincoln, ME 04457; 207-794-6002

SEASON: Year-round

ACCOMMODATIONS: Five cabins with outhouse, electric lights, refrigerator, gas stove, wood heat, porch; central bath and shower house; pets welcome

RATES: $30–73 per day per cabin; $215–511 per week per cabin

ACCESS: I-95 to exit 55 (Lincoln). In Lincoln, turn left at West Broadway, continue on Main Street, then turn right onto ME 6 east. Go 4.5 miles on ME 6; camps are on the left (sign).

Nesting Loon Cabins have a lived-in, year-round look. As you drive in, you pass a camper trailer, and a variety of other winter and summer, work and recreational vehicles. Construction work is progressing on a number of fronts around the small compound.

Sheila: "The original owner was Gerry Schrite from Pennsylvania, who built the biggest cabin, down by the water, around 1942 or 1943. We've been here since 1994. We liked the place because we could own our own land, it's only 10 minutes out of Lincoln, and it's within half an hour's drive of 13 lakes. We're on Caribou Pond, and only 4 miles to the Penobscot River for bass fishing. It's been written up in *Bassmasters* magazine. The Indian Nation has rights, I believe, to all the islands in the Penobscot. So it's fine for the public to go fishing in the river, but not to step foot on any of the islands, because that's Indian property. The Indian Nation we're talking about is located primarily in Old Town.

"Our camps are the only boat launch that's available for Caribou Pond, which is one of a chain of three ponds connected by waterways. There's Caribou, Egg, and Long Ponds. They cover about 825 acres and have a maximum depth of 46 feet, with smallmouth bass, white perch, and pickerel. All around the pond is paper-company land and on the pond there's a number of 'floating islands' of aquatic plant life where birds nest and flowers bloom. Our loon logo was designed by wildlife artist Bob Noonan and shows a loon nesting on one of these islands.

"In the fall we have guided hunts for bear, deer, and moose. There's also grouse, rabbit, and duck hunting that's good around here. For the winter, ITS 81 passes close by our cabins and only 4 miles farther east on Route 6 is Mount Jefferson for all-natural skiing. During the winter, we don't have running water in the cabins, but we provide water in plastic jugs, and our shower and bathhouse is heated and open year-round."

71. NICATOUS LODGE

AP/HK, SCA

OWNERS: Denise and Gary Betz Jr., Todd and Tim Twombly
ADDRESS: Box 100, Burlington, ME 04417; 207-732-4771
SEASON: Year-round
ACCOMMODATIONS: Nine log cabins with indoor plumbing and shower, gas lights, wood heat; four lodge rooms; pets welcome
RATES: $70 per person per day (AP); $70 per cabin per day (HK)
ACCESS: I-95 to exit 54 (Howland). Turn right onto ME 155 south. Cross US 2, then pick up ME 188 east to Burlington. Continue east on ME 188, following signs 14 miles to camp.

A gravel logging road bisects Nicatous: On one side is a lawn, complete with raised gardens, which leads to a long, wide dock and boats. An expanse of lake, dotted with islands, beckons beyond the cove. On the other side, perched at the top of a gentle incline, the generous front porch of the log main lodge offers a comfortable welcome. Beyond, nestled in a pine grove and fronting on Nicatous Stream, are the log cabins. The road leads across the stream and to another set of camps within view. It then continues dozens of miles into the wilderness again.

Todd: "Gary, Denise, and I talked about running something in the hospitality industry for years. We wanted to be in Maine, and I started looking in the Rangeley area." *Denise:* "Gary's dad found this, actually. He wanted us back East. With this being owned land we liked it." *Gary:* "Plus it has a year-round business. It just came up. Pete and Chris Norris, who'd bought the camps in 1984, were heading west. We flew out on April 28, 1997, and three weeks later we closed." *Denise:* "We decided immediately."

Todd: "We all are able to cook, and Gary is extremely handy outside. Denise and I take care of cooking and paperwork. Eventually we'll all do everything. We're all excited about getting out of working in a kitchen all the time."

Denise: "We've all been working in the hospitality industry. I also worked in a travel agency and cleaned condos—all stuff that leads up to this." *Gary:* "I grew up in a sporting camp, so I knew what to expect."

Todd: "The Norrises did a lot. They dug a well, kept the place up, so it was completely ready to go." *Denise:* "We're not going to change anything that drastic. I'm going to have a few theme rooms like moose, Indian, et cetera, upstairs here in the lodge for guests."

Todd: "A sporting camp in most people's minds is hunting and fishing, but we're expanding that a bit. We do the traditional, but branch out and offer rock climbing, mountain biking, cross-country skiing, ice climbing, to diversify our clientele. We also run specials. [Like the Norrises] we'll continue to put on weddings and special-occasion events, like a haunted hayride weekend in the fall and then Christmas get-togethers. We also do retreats, seminars, church groups, and family reunions. Recently we had a family game tournament and at the end they gave out trophies and we served prime rib. It was great! Then our lobster bake gets everyone at camp together."

Gary: "We're welcoming people from nearby [reservations required] who want to come in for dinner. We'll have this until the end of the fall. As for the recreation part, I hope to get my Master Guide license. We all hope to have recreational-guide licenses. I'm starting to put together a network of mountain-bike trails and will provide a map for people who want either easy, medium, or challenging rides."

Gary, Denise, Todd, and Tim requested that I use a previous interview with Chris and Pete Norris for background on the camps. *Gary:* "We're so new here, and they have such a long history with camping and with the place, they should really tell some of the story."

Chris: "Nicatous Lodge has been on this side of the stream and the other, over the wooden bridge, back and forth, a couple or three times since 1928. An old trapper used to live on the other side, at Porter Point, but it wasn't a business then. In 1953 Kate Chamberlain, the great-granddaughter of Horace Greeley, bought it for her husband's anniversary present. The people who owned the lodge over here became friendly with them, and to make a long story short, the Chamberlains ended up buying Nicatous Lodge. Then it was bought by the present owner of Porter Point Camps, Barry Tyne, who operated Nicatous from 1977 to 1984."

Pete: "At that point we were running Red River Camps. We sold Red River in 1979 when out-of-state people were buying up these businesses like crazy. A lot of camps went under; it was one of the most devastating times for the industry. Actually, that's partly why we all formed the Sporting Camp Association, to try to save the sporting-camp industry. I held various jobs after we sold, and Chris worked as well, but our son and daughter were becoming latchkey kids, and we didn't want that. One day, in 1984, I came home and said, 'I've had it. I've quit my job and we're going back into the woods.' Well, we told my parents that Nicatous was for sale. My father was sick at the time and he took my hand, looked right at me, and said, 'Don't let it get away.'"

Chris: "We came in and absolutely fell in love with the pine trees. You just don't see tall pines like this much anymore. Within a month we were here running the place. It was much better for our kids, Laura and Chuck, being together as a family."

Laura: "I don't know if you've spoken with any of the kids of sporting-camp owners, but when you live out in the woods, you don't have friends to go out and play with and stuff. So we had to entertain each other. We didn't have driver's licenses, but my parents had an old beat-up car and we'd drive around on these back dirt roads. We used to have a dump, and we'd go down about nine or ten o'clock, turn on the lights, and watch the bears feed. Just have the greatest time. You'd bring your friends in, 'Hey, let's go to the dump!' It was like going to the movies."

Pete: "The bottom line in this business is enjoyment. So if you can make people feel pleasure in the simple things, tell them stories and so on, then they'll relax, which is what they really want to do. My father was a sporting-camp owner for 20 years and a guide before that. And I don't think this really happened, but I like to say that it did. He sat me down and says, 'Well, son, I'll tell you this. If you want to have any chance for success in this business, you have to learn to tell a story. And remember, what you do is give 'em a 60/40 blend of truth and embellishment. And let them decide which part is true!'"

Lobster Pie

> 2 T butter, ¼ cup white wine, 1 well-packed cup lobster meat, ¾ cup thin cream, 3 T butter, 1 T flour, 2 egg yolks

In a small saucepan, add wine to 2 T butter; boil 1 minute. Add lobster and let stand. In a medium saucepan, melt 3 T butter, add flour, and stir until it bubbles. Remove from heat and slowly add cream, egg yolks, and wine drained from lobster. Place saucepan over hot water and cook, stirring constantly, until sauce is smooth and thick (the sauce may curdle if the water boils). Remove from heat and add lobster. Turn into a small pie dish and sprinkle with seasoned, crushed crackers or bread crumbs. Bake at 300 degrees for 10 minutes.

72. THE PINES

AP/HK, SCA

OWNERS: Steve and Nancy Norris

ADDRESS: PO Box 158, Grand Lake Stream, ME 04637; 207-796-5006
(summer, radio phone); 207-825-4431 (winter); web site: http//www.
thepineslodge.com

SEASON: May 1 through September 30

ACCOMMODATIONS: Five log cabins with outhouse (port-a-potty in cabin),
gas lights, woodstove, porch; two guest rooms in main lodge; two HK outpost cabins

RATES: $60 per person per day (AP); $380 per cabin per week (HK)

ACCESS: I-95 to exit 55. Proceed to Lincoln and go east on ME 6 to
Topsfield (about 40 miles). Take US 1 south about 15 miles. Turn right onto
the road to Grand Lake Stream, go about 10 miles to the village and then go
right at the Grand Lake Stream village store. Cross the bridge and take the
left fork. Go 11 miles to a left turn (sign). The last mile is a narrow driveway
along the shoreline of Lake Sysladobsis.

The Pines has the look of a homestead surrounded by tall pines and log
cabins. The main lodge is a two-story white-clapboard house with a
generous front lawn. The cabins are snug at the base of the pines out
on the peninsula or on the wooded side of the front yard. The Norris
children, Vanessa and Matthew, are an integral part of the camp scene.

Steve: "If you talk about the history of this place, it's been in one
family since 1938, and they had scrapbooks going back to 1891. The
original builders were the Shaw brothers from Canada." *Nancy:* "It was
built to be a sporting lodge. That was the original intent. It was fash-
ioned after a lodge up on the Miramichi River in Canada. Our guest
cabin on the point was the first to be built, in 1883, and then the lodge
was the year following. Can you imagine building a house like this
with no roads or anything in here? Boards all flat-sided, amazing!"
Steve: "They brought stuff in by a steamer that used to come down
from the head of this lake [Sysladobsis] to a big tannery in Grand Lake
Stream. I think they employed something like 2,000 people down
there, which at the time was just a metropolis. Now it's gone completely the other way and it's just a little fishing village."

Nancy: "Anyway, Shaw married a schoolteacher from Pennsylvania.
I bet she wondered what she was getting herself into!" *Steve:* "They
raised two little girls in here. The Shaws had it until the early 1900s.
Then the Chase family bought it and had it nearly 30 years. Then in

1938 the Lewis family purchased it and in '84 a niece of the Lewises' got it and kept it going until we purchased it in '91. The Lewises were 83 years old when they finished their last season, and in their later years—this is really intriguing—all the guests would come out back and help with the dishes. So our first year here a lot of the long-term guests returned, which we really appreciated. Well, all of a sudden they'd be up from the table, bringing their dishes out here, scraping them off, and we're thinking, what happened?! We weren't used to that because that was part of our service, you know. But they were such loyal guests, they wanted to help this old couple.

"Sysladobsis is a 9-mile lake with landlocked salmon in the spring and smallmouth bass the rest of the season. We have a remote pond you can hike to, and there are miles of interconnected lakes which make up what's called the Eastern Maine Canoe Trail.

"As far as our own history—you've heard the names Ruth and Charlie Norris many times, I'm sure. Briefly, Charlie, my dad, was a mechanic at the Boise Cascade mill, but he had a deep love for the woods and was a guide up at Pierce Pond Camps for years. His dream was that someday he'd own a set of camps. He and Floyd Cobb, Gary's father, were close friends and guided together. And old Floyd beat him to the punch by, I think, a day or two at buying Pierce Pond Camps. My dad was crushed. But as it turns out, years later, when he was 52, he decided to leave the mill—with eight children and hardly a penny in his pocket—to go to Kidney Pond in what is now Baxter State Park.

"At the time, 1968, Kidney Pond Camps didn't have the recognition, so it was a real risk. I was 8 years old then, the youngest, so I had the good fortune of growing up in the sporting-camp business. I was there the whole 20 years, except for a couple of years when I took a hiatus and stuck my toe into the outside world and didn't like it. I worked for the Farmers Home Administration—federal government, subsidized loans, forms in triplicate—working out of Caribou and Waterville [Maine]. I went to the University of Maine [Orono], Nancy went to University of Maine at Farmington." *Nancy:* "That's when we met. Steve's mother hired me as a waitress in '79 and I never left, basically! Steve and I got married in the meantime." *Steve:* "Woods romance." *Nancy:* "We got married in '83 at a church in East Millinocket, where I grew up, but we had our reception at Kidney Pond." *Steve:* "We closed camp a day or two early so we could make room for our wedding party. But Nancy organized that whole wedding with no phone, 30 miles from the nearest town, had—I don't know—a couple

Nancy and Steve Norris with their children at home at The Pines.

hundred people up there for the reception. It was great. It was crazy! I got thrown in off the camp dock by my brothers, tuxedo and all."

Nancy: "How we ended up here—it took five years of looking. We've flown, snowmobiled, walked, and driven into places." *Steve:* "We looked at 27 different sporting camps just to see what was on the market at different times. See, in '87 the state chose to revert Kidney Pond Camps, take it back. The family had leased it, so we had no equity. And they just didn't renew the lease, so we were basically left out in the cold. Mom and Dad were retirement age anyway and Dad was ill, but, we wanted to be at Kidney Pond. That's why we had put our time in. But it wasn't to be."

Nancy: "We had in our minds just the right place we wanted. We just didn't find it until we found this. We'd heard about The Pines from the previous owners. They were interested in having us manage it, so we thought we might as well go have a look. I said to Steve, 'You know what's going to happen? We're going to drive in and it's going to be the place we always wanted. And it's not going to be for sale.' And that's exactly what happened. We drove in and it was like, this is it! That was in 1990." *Steve:* "They wanted us to work for them, but we wanted equity." *Nancy:* "We didn't want to manage for someone else. If we're going to work this hard, we want to work for ourselves."

Steve: "We knew the business, we had clientele, we wanted to find our own place and get the ball rolling. I mean, each year that mailing list would stale on us a little bit more and people would go to other sporting camps. Fortunately, we were able to buy the place from them and start in. One point that's crucial for young couples like us, with limited funds, is that it's hard enough to buy a house, to say nothing of a big business with property. To go in and buy a property like this and operate with limited revenue, especially seasonally, is really a hard ticket."

Nancy: "We're doing our winter jobs to allow us to do our business in the summer. A lot of people find seasonal jobs in the summer. Our seasonal jobs are really in the winter."

Steve: "Our kids' grandparents spend time in here with us. My mother spent several summers here and loved it." *Nancy:* "Steve and I spent a lot of good years with her at Kidney Pond. But it's a hard business to be in if you're sick or of retirement age. The equity you earn, and then in order to realize it you have to sell, thus leaving what you love. It's really not quite right."

Steve: "We have a radio phone here, which runs off batteries that are charged by solar panels up on the roof, DC power. We can supplement that with the generator if we have a big stretch of cloudy weather. It's all pretty basic. A man is inclined to love this sporting-camp life and everything. But to find the girl that can come in behind the scenes and love the kind of life, too, that's a special woman." *Nancy:* "You have to have a man who's handy as well. It has to be the right combination for both."

Steve: "See this steep stairwell here in the kitchen? It was built back in the 1880s by Bill Shaw, the guy with the two little girls, right? Seems he went up the lake in the winter of 1907, and they found him the next spring, frozen in the ice. Left that family . . . Well, he used to come downstairs this way a lot, I guess. Now, this door here has a nice sturdy latch and all of a sudden, with no wind, no one walking on boards, without anything, it would just pop open. That's serious! We watched it happen couple of years ago for the first time." *Nancy:* "So now every time we see it we say, 'Hi, Bill. How ya doin'?' *Steve:* "Ever since 1907, first the Chases, then the Lewises, and now us, we've all seen it. I don't know, it's crazy. So now when old Caribou Bill Shaw comes down, we figure, well, here he is to check us out and see if we're running the place right."

246 IN THE MAINE WOODS

Ruth's Plain Doughnuts

Beat 2 eggs. Add 1 cup sugar and 2 T shortening and beat. Add 1 tsp. nutmeg, 1 tsp. vanilla, and 1 cup buttermilk and stir. Sift 2 tsp. baking soda, 1 tsp. cream of tartar, and 3½–4 cups flour, or enough to make the dough the consistency to roll out. Roll out, cut with doughnut cutter, and fry in hot fat on one side until brown. Turn and cook on the other side till brown.

73. PORTER POINT CAMPS

HK
OWNER: Barry Tyne
ADDRESS: Burlington, ME 04417; 207-866-7849
SEASON: Year-round
ACCOMMODATIONS: Five cabins with indoor plumbing and shower, gas lights, gas stove, gas refrigerator, wood heat, fireplace; one outpost camp with outhouse, hand water pump
RATES: $40–55 per day per cabin; $180–300 per week per cabin
ACCESS: I-95 to exit 54 (Howland). Take ME 155 north and then 188 east through Burlington. From Burlington, go 8 miles to the end of the paved road and another 6 miles on the gravel road.

B*arry:* "I was working as a lawyer with my father in New Jersey in the '70s when I brought my wife, Joan, and two kids, Mike and Jennifer, up to Maine for a vacation. We went to Mount Desert Island and spent 13 days at a campground in a tent and it rained the entire time. As we drove back on Route 2 through Farmington, the sun came out, and it was warm and beautiful. We'd had a great time, in spite of the rain, and I started to think, 'If I'm such a hotshot, I should be able to live where I want to.'

"By Washington's birthday, we were on a farm in Wilton. A big beautiful place. I was practicing law in a small Maine town. The toughest part was leaving my father. But after a time I found myself peering out the window a lot. One day I was standing at my office window on a sleeting day, looking at a town road truck go by, and I silently said to the driver, 'How lucky you are.' I really loved working outside. And it was then I realized that it wasn't a change of location, but of avocation, that I was looking for.

"Shortly after that, one Sunday morning in 1976, I was reading the paper and saw an ad for Nicatous Camps, on both sides of the

Barry and Mike Tyne

stream, for sale. On Monday we took a ride in and in February 1977 we closed. I sold my law practice and we moved in. In 1984, when Brian was born, Joan said, 'I'm out of the kitchen.' The kitchen was really a job. So we sold Nicatous to Chris and Pete Norris and signed keeping. I have my own set of loyal guests, so it really isn't a problem. We're on the northern end of Nicatous Lake here, at the outlet where there's a dam and fishway. The lake is stocked with salmon. The Maine Coast Heritage Trust owns 500 feet back from the shoreline around the lake, so it's very pristine. Maine natives have the right of access onto the lake.

"Mike and Jennifer went to school from here. I'd drive out 12 miles for the bus each morning and then they'd have another 18 miles to go. It got hectic, with all the sports and no phone communication. Sometimes they'd get home at 9 o'clock. Sometimes I didn't know when they'd be getting home. I always brought a book in case I had to wait hours for them. They were both great students. Mike played football and at 14 left home to board at Maine Central Institute in Pittsfield. From there he went to Dartmouth and Yale Divinity School. He taught a couple of years, wrote a novel, and is a teaching assistant at the University of Maine [in Orono]. Jennifer went to Smith College and New England Law School and is a district attorney in Massachusetts. When they were kids they ran the little general store, which is the cabin nearest the logging road.

"We home-schooled Brian. Now it's just Brian and me here. Joan passed away in 1994. She was wonderful, a real trouper. She was willing to do anything. It's sad in here without her. When we were all in here together and owned the whole place, it seemed like our own little town. I'd go up and shovel roofs. I'd plow the road at 2 in the morning and see nothing but fox tracks go up the middle of the road. See the moon shining through the glistening trees. It was great! This life is very satisfying, very personal. I'm my own boss, the only one who has to be satisfied with my work."

74. RIDEOUT'S

AP/MAP/HK

OWNER: Bob and Anna Lorigan and Bob Lorigan Jr.

ADDRESS: East Grand Lake, Danforth, ME 04424; 207-448-2440

SEASON: May 1 through September 30

ACCOMMODATIONS: 20 cabins with indoor plumbing and shower, hot-water or propane-furnace heat, electric lights, some with porch; HK cabins have gas or electric stove, electric refrigerator; pets welcome

RATES: $70 per person per day (AP); $400–450 per cabin per week (HK)

ACCESS: I-95 to exit 55 to Lincoln, then ME 6 east to Springfield. From Springfield, take ME 169 to Danforth and then go 3 miles north on US 1 to the camp sign and driveway, on the right-hand side of the road.

As you drive into Rideout's you pass under a huge sign tacked up on a pine tree. A little village of cabins is to the right of the driveway and a large salmon-colored main lodge is to the left, right down at the water's edge and beside an expansive boat dock. Farther down the driveway and cove, and separated slightly from this main compound, is another set of cabins for guests going the housekeeping route. The main lodge's honey-colored, wood-paneled dining room has large picture windows looking out onto Grand Lake.

Bob Sr.: "We're right in the center of Grand Lake here, at Davenport Cove, and you look out these windows right into Canada [New Brunswick]. Larry Rideout was the first owner of these camps, and he developed 90 percent of what we do today. When he was in business, he catered to a lot of professionals and rich people. The president of L.L. Bean would come up frequently. [Rideout] owned it until 1964, when he sold to George Graham, who had it from '64 to '84, when he sold to us. We stayed only from '84 to '86, because we had two small kids at the time and it was too confining and demanding of our time. We lived at the place on the lake we've had since 1970 and sold the camps to a group of people who ran it until '95, when we got it back.

"We're from Pennsylvania and have five kids and nine grandchildren. I'm an ex-military man, and we've been in the area, like I say, since 1970. This is a demanding business. You open up at 6 AM and finish most days in season around 10:30. I'm in the senior-citizen category, so we appreciate the help our kids have given us. Plus we have six full-time and four part-time staff.

"I've seen some differences in things over the years we've been here. The last 10 years or so we've seen a 50 percent drop in boat rentals, so we're having to charge a dock-rental fee, for people bringing their own boats. Another thing is we're ending up with more and more in the middle-income group, who tend toward the housekeeping. And the third change regards help. The cost of doing business now is out of sight. Workmen's comp and insurance costs are terrible. It just all adds up. And then there's the paperwork that's now required. I spend four hours a day on paperwork, and that's no joke. So in order to keep our costs down, so we can keep the cost down for our guests, we're never operating with everyone we need.

Food at Maine sporting camps is famous. Here, baking bread at Rideout's.

"We serve the general public out of our restaurant [for dinner only, by reservation]. It's Down East cooking and basically the menu hasn't changed in 40 years—New England boiled dinner, rib-eye steaks cooked on the open fire, roast pork, which I guess we're famous for, because you can't get a seat in here most Wednesday nights. We also serve barbecued chicken, baked ham, pot roast, and every Sunday we have a traditional Thanksgiving dinner.

"We're here because we appreciate the area and our guests. We have some coming over 24 years who are real practical jokers and the whole camp does nothing but laugh the whole time." *Buck Plummer (Guide):* "To give you an example, one guest came into the lodge here at 3 AM and put teaspoons on every blade of our ceiling fans. When the girls came in and turned on the switch, they got rained on by a bunch of teaspoons! Then these folks, Vinnie and Ginny, dress up in costume— one year we had a George and Martha Washington outfit—and go cruising around the lake. You see the big iron skillet hanging on the wall? We have our meals at certain hours and our evening meal is at 6. Well, Vinnie had set an alarm clock in there to go off a little after 6. Of course, nobody knew where it was coming from. The whole dining room went quiet. 'Course he was deadpan, looking around just like everyone else. The cabin girls get in on the practical jokes, too, of course. And one time they sewed lace on a pair of his underpants. Not to be outdone, he wore them over his regular pants into the dining room for dinner. Say he's down in English Cove and the fishing's slow, he'll just reel in and take off full speed across the lake looking for people. A couple of years ago he saw some people over in Haley Cove, went all the way up to them practically full throttle—the waves are going and the guys in the boat are looking like, oh my God, what's the matter—you know. He leans over, looks at them, and says, 'Excuse me. Do you have any Grey Poupon on board?' The two poor fellows were just standing there, holding their arms up, 'Well, no . . .' 'Thank you,' he says, and tears off to the other side of the lake! That same day he lost his bait pail—this gets so involved, talking about Vinnie and Ginny. They usually have a theme when they come up. That year it was Christmas. They came into camp and put a big wreath in the dining room and hung Christmas bells and everything outside their cabin. So everyone knew, well, this year is Christmas. So after they did the Grey Poupon thing, and lost the bait pail, I dressed up in a Santa Claus outfit and went out on the lake looking for them. It was over 85 degrees out, and the girls all had elf suits on and of course there were a lot of boaters out on the lake, fishing. Well, we're just going along waving at everybody, and here it is June! We finally found Vinnie and Ginny and gave them their Christmas present, which they thoroughly appreciated.

"Then there was the famous bird routine. There was a couple—we haven't seen them for a number of years now, and I hope this didn't have anything to do with that!—but the lady was an avid birdwatcher. Every morning she'd go out birding. Well, Vinnie had this little artificial bird that was a thousand different colors. Strangest thing you ever saw. He got me to put it up in this tree for him, way at the top. And every morning he'd come into the dining room and tell this lady about this particular bird he'd seen. She was wracking her brain, going nuts because she didn't know this bird he was describing. Well, he fed her this information for a week and she walked underneath that tree, right by the lodge, and never looked up in it. So finally, the last day, he goes out and says, 'Aha! I see the bird,' and shows it to her. But that gives you an idea. And we can dish it out, too. Screw a quarter into the floor of their cabin, tie their chairs to the dining room table, that kind of thing.

"One year I made snowballs during the winter and saved them in the freezer. We lined up on the dock and when they came in, we pelted him with snowballs. Same thing with water balloons."

Bob: "People have such a good time, that's why we're here. They're not here just to fish, but to see old friends, and that's a big part of the atmosphere. It's like a class reunion. Basically, we think we're reasonably priced, clean, have a good restaurant, and a beautiful spot."

Oatmeal Bread

The Lorigans say: "This bread recipe has been handed down and doctored up here and there. People come from all around and ask for it. They'll order loaves of it when they come in for dinner."

> 2 cups oatmeal, 1 cup molasses, ¼ cup sugar, 2 T salt, ⅓ cup oil, 4 cups boiling water, 10 cups bread flour, 4 T dry yeast

Put first five ingredients in a large, heat-proof bowl and pour the boiling water over everything. Stir and let set 45 minutes until lukewarm. Meanwhile, put yeast into ½ cup lukewarm water (it will rise and bubble up). Add this to the lukewarm first mixture. Add the flour and mix well (we use a machine, so 10 cups works for us). Knead until smooth, and place in a greased bowl. Cover or let set away from cold drafts until the dough has doubled in bulk. Punch down, divide into eight equal balls, and place two balls per greased loaf pan. Cover until risen over the top of the bread pan. Bake at 350 degrees for 35–40 minutes, until golden and bread sounds hollow. Take out of the oven and butter the tops of the bread. Makes 4 loaves.

75. SPRUCE LODGE CAMPS

MAP/HK/AP

OWNERS: Ron and Kat Bradford

ADDRESS: RR 1, Box 716, Springfield, ME 04487; 207-738-3701

SEASON: May through November; January through March

ACCOMMODATIONS: Four log cabins with indoor plumbing, shower, electric lights, automatic heat, woodstove (in one cabin), gas stoves, refrigerators; pets allowed

RATES: $25–65 per person per day; $350 per cabin per day

ACCESS: I-95 to exit 55 and bear right onto the access road (cross the Penobscot River). When you come to the flashing red light, turn left onto Route 2. Follow Route 2 through Lincoln to the traffic light/monument. Turn left at the stop light. Go ⅛ mile to a fork and bear right onto Route 6. Go about 20 miles, through Springfield. At the top of a hill, turn right (camp sign on right). Go 6 miles, then turn right onto a dirt road (at camp sign). Go 2 miles to the camp driveway.

Spruce Lodge Camps form a small compound at the head of Lower Sysladobsis ("Dobsis") Lake.

Kat: "These camps have been in operation nearly a hundred years. They were called Bayview Camps originally, and we have the old brochure from when Joseph Patten was the owner." A quote from the brochure describes the camps much as they would be described today: ". . . situated on high land on the shore of the lake, and consisting of the main house and a separate building or annex containing five good rooms, and several log cabins. The sleeping rooms and cabins are all furnished with good spring beds, mattresses and easy chairs. The camps have open fires and there is a parlor or living room for guests."

Kat: "Dobsis Lake is 11 miles long and is part of a huge waterway that was used by the Penobscot Indians when they traveled from the Atlantic Ocean to the Great Lakes. We have lake and stream fishing here with landlocked salmon, smallmouth bass, white perch, pickerel, and brook trout. The wildlife around here is amazing: loons, eagles, osprey, cormorants, and ducks. Sometimes in the early morning you can see a beaver or muskrat swimming around the docks. Deer and moose are also around here, because we have apple trees and berry bushes.

"We have housekeeping cabins, which are great for families—and we get a lot of families. But we also serve meals in our dining room for those who don't want to do all their own cooking. For those who do, and need supplies, Smith's Grocery Store is 8 miles from camp on good roads.

"In our main lodge we have a mounted rack of what we believe to be the largest white-tail deer ever taken in the State of Maine. It has a modest rack—13 points—but holds the state record and has been written up in the newspaper as holding the national record for the largest deer. It dressed out at 463 pounds: My husband's grandmother and grandfather got it in the mid-fifties!

"Also in the lodge we have a telephone for our guests, and we provide daily mail service. We're close to churches, a hospital, and major tourist attractions such as Baxter State Park, and yet we're tucked off here in this cover where it feels like there isn't anyone else in the world."

76. VILLAGE CAMPS

HK

OWNERS: Lance and Georgie Wheaton

ADDRESS: HC 81, Box 101, Forest City, ME 04413; 207-448-7726; fax: 207-448-7726; Web site: http://www.mainerec.com/village2.html

SEASON: Year-round

ACCOMMODATIONS: Six log cabins (one or two bedrooms) with electric lights, well water, indoor plumbing and shower, gas furnace or wood heat, gas or electric stove

RATES: Spring and summer $27–75 per cabin per day; $340–450 per cabin per week

ACCESS: I-95 to exit 55 (Lincoln). From Lincoln, take ME 6 east to Topsfield (40 miles). Turn left at Topsfield onto US 1 north to Brookton (8 miles). Turn right at the sign to Forest City and go 12 miles. Camps are on the left; there's a sign in front of the white house.

The Village Camps line either side of the driveway behind Lance and Georgie Wheaton's white clapboard house. Cabins lead down to a small quite cove where guests can look out over East Grand Lake at the sunsets. Although they are next door to the camps owned by Lance's brother Dale (Wheaton's Lodge), you cannot see one from the other because of the cove. In addition, each camp has a distinct feel and look all its own. Wheaton's cabins are gray clapboard; the Village Camps' are dark-stained log. Wheaton's is a larger, American Plan seasonal operation with many guides; the Village Camps is a smaller, housekeeping, year-round business.

Georgie: "This place was built as housekeeping cottages in the '50s by a couple of buddies and were originally called the Ed and Don Cottages. We've been here since April 1969. My husband, Lance, was born and brought up right down the road, where Dale and Jana [Wheaton] are. He's the middle of the three brothers; the oldest is a vice president of Remington Arms. We'd been married about a year and a half, were working in Connecticut, and had just come back to Forest City from a fishing trip when Lance's folks said this place was for sale. I was young and foolish, so here we are! I knew practically nothing about fishing. I'm from Sherman, so I do know the out-of-doors, and my brothers were into fishing, but I never was. So when we started running the camps I was doing things like calling fishing rods 'fishing poles' until Lance said, 'Look, if you're going to be running a sporting camp, you'd better start learning what these things are

Georgie and Lance Wheaton and one of Lance's handcrafted Grand Lakes canoes

called.' Which I did. And I also learned the names of the various flies right off.

"We raised three daughters here, and it really was good for them in many ways. It's a safe, healthy environment, and they're very people-oriented because they've been around a lot of people all their lives. The downside has been that we're so far from 'civilization.' They had to travel 24 miles, one way, to school each day. And they had to miss out on a lot of events. But I think it has made them stronger and more self-reliant. Because we live in an unorganized territory, the state provides tuition for the school of our choice plus gives transportation money, which can then be applied toward boarding a student. This is what we're doing with our youngest daughter now.

"I'm happy that we can offer people the option of housekeeping cottages. We have a lot of professional people coming here, so it's not simply a matter of money. Some guests just don't like to be confined by certain eating hours. They figure, if the fish are biting, they don't want to have to hurry back for a meal. For guests going out with a guide, we prepare a shore dinner and sometimes when we have families in during the summer, we'll have a camp potluck supper down by the rec hall cookout area.

Lance: "We're a four-season place here. In the winter we actually

have more ice fishing than snowmobiling. I spend my time stocking
our ice shacks with wood for guests. It's good fishing here, as always—
some of the best anywhere. In the fall there's hunting. Although, I have
to say, the deer population is down due to the wood cutting and the
coyotes. I go out and do some bird hunting. We don't kill many birds
generally, but we have a lot of fun just wandering around in the woods.
I mean, there's more to hunting than killing. It's not like fishing, catch-
and-release. There's no such thing as shoot-and-release. So most of
us just enjoy the chance to be outside on a nice fall day.

"My grandfather, Arthur, built canoes, and my father built canoes,
so I figured I might as well. I've been making 21-foot Grand Laker canoes, 52 of them so far. I'm old-fashioned and stubborn and never
wanted to copy what anyone else had done, so I built a mold myself.
But I hated the canoe, the way it handled, so I made a second mold the
next winter. I changed it seven times until I got what I wanted. No
more changes now, it's a dream—rides well and is safe with a load. I
want a canoe that can do the job for the guides, one they can afford
and use without a lot of repairs. My canoes are all handmade. The
ribs and lining are northern white cedar, the thwarts are ash, the gun-
whales are spruce, because they hold their shape, and the heel, stern,
and stem are out of white oak. I'll use about 4 or 5 pounds of tacks
for a canoe. My bows are indented slightly to split the water in a clean
arch. To make it, you 'strake'—or cut, trim, and plane—all the individual pieces of wood to a different taper to lay and fit into the bow.
A Grand Laker canoe has a square stern, is generally 18 to 21 feet
long, with a 40- to 44-inch beam, and 16 to 20 feet deep. It is rib-built,
which means there are pieces of northern white cedar that are bent to
go all the way around the canoe for strength. When I take an order for
a canoe, I tell my customer, 'I do this because I love to, and I make
canoes when I have the time. I know you're on the list, and every
time you call to ask me when I'm going to be done, I'll add $100 to
the price.' That usually lets me do my work in peace. Then, when
I've finished a canoe and hand it over to my client, I tell them with a
grin, 'Don't forget, the green side goes down!'"

Lance has been putting down some of his remembrances and
someday hopes to compile them into a book. In the meantime, here are
two of his stories:

"One day my father and I were in the shop when a fellow stopped by
to say hello. While we were talking, the man looked over to a rack of
axes we had on the wall. He said that the ax on the bottom of the rack

looked really old, and father said that it had been in our family for over a hundred years. 'I've had to change the head on it three times,' my father added, 'and the handle nine times.' The man nodded and left the shop. We don't know if he ever realized that it wasn't a very old ax!

"Another time, I was guiding a couple from New York City and we were out fishing for salmon on East Grand Lake. It was an overcast day in early spring with light mist in the air. The water was flat calm. If any of you have ever fished on that kind of day, you'll know what I'm talking about. The water with the mist had streaks across the top of it. Now, what makes these streaks is beyond me, but I've seen them a million times. About midmorning the lady in the party keeps looking at the lake and finally turns around and asks me, 'Lance, what are those streaks out on the water?' Without thinking I answered, 'Oh, that's where a car drove on the ice last winter.' She looked around for a moment and then said, 'Isn't that amazing they would stay there that long.' With that I was in so deep, I didn't dare reply!"

77. WEATHERBY'S

AP/MAP, SCA

OWNERS: Charlene and Ken Sassi
CAMP ADDRESS: Grand Lake Stream, ME 04637; 207-796-6668
WINTER ADDRESS: RR 1, Box 2272, Kingfield, ME 04947-9729; 207-237-2911
SEASON: May 1 through October 1
ACCOMMODATIONS: 15 log cabins with indoor plumbing and shower, gas or electric lights, screened-in porch, gas heat
RATES: $95–120 per person per day (AP); $85–110 per person per day (MAP)
ACCESS: I-95 to exit 55 (Lincoln). From Lincoln, take ME 6 east to Topsfield. Turn right and take US 1 south for about 15 miles. Turn right onto Grand Lake Stream Road and go about 10 miles to Grand Lake Stream. The camps will be on your right when you reach the village (sign).

Weatherby's is set back on a knoll in the center of the village of Grand Lake Stream. A gracious white farmhouse with wraparound porch welcomes guests. The cabins, a mixture of shapes and styles, range around the top and one side of the knoll. The camps are within walking distance of the village store, the stream, and the boat landing for the lake.

Charlene: "Weatherby's originally was built because the largest tannery in the world was here in Grand Lake Stream. The tannic acid from the hemlock bark was very plentiful in the area and people would come to Grand Lake to have their hides tanned. Places like Weatherby's, which originally was called the White House in the Birches, were built in the late 1800s to house the people who'd come and have to wait four to six months for their hides to be tanned. They would come and, you know, leave a little bit in the area. The English and Scottish ancestry is strong, although now there's no particular ethnic group."

According to historian Minnie Atkinson's book *Hinckley Township:*

> The tannery was built in 1870 and bark camps were established on the shores of the upper lakes. Two or three hundred men were employed at these camps in a summer season as well as 400 pairs of horses for bark hauling. Forty cords of bark were consumed in a single day as well as 25 barge-loads of imported tan extract per week. Another 200 to 300 men worked at the tannery itself. Sometimes 1200 hides would be finished in a day. On May 11, 1887, fanned by a tremendous wind, four main tannery buildings were flat ruins in 45 minutes and ice in the lake, still a foot and a half thick, was broken and driven to the foot of the lake. In 1898 the tannery was closed. The White House, which had accommodated a few sportsmen, was sold in 1895 to Stephen Yates, son of the first pioneer in the area, and the number of sportsmen visiting increased.

Charlene: "My involvement with sporting camps goes back to my parents, Ruth and Charlie Norris, who were in the business at Kidney Pond Camps at Baxter State Park. Back in 1901, the Balls from Massachusetts bought the camps and put in cabins and a garage. It was called Balls Camps for many years. Then Mr. Rutherford Weatherby from New Brunswick bought it and ran it for 33 years. His son, Beverly Weatherby, the gentleman we bought it from, had it for 25 years. When we first bought the place, in 1974, we didn't have much money. We signed the papers in September and had a couple of weeks' work. But we had no business all winter. None. I mean, no food, nothing! We wondered what we had done. Ken's an engineer and he had dropped all that to go into the woods. It was a little scary that first winter, believe me, living in this big old place, with two kids, and trying to heat it. Our daughter, Jessica, was 12 and our son, Mark, 6 at the time. So it was a little tough for them. They bused 23 miles to the town of Woodland for school. We were just waiting for our first

An evening's entertainment with friends at Weatherby's

season—couldn't wait to see what would happen!

"That first winter, nobody came to visit. I was shocked! I thought in a little town people would love to meet the new folks. They didn't. I'd stand in the post office and say, 'Isn't anyone my neighbor?' That's the truth! Really, I was terrible. We all laugh about it now. People are very skeptical, you know—new people, oh! Well, the neat part was that we were Mainers, you see. And that's what saved us all these years, even in the town. After a few years they finally accepted us, and now we're perfectly accepted. They can't wait to see how the summer will be, because if they work or don't depends on how our business is. Both our children will be coming into the business as limited partners to continue what we've been doing here all these years. So this provides the family traditions and continuity for our guests.

"I do all the cooking. For breakfast, I'll go into my special pastry room, with its baking oven, and start to make muffins and cook bacon or sausage. When we're cooking for 40 and want to get it done, if the guests come right in, I can feed them in 20 minutes—and that's to order, anything they want! After breakfast we have a staff meeting and plan our day. We have to be very organized so that we have time in the middle of the day, because there are no days off. Sometimes we don't know—other than that the menu changes—what day it is! Some weeks I don't go off this lot, and that's the truth. I love to garden. So when everyone's off and I have a few minutes, I go into my flower garden—that's my time.

"For the past few years we've had the intermediate L.L. Bean fly-fishing school here. They come in on a Thursday and it finishes up late Monday afternoon. It's for stream fishing mostly and they give people a day out on the lake as well. It's for 12 to 14 students with four instructors. A couple of the instructors come up early to see what's going on in the stream, to check the amount of water coming through the dam."

Ken: "There's a salmon hatchery here. They run cold water through it, which helps keep the stream a little cooler. I've been working with Georgia-Pacific to regulate the water flow. The paper companies are becoming aware that they affect a lot of people when they change the flow pattern. As the temperature of the water gets hotter, the trout and salmon become stressed and it's harder to catch them. A few years ago, between the seasons of the school, we had a really major change where the paper company opened up two gates in the dam and the water went up by about a foot and a half. It really made it hard for the fish and for the students until things got settled in. Right below the hatchery is a well-known pool, Hatchery Pool, and it gets fished a lot.

"We have 25 or 30 registered Maine guides, the most of any sporting camp. And they all have to be approved by me. Grand Lake is one of the best fishing areas in the Northeast. We have landlocked salmon, lake and brook trout, smallmouth bass, white perch, and pickerel. You can have a pack lunch or go out with a guide in one of our Grand Lake canoes and enjoy a guide's cookout. We have a monument right in town that's dedicated to our guides from Grand Lake, and every last weekend in July we have a folk art festival dedicated to the Grand Laker canoe."

Guide's Cookout: Fish with Hush Puppies

Fish cooked in tinfoil: Use 1–2 pounds of fish (any kind). Scale and clean the fish. Remove the eyes. Salt and pepper the stomach cavity. Add two slices of lemon. Fold the tinfoil over the fish and cook it slowly over hot coals 15 minutes on each side. Serve with hush puppies.

Hush Puppies: Mix 1 egg and 1 cup cornmeal with enough water to make a mixture thick enough to drop off a spoon. Heat fat in frying pan over an open fire. Drop the batter by spoonful into the fat and fry until golden on each side.

78. WHEATON'S LODGE AND CAMPS

AP, SCA

OWNERS: Dale and Jana Wheaton
CAMP ADDRESS: Forest City, ME 04413; 207-448-7723
WINTER ADDRESS: PO Box 261, East Holden, ME 04429; 207-843-5732
SEASON: May through September
ACCOMMODATIONS: 10 cabins, indoor plumbing and shower, electric lights, automatic heat, screened-in porch
RATES: $78 per person per day
ACCESS: I-95 to exit 55 (Lincoln). From Lincoln, take ME 6 east to Topsfield (40 miles). In Topsfield, turn left onto US 1 and go north to Brookton (8 miles). Turn right at the sign to Forest City and go 12 miles. The camps are at the end of the road through the village.

D*ale:* "My father, Woody Wheaton, started these camps in 1952. He was quite a well-known guide and his roots go to Grand Lake Stream. My mother's sister was Alice Weatherby, and they sold Weatherby's to Ken and Charlene Sassi. My uncle Bev's father, Rutherford Weatherby, was one of the original owners of Grand Lake Stream—my father guided for him. Then Bev Weatherby came up here and guided for my father and now me. So my family's been in the sporting-camp business for what must be 65 years.

"My mother graduated from Massachusetts College of Art and taught painting. You'd never know she was a sporting-camp person, but she's strong on the inside work. Every good sporting camp involves a strong woman—it has to. I was 2 when my folks started Wheaton's and I have two brothers. We all grew up in the stern seat of a canoe. We got on the map in the late '50s by virtue of some articles in *Outdoor Life*. At that time Spednic Lake was regarded as the best smallmouth bass lake in the world. As you market yourself in the accommodations business, you have to carve out what your strength is and specialize. And our strength is fishing, splendid fishing. You can get bass one day and landlocked salmon the next. We've been written up by *Sports Afield* as one of the best fishing lodges in North America. A 4-pound smallmouth bass is considered a trophy fish in every state in the union and we catch 25 or 30 at our lodge every year, almost all of which are released. The lake we're on, East Grand Lake, is 18 miles long and flows into Spednic, which is 25 miles long. They're the largest of the Chiputneticook chain of lakes, which form the boundary with Canada. In the course of a summer we'll fish 10 or 12 different lakes."

Jana: "We met at the University of Maine. I never really went out with Dale until the night before graduation, so it was a near miss. I went on to teach physical education, and he was writing his thesis in economics at the University of Nottingham, England. His folks, when they were ready to sell, approached all the 'kids' to see if we were interested. At that point, none of us were. We were kind of young and I don't think ready for that kind of responsibility. Maybe we realized that somehow." *Dale:* "The sporting-camp business puts quite a strain on a marriage, particularly if you're young and just crawling out of college, when kids are little." *Jana:* "Anyway, his folks sold to a young couple, and they ran it for three years, and that ended in divorce. At that point, in early '79, we decided we wanted to get into it. The first year was difficult, trying to learn the business, being a manager, and trying to keep everyone happy. There were many nights I went to bed in tears and Dale had to deal with that on top of a day of guiding and all." *Dale:* "There are really only two or three of us with sporting camps that guide full time. It's probably not fair to Jana, but that's my first love, being in a canoe. We usually have a chore boy, but if something breaks down, it falls back to me." *Jana:* "When he gets in. Otherwise I deal with it, too."

Dale: "For example, we've got regular commercial power." *Jana:* "But we were forever losing it—a bird landing on the wire in Canada, where we get the power—it wouldn't take much." *Dale:* "So Jana finally laid down the law: 'I want a generator, I want dug wells. I'm outta here without this stuff.'" *Jana:* "I found that worked nicely. If I threatened to leave and never come back, things somehow seemed to get done."

Dale: "At least they got way up on the list!"

Dale: "Jana's got a good crew of six or eight people and most of them have been with us at least 14 years. And I have up to 10 or 12 guides a day. My guides are loyal to me and very competent. One of the biggest roles I do at camp, and one that's very obscure, is to match guides to guests. I never assign anyone until I've sat down and talked with people, what their expectations are, what their skill levels are, to see if I can match them in personality with the guide. Some guides are tuned into the fishery, some are tremendous with kids, some are conversant on an intellectual level, and some are happy-go-lucky. If I can match that up and then let that sail, things take care of themselves. Each guide carries his own, as the Indian called it, wanigan bag and his ax. He's self-contained. Most guides nowadays carry a little wood with them, although my father would've kicked my ass until my nose bled if I'd ever done anything like that! In a wanigan bag you've got seven articles—a long-handled, large tin fry pan, a small fry pan, a potato pot with a cover, two broilers or grills, and a coffeepot. The guides cook a full meal every day—steaks, chops, or chicken, plus the fish caught in the morning, potatoes and onions, and coffee. Plus the camp cook makes homemade bread and pie, so it's a big meal. It's a case of pride that the guide cooks fish for his meal.

"You know what the dingle was in the old logging camps? It was the building or shed that went from where the men slept to where they ate, and was where they stored food outside."

Mark Danforth (Guide): "The 'dingle stick' is a long stick that hangs off a campfire to hold the pots and pans. It's made out of a hardwood, mostly green so that it doesn't catch fire. And you make a small, hot fire, not what the Indians called a white man's fire, which was so big you can't get close to it to get warm. The other thing we use is a hookeroon. That's a stick with a branch cut off short at the bottom to pick up your pots when the handles are hot." *Dale:* "You always use the hookeroon to take the grub off the dingle stick." *Alice:* "This is great! So what do you call the thing you use to turn the fish?" *Dale:* "A fork."

Mark: "I started guiding in the summer of '86. What Dale does with his young, green guides is he sends you out in parties where there might be six people in a group and two veteran guides along. That way the younger guide, especially at lunch, gets a little practice and learns how to do things 'Dale Wheaton's Way,' which is usually the right way. He'll do that maybe six or eight times, and then [the guide is] out on his own. Normally, his first time out, Dale will give him a

Mark Danforth prepares a Guides' Lunch at Wheaton's

veteran client, someone who's been here before and can keep a green guide straight and who's understanding. Dale has very good judgment and knows what he's looking for in a guide. The focus is on the traditional ways—nothing high-tech. We do things different in Forest City than they do in Grand Lake Stream, even though there's only about 40 miles separating us. The way we fillet a perch, for example—they wouldn't take the bones out, they'd take the ribs out. This jackknife here's a guide's most valuable tool. With that and an ax, you can do just about anything. But you don't want to pick up another man's ax. It's a superstition, I suppose, but a strong one. Dale and Jana are a great team. Jana is one of the biggest reasons Wheaton's is successful, because she does most of the work around the camp."

Jana: "Well, I guess I'll tell you the story of the blueberry buckle. That was during the hard times, the early years. Sometimes we'd only have five or six people in camp, but it would run us ragged because the two of us were covering all the bases. Anyway, I was cooking and we had some unexpected company. I had just cleaned the oven and put a blueberry buckle in to cook. I had all kinds of things on my mind and was trying to be cordial to these people. Well, about the time Dale got in off the lake, my blueberry buckle boiled over." *Dale:* "It buckled." *Jana:* "All over my clean oven. I was at the end of my rope. Well, I went out on the back porch and chucked that buckle as far as I could chuck it. I mean, blueberry all over everything—the tree, the porch. Then I had a few choice words for Dale. Then I got into our Volkswagen—this is before kids—and went hell-bent for election out the road. Well, I got 5 miles out of town and started feeling sorry for Dale, because dinner was about an hour and a half away and I had left him high and dry. So I turned around and came back. Dale was standing in the kitchen with a cookbook open, wondering how he was going to put a meal together."

Dale: "If you're going to be a successful sporting-camp operator, you have to commit yourself for a lifetime. It's your first love. I'm on the advisory committee to the Northern Forests Land Council, which is trying to protect the band of woods that runs across from eastern Maine to the Adirondacks. And we've established the Woody Wheaton Land Trust to protect our beautiful environment around here. The main point is that everyone has to have a reverence for what's out there, because it will slip away very quickly.

"I think the key to our business is to make it fun. Not just for the people, but the staff, too, and with that kind of attitude you can have a great time. We say with a grin that people come to sporting camps for a change and to rest—the camp gets the change and the guide gets the rest! But it's completely true that people come back here— decades, some—mostly just to unwind and have a good time. Now, I bet your readers would like to know how to earn a small sporting-camp business." *Alice:* "Sure!" *Dale:* "Well, first you start out with a small fortune . . ."

Blueberry Buckle

> ¾ cup sugar, ½ cup shortening, 1 egg, 2½ cups flour, 2½ tsp. baking powder, ½ tsp. salt, ½ cup milk, 2 cups blueberries, ½ cup sugar, ½ tsp. cinnamon, ¼ cup butter

Beat sugar and shortening until fluffy. Add egg and beat well. Combine 2 cups flour, baking powder, and the salt. Add flour mixture and milk alternately to batter and beat until smooth after each addition. Spread in a greased 8x8x2-inch pan. Top with blueberries. Combine remaining ½ cup flour, ½ cup sugar, and cinnamon. Cut in butter (or margarine) until crumbly. Sprinkle over blueberries. Bake at 350 degrees for 45 minutes.

FURTHER READING

Listed below are books and reference materials that were either mentioned to me during my interviews with sporting-camp owners, were available at the sporting camps I visited, or were used in connection with compiling this book.

Anderson, Gareth, and John F. Marsh. *You Alone in the Maine Woods: The Lost Hunter's Guide.* Augusta, Me.: Maine Department of Inland Fisheries and Wildlife, 1983.

The Appalachian Mountain Club. *AMC Maine Mountain Guide.* Boston: Appalachian Mountain Club, 1995.

Atkinson, Minnie. *Hinckley Township or Grand Lake Stream Plantation.* Newburyport, Mass.: Newburyport Press, c. 1918.

Bennett, Dean. *Maine's Natural Heritage: Rare Species and Unique Natural Features.* Camden, Me.: Down East Books, 1988.

Clark, Stephen. *Katahdin: A Guide to Baxter State Park and Katahdin.* Thorndike, Me.: Thorndike Press, 1985.

Coatsworth, Elizabeth. *The Enchanted: An Incredible Tale.* Nobleboro, Me.: Blackberry Books, 1992.

Cobb, Gary, and Alfred H. Fenton. *The History of Pierce Pond Camps* (1992) Gary Cobb, North New Portland, Me. 04961.

Cole, Stephen A. *Maine Sporting Camps.* Manuscript on file with the Maine Historic Preservation Commission, 55 Capitol Street, Augusta, Me. 04330.

Eckstorm, Fannie Hardy. *The Penobscot Man.* Juniper Press, 1978.

Farrar, Charles A.J. *Farrar's Illustrated Guide Book to the Androscoggin Lakes.* New York: Charles T. Dillingham, 1881.

Fendler, Donn, as told to Joseph B. Egan. *Lost on a Mountain in Maine.* New York: Beech Tree Books, 1978.

Gagnon, Lana. *Chesuncook Memories.* Greenville, Me.: Chesuncook Village Church Committee, 1989.

Gramly, Richard M. *The Atkins Site: A Paleo-Indian Habitation.* Persimmon Press, 1988.

Hamlin, Helen. *Nine Mile Bridge.* New York: W. W. Norton & Co., 1945.

Hart, Robert Thompson. *The Nicatous History.* (c. 1978), available at Nicatous Lodge.

Holbrook, Stewart. *Yankee Logger: A Recollection of Woodsmen, Cooks and River Drivers.* International Paper Company, 1961.

Howe, Anne. *Bully, My Third Child*, 1985. Available from Anne Howe, Thorndike, Me. 04986.

Huber, J. Parker. *The Wildest Country: A Guide to Thoreau's Maine.* Boston: Appalachian Mountain Club, 1981.

Humphrey, Bob. *Bobby Goes to Maine* (children's book), 1989. Available at Wilderness Island.

Hutchinson, Doug. *The Rumford Falls and Rangeley Lakes Railroad.* Dixfield, Me.: Partridge Lane Publications, 1989.

Kauffman, John Michael, and Jean Powers Paradis. *Dear Old Kennebago. A Pictorial History of a Maine Lake, 1862–1992.* (1992), available from Kennebago Lake Owner's Association, PO Box 18, Oquossoc, Me. 04964.

Kidney, Dorothy Boone. *Away From It All.* New Jersey/London: A.S. Barnes & Co., 1969.

Lansky, Mitch. *Beyond the Beauty Strip.* Vancouver, B.C.: Terrapin Press, 1992.

Libby, Ellen. *Sharing Our Best: Libby Camp Cooks.* Nebraska: Morris Press, 1995.

Lynch, Jim "Grizzly." *An Old Guide's Tales of the Maine Woods.* (1986), c/o Florence Chapman, Portage, Me. 04768.

Macdougall, Arthur R. Jr. *Dud Dean and the Enchanted* (also *Dud Dean and His Country; Where Flows the Kennebec; Doc Blakesly, Angler*). Manchester, Me.: Falmouth Publishing House, 1954.

Maine Sporting Camp Association. *Cooking with the Maine Sporting Camp Association.* Kansas: Cookbook Publishers, Inc., 1993. Available from Maine Sporting Camp Association, PO Box 89, Jay, Me. 04239.

The Maine Sporting Camps Association Guide. Booklet, PO Box 89, Jay, Me. 04239.

Marchand, Peter J. *North Woods: An Inside Look at the Nature of Forests in the Northeast.* Boston: Appalachian Mountain Club, 1987.

Martin, Al. *Three Maine Woodland Stories.* Brattleboro, Vt.: A.C. Hood & Co.

McPhee, John. *The Survival of the Bark Canoe.* New York: Farrar, Straus & Giroux, 1975.

McPhee, John. *Table of Contents.* New York: Farrar, Straus & Giroux, 1980.

Mithee, Viola. *Living at Katahdin.* Milo, Me.: Milo Printing Co.

Packard, Marlborough. *A History of Packard's Camps: 1894–1916.* (1974), available from Maine State Library.

Raychard, Al. *Trout and Salmon Fishing in Northern New England.* Thorndike, Me.: North Country Press, 1982.

Rich, Louise Dickinson. *We Took to the Woods.* Camden, Maine: Down East Books, 1942.

St. Croix Waterway Map, also *St. Croix Management Plan.* St. Croix International Waterway Commission, Box 610, Calais, Me. 04619.

Sawtell, William R. *Katahdin Iron Works, Boom to Bust (*also *KIW Revisited and KIW III*). William R. Sawtell, Box 272, Brownville, Me. 04414.

Seal, Cheryl. *Thoreau's Maine Woods, Then and Now.* Hanover, NH: Yankee Books, 1992.

Thoreau, Henry David. *The Maine Woods.* Originally published in 1864. New York: Harper and Row, 1987.

Tree, Christina, and Elizabeth Roundy. *Maine, An Explorer's Guide,* 8th Edition. Woodstock, Vt.: The Countryman Press, 1997.

Varney, Susan. *Take a Hike: Featuring the Appalachian Mountains in the Upper Kennebec Valley Region of Maine.* The Forks, Me.: Bread and Water Books, 1990.

Verde, Thomas. *Cornelia "Fly Rod" Thurza Crosby.* Phillips Historical Society, Phillips, Me. 04966.

Wight, Eric. *Maine Game Wardens.* (1983), Maine Warden Service Relief Association, available from Eric Wight, Bethel, Me. 04217.

RECIPE INDEX

Recipes featured in this book come from the American Plan camps (serve all three meals) rather than those that are primarily Modified American Plan (two meals) or Housekeeping (cook for yourself). Maine sporting camps pride themselves on their food, and so they should; the quality is uniformly excellent. The planning, care, and time that go into the preparation of food is prodigious, since most cooks are miles from a grocery store and must cook without the benefit of electricity or modern conveniences year after year. Delicious, simple food—homemade and cooked the slow way—is part of what makes the camps authentic.

Recipes with an asterisk (*) are printed, with permission, from *Cooking with the Maine Sporting Camp Association;* Tunnel of Fudge Cake is from *Treasured Recipes,* Ashland Advent Christian Church.

Books from The Countryman Press

A selection of our books about Maine and the Northeast

25 Bicycle Tours in Maine
50 Hikes in the Maine Mountains
50 Hikes in Southern and Coastal Maine
In-Line Skate New England
The Architecture of the Shakers
Seasoned with Grace: My Generation of Shaker Cooking
The Story of the Shakers
Blue Ribbons and Burlesque: A Book of Country Fairs
The New England Herb Gardener
Living with Herbs
Wild Game Cookery

Explorer's Guides

The alternative to mass-market guides with their paid listings, Explorer's Guides focus on independently owned inns, B&Bs, and restaurants, and on family and cultural activities reflecting the character and unique qualities of the area.

Cape Cod: An Explorer's Guide Second Edition
Connecticut: An Explorer's Guide Second Edition
Maine: An Explorer's Guide Eighth Edition
Massachusetts: An Explorer's Guide Second Edition
New Hampshire: An Explorer's Guide Third Edition
Vermont: An Explorer's Guide Seventh Edition
Rhode Island: An Explorer's Guide Second Edition

We offer many more books on hiking, fly-fishing, travel, nature, and other subjects. Our books are available at bookstores and outdoor stores everywhere. For more information or a free catalog, please call 1-800-245-4151 or write to us at The Countryman Press, PO Box 748, Woodstock, Vermont 05091. You can find us on the Internet at www.countrymanpress.com.